PROMOTING MINORITIES & WOMEN

A Practical Guide to Affirmative Action for the 1990s

Copyright © 1989
The Bureau of National Affairs, Inc.
1231 25th St., N.W.
Washington, D.C. 20037

International Standard Book Number: 1-55871-142-2

Table of Contents

Introduction

In the 1990s and thereafter, the success of U.S. companies will depend largely on how well they handle emerging issues related to competitiveness and workforce productivity.

In the marketplace, U.S. companies face stiff challenges from economic powers like Japan. At the same time, a changing workforce will mean tighter competition for workers at all levels but particularly for highly skilled and highly educated workers who can fill management and other upper-level positions.

In addition to competing for fewer available workers, employers will be choosing from a labor pool that will include a greater proportion of women and minorities. According to the federal government and private researchers, white males, who made up 45 percent of the labor force in 1986, will represent only about 10 percent of labor force growth in the 1990s.

There is no indication, however, that white males will be displaced from the majority of management and upper-level positions. But blacks, other minorities, and women increasingly are seeking greater access to these jobs. Also, because of government pressure, market considerations, and commitment to workforce diversity by some top-level managers, more and more companies are making efforts to help advance and promote female, black, Asian, and Hispanic workers. These efforts include recruiting and training efforts targeting these groups, specific hiring and promotion goals, and increased monitoring to ensure affirmative action progress.

"In the decade of the 1990s, employers will have no choice. They will have to reach out to a labor pool that includes more women and minorities," said Phyllis A. Wallace, professor emerita of management at the Sloan School of Massachusetts Institute of Technology.

DEMOGRAPHIC CHANGES

Demographic trends indicate that during the 1990s, women, minorities, and immigrants will comprise two-thirds of the U.S. workforce, Wallace told BNA.

According to *Opportunity 2000*, a Department of Labor report released in 1988 on upcoming changes in the workforce, "These trends will persist for the remainder of the century. Thus between 1985 and 2000, white males, who only a generation ago made up the dominant segment of the labor market, will comprise only 15 percent of the net additions to the workforce. The majority of new entrants will be women and minorities. By the year 2000, about 47 percent of the workforce will be women and 61 percent of all American women will be employed."

Assistant Secretary of Labor William Brooks told BNA that employers need to take steps to provide genuine advancement opportunities for women and minorities.

"I especially think that as we move to the year 2000, it's in a company's best interest ... to move minorities and women into 'real' management jobs," Brooks said.

"The customer force is going to look a lot like the workforce," Brooks said. "If you just put supply and demand into the equation, along with the demographics of the country, all people are going to be needed ... if you want to be globally competitive."

To respond to these developments, companies will place greater emphasis on training, he said. Stepped-up training efforts will be vital in the 1990s because the skills of many people in the workforce will fall far below those that will be required by many industries, he added.

LEGAL AND LEGISLATIVE DEVELOPMENTS

Employers had a clear picture of workforce demographics into the next century, but recent developments in the courts and in Congress have made future legal requirements less certain. Throughout 1989, much of the debate on equal employment and affirmative action centered on controversial U.S. Supreme Court rulings in affirmative action cases.

For example, in *Wards Cove v. Atonio*, 490 U.S. ___, 104 L.Ed.2d 733, 109 S.Ct. 2115, 49 FEP Cases 1519 (1989), the justices ruled, in a 5-4 vote, that the ultimate burden of persuasion under Title VII of the Civil Rights Act of 1964 remains with the minority workers throughout the litigation. The court also held that racial imbalance in one segment of the workforce does not, alone, prove that an employer's hiring and promotion policies have a disparate impact on minorities in the employer's entire workforce.

In *Lorance v. AT&T Technologies*, 490 U.S. ___, 104 L.Ed.2d 961, 109 S.Ct. 2261, 49 FEP Cases 1656 (1989), the court barred a suit by female employees seeking to invalidate a seniority system after the women discovered that the company and the union had instituted the system to give male workers an advantage over their female co-workers.

In *Martin v. Wilks*, 490 U.S. ___, 104 L.Ed.2d 835, 109 S.Ct. 2180, 49 FEP Cases 1641 (1989), the court ruled that white males who claim they were affected adversely by an affirmative remedy and a civil rights consent decree can sue their employer whenever that remedy harms their position.

In *Patterson v. McLean Credit Union*, 491 U.S. ___, 105 L.Ed.2d 132, 109 S.Ct. 2363, 49 FEP Cases 1814 (1989), the court said an 1866 civil rights law that prohibits race discrimination in the making of a contract "extends only to the formation of a contract but not to problems that may arise later from the conditions of continuing employment."

In November 1989, the NAACP Legal Defense and Educational fund released a study reporting that at least 96 racial discrimination claims had been dismissed in lower federal courts because of the June 15, 1989, *Patterson* ruling. "Although the central holding of *Patterson* was that racial harassment was not forbidden by [the civil rights law], most of the dismissals have involved forms of discrimination other than racial harassment," the study said.

The 96 dismissals, involving 50 cases, came as a result of discrimination claims by black, Hispanic, Chinese, Filipino, Hawaiian, and Jewish plaintiffs.

In the 1989 rulings, "the Supreme Court has substantially limited the reach of the fair employment laws," said Barry Goldstein, a civil rights lawyer who formerly served with the NAACP Legal Defense and Educational Fund. He told BNA that the decisions also limit "the scope of the remedies available and the ability of the parties to develop consent plans that would resolve discriminatory practices."

Benjamin Hooks, executive director of the National Association for the Advancement of Colored People, called the rulings a "diabolical plan to rob minorities of gains we thought we had." In August 1989, the NAACP and other civil rights organizations led thousands of demonstrators on a "silent march" in Washington to protest those Supreme Court rulings on affirmative action.

Bills Introduced

By the autumn of 1989, congressional action was under way to nullify the controversial Supreme Court decisions. Sen. Howard M. Metzenbaum (D-Ohio) and Rep. Thomas J. Campbell (R-Calif) introduced bills (S 1261 and HR 3455) designed to uphold the "adverse impact doctrine," under which statistical data can be used to prove racial or gender discrimination. In October 1989, Sen. Edward Kennedy (D-Mass) announced his plans "to introduce comprehensive legislation to repair the damage caused by" several of the most recent Supreme Court decisions on EEO and affirmative action.

"The bill will overrule the *Wards Cove* decision and restore the prior law that employers, not the victims of job discrimination, must bear the burden of proof when minorities and women are unfairly excluded from the workplace," Kennedy said at a civil rights conference in Boston. "The bill will overrule the *Martin v. Wilks* decision and establish fair procedures to ensure that consent decrees settling job discrimination cases will not be subject to endless further litigation," he added.

Former EEOC Chair Denounces Rulings

A former head of the Equal Employment Opportunity Commission also criticized the decisions and called on Congress to pass legislation that would nullify them.

"The court has decimated equal employment law," said Eleanor Holmes Norton, professor of law at Georgetown University Law Center in Washington, D.C. Norton, who headed the EEOC from 1977 to 1981, told BNA that it now is "up to the Congress to re-establish" the legal principles established by previous Supreme Court decisions.

The rulings notwithstanding, Norton said employers will continue their equal employment efforts and will keep "in place machinery for affirmative action."

Employers have continued to demonstrate a commitment to these policies, she said. "During the 1980s, employers have done a better job with affirmative action than the government has with enforcing it."

"Employers have a powerful demographic incentive that was not there when the [equal employment] statute was passed," she said. Companies that abandon equal employment or affirmative action might find themselves short of skilled workers and will be in violation of the law, Norton said.

Support for Rulings

Despite such criticisms from Capitol Hill and elsewhere, the Supreme Court rulings won outspoken support from William Allen, chairman of the U.S. Commission on Civil Rights. He said any effort to counteract the rulings on affirmative action would be unwarranted.

In remarks at a Heritage Foundation policy seminar in August 1989, Allen said such legislative action would "establish different rules of evidence and different standards of justice, by race and gender, for the enforcement of civil rights laws." The proposed legislation would "lead [the] country deeper into the hell of race-conscious social remedies and a society divided by racial terms of reference," Allen said.

Some private organizations also were beginning to speak out against proposed legislation. Clint Bolick, director of the conservative-oriented Center for Civil Rights, called on President Bush to resist congressional challenges.

"The recent Supreme Court decisions were a triumph for civil rights," Bolick told BNA. He said the decisions show that under the current court, EEO and affirmative action policies will face the "highest Constitutional scrutiny."

SCOPE OF THIS REPORT

This BNA special report examines these and other equal employment and affirmative action issues surrounding the advancement of minority and female employees, particularly those working at major U.S. corporations.

Chapter I of the report highlights corporate and government efforts aimed at achieving further equal employment progress for women and minorities.

Chapter II discusses past progress in hiring and promoting minorities and women and the historical factors that led to it. The chapter also examines how discrimination continues to block women and minorities from moving up in corporations.

In Chapter III, corporate and government EEO officials provide their perspectives on affirmative action and EEO policies. These officials discuss the roles of employers and the federal government in pursuing these policies.

In Chapter IV, author Edward W. Jones Jr. recommends how corporations can expand employment opportunities, particularly for highly trained minorities. The chapter also points out that increasing workforce diversity will require greater attention to EEO.

Chapter V analyzes enforcement initiatives issued by the Office of Federal Contract Compliance Programs. The author, Edmund D. Cooke Jr., also describes policies of the Equal Employment Opportunity Commission related to promoting minorities and women.

In Chapter VI, authors William J. Kilberg and Stephen E. Tallent examine how the 1989 Supreme Court rulings on affirmative action and equal employment could affect the use of subjective criteria in promotion decisions. The authors also discuss the outlook for the disparate treatment and disparate impact standards in employment discrimination cases.

In Chapter VII, Richard T. Seymour discusses how the decisions on affirmative action and equal employment have affected civil rights laws and their enforcement.

Chapter VIII outlines the efforts of companies that have been recognized for their progress in hiring and promoting women and minorities, including Gannett Co. Inc., US West Inc., Aetna Life & Casualty, Xerox Corp., American Telephone & Telegraph, and Chase Manhattan Corp.

Appendix A contains the 1988 OFCCP Directive on "Corporate-Level Selection Decisions."

Appendix B provides the text of: *Lorance v. AT&T Technologies*, *Martin v. Wilks*, and *Wards Cove Packing Co. v. Atonio*.

Appendix C contains corporate equal employment and affirmative action plans. The plans described are from Gannett Co. Inc., Xerox Corp., and Aetna Life & Casualty.

Appendix D contains the questionnaire used in the informal poll examined in Chapter III. This appendix also includes excerpts from surveys by Korn/Ferry International, the executive recruiting firm, and by Sirota, Alper & Pfau, the management consulting firm.

Appendix E provides text of an analysis on the impact of *Patterson v. McLean Credit Union* by the NAACP Legal Defense and Educational Fund.

ACKNOWLEDGMENTS

This special report was prepared by the BNA PLUS Research and Special Projects Unit of the Bureau of National Affairs, Inc. Drew Douglas, managing editor, supervised the project. Mark Williams, staff editor, served as editorial coordinator and wrote the Introduction, Chapters I-III, and the Gannett Co. Inc. case study.

Edward W. Jones Jr., author of Chapter IV, is president of Corporate Organizational Dynamics Inc. in South Orange, N.J. Jones advises senior corporate executives on how to build productive organizations.

Edmund D. Cooke Jr., author of Chapter V, is a partner in the Washington, D.C., office of the law firm of Epstein, Becker & Green. Cooke served formerly as counsel to the House Education and Labor Committee.

The authors of Chapter VI are William J. Kilberg and Stephen E. Tallent. Kilberg is a partner in the Washington office of the law firm of Gibson, Dunn & Crutcher. He has served as solicitor for the U.S. Department of Labor and as special assistant to the secretary of labor. Tallent is a senior partner with Gibson, Dunn & Crutcher and a member of the firm's executive committee. He specializes in labor and employment law and has written and lectured extensively on those topics. Peter D. Coffman, a member of the University of Michigan Law School class of 1990, assisted Kilberg and Tallent.

Richard T. Seymour, author of Chapter VII, is director of the employment discrimination project of the Lawyers' Committee for Civil Rights Under Law, in Washington, D.C. He has extensive experience in handling plaintiffs' class actions alleging racial and sexual discrimination in employment.

BNA staff researcher Loretta Kotzin coordinated production of the report. Staff correspondent Martha Kessler wrote the case studies on Aetna Life & Casualty and Xerox Corp. Staff correspondent Karen Breslin wrote the case study on US West Inc. BNA special correspondent Suzy Parker wrote the case studies on AT&T and Chase Manhattan Corp.

Other BNA editors who assisted with planning and preparing this special report include: Roger Feinthel, BNA Special Projects senior copy editor; Karen Ott-Worrow, staff editor; J. Michael Reidy, director of surveys; and Michael Levin-Epstein, associate editor for New Product Development. Bernard Lott, assistant to the president of BNA for equal employment opportunity, served as an adviser to the editorial staff.

* * *

Highlights

Recognizing that women and minorities will comprise two-thirds of the 1990s workforce, many U.S. employers have begun to expand or revamp employment programs and policies aimed at attracting these workers or retaining them through advancement.

Some employers have set specific goals for hiring and promoting blacks, other minorities, and women. Others have established less formal methods, such as instructing managers to make sure they seek out minority and female candidates for each job opening. Still others ask minority and female employees to recommend job candidates.

Some employers have stepped up recruiting efforts on the campuses of historically black, or predominately female colleges. Some also have tried other methods such as targeting job advertisements to publications that serve mainly black, Spanish-speaking, or Asian communities.

The success of these kinds of efforts is the subject of continuing debate among corporate managers, government officials, employees, consultants, and researchers. During the past 25 years of equal opportunity law, progress was made in moving women and minorities into entry-level jobs and lower-level management. But today these groups are seeking greater economic and social advancement through promotion into management and other supervisory jobs.

In recent years, women have moved in large numbers into lower-level management positions. But many say they have been largely unable to advance further. Blacks also have made progress in gaining management jobs, but many fear that the focus of affirmative action efforts are turning away from them to white women, Asians, and Hispanics.

Discussions of these issues are among the highlights of this BNA special report. Among the findings:

- Women made up 45 percent of the U.S. workforce in 1989. Minorities comprised more than 20 percent of the workforce. Together, these groups will account for 90 percent of workforce growth in the 1990s, demographic experts say.

- Upper-level corporate management continued to comprise white males almost exclusively. A survey of 1,362 *Fortune* 500 senior executives found that 29 (or 2 percent) were women. Minority representation totaled less than 1 percent—consisting of four blacks, six Asians, and three Hispanics, according to the survey by Korn/Ferry International, a leading executive recruiting firm.

- Stereotypes continue to create obstacles for women and minorities. According to workplace research, blacks continue to face being characterized as lazy, arrogant, and intimidating. Assertive women are viewed as "too aggressive," while women who exhibit "stereotypical female behavior," are viewed as too weak. Women also are denied promotions because of their family responsibilities. "Women are still being penalized for being able to have children," said Claudia Withers of the Women's Legal Defense Fund.

- Many attorneys say they are finding it more difficult to plan and try cases because of changes in liability standards in employment discrimination actions. The Supreme Court's 1989 decisions may leave employers and workers to face sweeping changes. The NAACP Legal Defense and Educational Fund reported that a rash of discrimination claims were dismissed following the Supreme Court ruling in *Patterson v. McLean Credit Union,* one of those controversial decisions.

- Advocacy groups and members of Congress are working to nullify the 1989 Supreme Court decisions on affirmative action. They say the decisions could roll back employment progress made by minorities and women since the enactment of equal employment laws in the 1960s.

- EEO officers, representing public and private sector employers, say increased federal government involvement would help ensure that minorities and women have advancement opportunities. Among the efforts suggested were increased funding for education and training and expanded programs for minority-owned businesses and contractors.

- Success in achieving workforce diversity requires strong commitment from top-level executives, according to executives, consultants, and EEO officials. They said tying managers' pay increases, bonuses, and promotions to affirmative action progress is one of the best ways to demonstrate this commitment. "When it affects their pocketbooks, they'll pay attention," Madelyn P. Jennings, senior vice president for personnel at Gannett Co. Inc., told BNA.

Also examined are specifics of affirmative action and equal employment programs at six companies:

- Gannett Co. Inc., which closely monitors the affirmative action efforts in each of its units and ties such progress to management bonuses.

- US West Inc., whose efforts include an intensive training program aimed at preparing minority women for management.

- Aetna Life & Casualty, which emphasizes workforce diversity in efforts such as the "Consulting Pairs" program, in which pairs of employees of different racial or ethnic backgrounds address diversity issues.

- Xerox Corp., which offers managerial training programs that examine workforce diversity issues. Minority and female employees also have formed more than 100 support groups to help address their concerns.

- American Telephone & Telegraph, in an effort to attract more minorities, allows employees to serve as visiting professors at historically black universities. Students from those schools also get an opportunity to spend summers at Bell Labs.

- Chase Manhattan Corp., which sponsors a minority summer internship program that includes six weeks of business training alongside entry-level, full-time employees.

* * *

Background

By a variety of measures, women and minorities have increased their representation in management positions since the 1960s.

As the 1980s drew to a close, women held 39 percent of the public and private sector jobs included in the Department categories of executive, administrative, and management. That figure was up from 15 percent in 1966, according to the Department of Labor (DOL). Overall, women made up 45 percent of the work force in 1989, compared with 38 percent in 1970. By 2000, women were expected to represent almost half the labor force.

In 1965, minorities made up about 3 percent of the executive, managerial, and administrative employees in the United States, according to the Bureau of Labor Statistics. By 1984, the proportion of minority managers had risen to 8.4 percent. The BLS "officials and managers" category includes those in all levels of government, the private sector, and self-employed people.

Much of this progress began after the signing of equal opportunity and affirmative action laws and orders in the 1960s. One of the most far-reaching of these was Executive Order 11246, signed by President Johnson in 1965. It required federal contractors to take affirmative action to hire minority group members, women, and other protected groups. In this way it exceeded the provisions of Title VII of the Civil Rights Act of 1964, which prohibits employers from discriminating on the basis of race, color, religion, sex, or national origin.

The policy was expanded in 1972. Congress amended Title VII to include a section stating that a court could order an employer to take broad affirmative action after a finding of discrimination.

ADVANCEMENT OF WOMEN

Despite the significant overall increases in the proportion of women in the workforce and in management positions, few of these women had been able to reach the senior management level.

In 1989, women filled only 3 percent of the most coveted top management positions at the country's largest publicly traded corporations, a figure expected to rise to 16 percent by the year 2000, according to data from a survey of senior executives that was being prepared by Korn/Ferry International, a leading executive search firm.

Employment researchers such as Phyllis Wallace, of the Sloan School of Massachusetts Institute of Technology, describe obstacles women managers have faced in obtaining equal rewards and opportunities for promotion. Wallace's books on employment and equal opportunity issues include *MBAs on the Fast Track*, published in 1989. In that book, she wrote that "success in management for women has been difficult as they have aspired to senior positions. Although women managers at entry level and middle management positions may have overcome many hurdles, they appear to have to confront more barriers than their male peers as they compete for the top jobs."

Obstacles Still Exist

At all levels of employment, "employers could be doing a lot better" to remove obstacles that keep women from advancing, said Claudia Withers, deputy director for employment programs at the Women's Legal Defense Fund.

"Women are still being penalized for being able to have children," Withers told BNA. She said having family responsibilities, such as child care or care of elderly family members, continues to be treated as a disadvantage for female and male employees.

While employment statistics show that women have made substantial progress in moving into lower-level management, other research indicates that prospective women managers still are likely to face greater obstacles than their male counterparts.

"There are still a lot of stereotypes about women" that make their advancement more difficult, said John Fernandez, president of Advance Research Management Consultants. His books on how women and minorities are faring in the corporate world include *Survival in the Corporate Fishbowl* and *Racism and Sexism in Corporate Life*.

In *Survival in the Corporate Fishbowl*, Fernandez wrote that attitudes regarding women in corporations remain a major barrier: "The pervasive sexist stereotypes and attitudes of society in general and corporate America in particular translate into special difficulties that corporate women must face, over and above the normal bureaucratic problems, concerns, and difficulties encountered by all employees. As women move up the corporate hierarchy, the intensity of these problems increases."

Fernandez gathered responses from more than 12,000 management and non-management employees in 13 companies. Those responses included frequent expressions of negative, stereotypical attitudes: Some employees said they did not believe women belonged in the workforce; others, male and female, said women used sex to get ahead; still others said women were lazy, weak, or lacking in managerial ability.

Withers said assertive women often are viewed as "too aggressive," while women who exhibit "stereotypical female behavior" are viewed as too weak.

Fernandez also found that women were perceived in the late 1980s as having less opportunity for advancement than they were in a survey he completed in 1978.

"In 1976-78, 19 percent of the women and 47 percent of the white men believed their gender was harmful to their career advancement. In 1986, 43 percent of minority women, 30 percent of white women, and 29 percent of white men believed their gender was harmful," Fernandez wrote. "This is a clear sign that affirmative action efforts have slipped under the Reagan administration, and that white males are feeling less threatened by even a perceived emphasis on preferential treatment for women."

In *MBAs on the Fast Track*, Wallace tracked periods early in the careers of 1975-1979 male and female graduates of the Sloan School's Master of Science in Management program. While salary differences between these graduates were small, women reported "paying a higher price for an equivalent level of success," Wallace wrote.

"Our conclusion was that women after two years earned the same mean salaries as their male peers from Sloan, but also reported greater psychic costs such as more problems in integrating their work and non-work activity; a high negative spillover of their jobs into their personal lives; and job stress, whereas the men did not."

Further advancement for women may depend largely on how well "psychic costs" can be reduced, Wallace told BNA. Companies are starting to help women and men achieve a greater balance between their work and their family and social activities, she said.

"More employers are realizing that they have to take into account what happens in their [employees'] personal lives," Wallace observed.

Employers that do not adopt such policies will be more likely to lose women managers to entrepreneurial ventures and to other companies with more flexible policies, Wallace said.

MINORITY ADVANCEMENT

Minorities held 9 percent of managerial and 12 percent of professional jobs in 1987, according to the Equal Employment Opportunity Commission (EEOC). Overall minority participation in the workforce was 21 percent.

Wallace wrote that progress for minority managers, particularly blacks, remained limited.

"Although many companies, under some external pressures, have hired black managers, these employees remain in the lower ranks and their promotions lag considerably behind those for their white male peers," Wallace wrote in *MBAs on the Fast Track.*

Among the most widely read articles on black managers' experiences inside corporations have been, "What it's Like to be a Black Manager," and "Black Managers: The Dream Deferred," both written by consultant Edward W. Jones and published 13 years apart in *Harvard Business Review.* (Jones is the author of Chapter IV of this special report.)

In "What it's Like to be a Black Manager," published in 1973, Jones detailed his experiences at a large company and discussed the pervasiveness of racial stereotypes and how they affect black managers.

"I was probably guilty of many of the subjective shortcomings noted in my appraisals. But I do feel that the difficulties I experienced were amplified by my lack of compatibility with the informal organization. Because of it, many of the people I had problems with could not differentiate between objective ability and performance and subjective dislike for me, or discomfort with me," Jones wrote. ... I cannot fully differentiate between problems attributable to me as a person, to me as a manager, or to me as a black man."

When this article was published, Jones was a division manager at New York Telephone Co. He moved on from there to AT&T, where he oversaw media planning and initiated the company's satellite strategy. He established a consulting firm, Organizational Dynamics Inc., in 1984.

Jones updated his findings in "Black Managers: The Dream Deferred," published in 1986 as an assessment of the progress of black managers.

"In conversations with black managers, I hear expressions of disappointment, dismay, frustration, and anger because they have not gained acceptance on a par with their white peers," Jones wrote. "They find their careers stymied and they are increasingly disillusioned about their chances for ultimate success. They feel at best tolerated; they often feel ignored."

Racial discrimination remains a major obstacle to the advancement of minority employees, Fernandez said. In his research for *Survival in the Corporate Fishbowl*, he found that employees were not reluctant to express views about minorities — particularly blacks — that were filled with negative stereotypes. Blacks frequently were characterized as lazy, arrogant, intimidating, and selfish and were said to habitually "cry discrimination" and to "stick together."

Top-level leaders can help change negative attitudes and behavior toward female and minority employees, Fernandez said. Otherwise, "people will fall back into their old beliefs." When top management does not speak out strongly against racist or sexist views or behavior, it is, in effect, condoning such behavior, Fernandez said.

"Leadership has to have sanctioned these views or [employees] wouldn't express them," he maintained.

FEW REACH UPPER MANAGEMENT

Despite progress in breaking into some levels of management, women and minorities at companies rarely have reached senior management positions, according to corporate surveys.

A 1986 survey of senior executives by Korn/Ferry International revealed that upper-level management continued to comprise white males almost exclusively.

Of the 1,362 respondents, all *Fortune* 500 senior executives, 29 (or 2 percent) were women. In a similar 1979 survey by Korn/Ferry, less than 1 percent of the respondents were women.

"In 1979, we observed that the country's very largest companies had not made a dent in solving the problem of women and minority representation at the senior corporate level. Six years later, despite industry and government efforts to promote opportunities for women and minority executives, the progress in this area is minimal," the firm said in its 1986 survey, *Korn/Ferry International's Executive Profile: A Survey of Corporate Leaders in the Eighties.*

Among the 1,362 executives in the 1986 survey were four blacks, six Asians, and three Hispanics.

"As in 1979, all non-white respondents taken together still constitute less than 1 percent of the total," the survey reported.

In placing representative numbers of women and minorities in middle and upper management, "companies, for the most part, are still not there," said Fred Rasheed, director of economic development programs at the NAACP. Most black employees, in particular, still find themselves at the bottom of a "corporate pyramid," with limited opportunity at the top for everyone and almost none there for blacks, Rasheed told BNA. The few who have reached middle or upper-level management often are confined to "non-operative areas," such as public affairs or personnel, Rasheed said.

"You really have to look at what that means in terms of responsibility," he said.

Rasheed's responsibilities include negotiating the NAACPs "fair share" agreements with corporations. Under these agreements, the NAACP cites black consumer spending to help obtain companies' assurances that they will hire and promote more blacks and that they will provide vending and subcontracting opportunities for blacks. By 1989, nearly 50 companies had signed such agreements, including Chrysler Corp., General Motors Corp., Adolph Coors Co., and K mart, Rasheed said.

* * *

Interviews with EEO Officials

Increased federal government action is needed to ensure that minorities and women are allowed to move up in the nation's corporations and in other places of employment, equal employment officials representing corporate and government employers told BNA.

This view was expressed by corporate and public officials contacted at a gathering of EEO professionals in September 1989. Twenty-two of these officials answered a BNA questionnaire on promoting minorities and women, and six of the officials participated in follow-up interviews. (Text of the questionnaire appears in Appendix D.) The issues covered in the questionnaire and interviews included:

- How the federal government could help ensure the advancement of minorities and women in employment.
- The level of commitment of employers in helping minorities and women move up.
- The degree to which sexism and racism in the workplace remain obstacles to the advancement of minority and female employees.
- How to design and implement specific policies aimed at helping minority and female employees advance.

Aggressive affirmative action policy "trickles down from the very top," said a state equal opportunity officer from the Mid-Atlantic region. He told BNA that public and private-sector employers follow the federal government's lead in their own approaches to affirmative action policy. Thus, employers are more likely to relax their efforts if they see that the "federal government does not exert the effort to enforce these laws that are on the books," he said.

The official also called on the government to expand programs for minority-owned businesses and contractors as a way to increase employment and promotion opportunities for minorities.

In another interview, an administrator for a public utility in the Northeast said the best way for the federal government to help minorities and women advance would be to increase funding for education and training. The availability of more government-sponsored programs would prompt more people to develop the skills they need to advance, he said. "It doesn't hurt to have an incentive," he said.

GOVERNMENT EFFORTS

In the BNA questionnaire, the EEO officials were asked to select answers that best reflected their opinions about programs and policies to help minorities and women advance. There was strong agreement regarding the federal government's role:

- Nineteen of the officials answered that the "federal government should increase its efforts" to ensure the advancement of minorities;
- Two said the "federal government's role should remain about the same"; and
- One said the "federal government should decrease its efforts."

Concerning advancement opportunities for women:

- Nineteen said the "federal government should increase its efforts";
- Three said the "federal government's role should remain about the same"; and
- None said the "federal government should decrease its efforts."

The officials were contacted at a September 1989 meeting of the National Institute for Employment Equity (NIFEE) in Columbus, Ohio. The 300-member organization sponsors symposiums and other educational programs on equal employment and affirmative action issues.

EMPLOYER POLICIES RATED

The officials also described policies that could better enable employers to reach affirmative action objectives. These policies include:

- Development of affirmative action policy that ties progress in this area to management pay raises, promotions, and bonuses.
- Counteracting racism and sexism through direct attention to such problems by top-level management.
- Better use of minority and female role models and mentors.

The public utility administrator emphasized the importance of female and minority role models in private and public sector employment.

Employers need to make it possible for more minorities and women to be "seen in the role of policy-maker and decision-maker," he said.

In responding to the questionnaire, the EEO officials gave differing assessments on their employers' efforts to promote women and minorities.

When asked to rate their organizations' records on promoting minorities:

- Eleven said their organizations were about the same as other employers;
- Five rated their organizations as much better;
- Two said somewhat better; and
- Four said much worse.

When asked to rate their organizations' records on promoting women:

- Thirteen said their organizations were about the same as other employers;
- Three said much better;
- Five said somewhat better; and
- One marked "no basis for judgment/don't know."

A county affirmative action officer from the Northeast said employers should provide promotion opportunities to a wider range of employees. "If people are producing, move them up the ladder," he said.

When it came to seeking and training minorities for management positions:

- Nine of the officials said their organizations were "not very aggressive";
- Five described their companies as "somewhat aggressive";
- Five said "very aggressive"; and
- Three said "not at all aggressive."

When it came to seeking and training women for management positions:

- Ten called their organizations "not very aggressive";
- Eight described their companies as "somewhat aggressive";
- Three said "very aggressive"; and
- One said "not at all aggressive."

Racism and Sexism

A human resources director for an industry association in the Midwest said counteracting racism and sexism remains a high priority for firms her organization represents. She said top-level management must "deal with incidents forcefully" to demonstrate that such behavior would not be tolerated. She gave as an example of such action a company executive who took a work day to meet with workers after a dispute between a male and a female employee.

A state personnel officer from the Midwest agreed that there is a "need for the right kind of commitment from top management" in pursuing workforce diversity. "Everything else flows from that," he said.

He said this commitment needs to be "backed up by a decision to hit people in the wallet." Pay increases, bonuses, and promotions should be tied to managers' effectiveness in hiring and promoting women and minorities, he said. "This should be assessed and evaluated the same way as meeting production goals."

In responding to the questionnaire:

- Twelve of the EEO officials said they believed racism was "to some extent" an obstacle to advancement of minorities at their organizations, while nine said they believed sexism was "to some extent" an obstacle to the advancement of women;

- Five said racism was an obstacle "to a great extent," and four found sexism to be that kind of obstacle to the advancement of women;

- Three said racism was "to little extent" an obstacle, while seven had the same view of sexism;

- Two answered that racism was "not at all" an obstacle for minorities, and the same number also believed sexism was "not at all" an obstacle for women.

An EEO officer for a state agency in the Midwest said racism and sexism are "just as vicious" as before the enactment of equal opportunity laws but are acted on in a more "covert" manner. When racial problems exist, companies have a responsibility to "open a dialogue with minority employees," she said. She said employers can better manage workforce diversity if they "recognize fundamental psychological differences" between the sexes and among racial and ethnic groups.

* * *

Workforce Diversity: A Consultant's Analysis After 25 Years of EEO

By Edward W. Jones Jr.*

The nature of American work is changing rapidly, with shifts in the composition of the workforce, intensifying global competition, and increasing dependence on minorities and women to assume greater levels of responsibility and leadership. Success in handling these issues will be closely linked to the future of equal employment policy and where America stands in achieving the national ideal of equal opportunity.

This chapter will assess the status of the nation and its employers in realizing equal opportunity. This chapter presents the perspectives of an organizational consultant, researcher, and trainer of executives and managers. The discussion includes requirements for continued progress and suggests how to realize more effective policies for managing diverse and productive organizations. Success for U.S. companies in the coming decades will depend largely upon how well corporate leaders understand and develop such policies.

Accelerating technological change is fueling an increasing demand for highly educated white-collar workers. The future of American companies in intensely competitive global markets depends upon their success in achieving unprecedented productivity. Given equal technology, the most productive workforce will prevail. This expansion of national and international competition comes at a time when the nation's workforce is becoming increasingly diverse.

---

*Edward W. Jones Jr. is president of Corporate Organizational Dynamics Inc. He advises senior corporate executives on how to build productive organizations.

The Hudson Institute Reports in *Workforce 2000* that white men no longer make up a majority of the U.S. workforce but that they will continue indefinitely to be key participants. Blacks, Hispanics, and Asians will constitute 26 percent of workers and 57 percent of the growth to the year 2000. White women and minorities combined exceed 90 percent of all growth.

EMPHASIS ON EDUCATION NEEDED

The next generation of American workers will need more and better education, and the nation's leaders are searching for better programs with which to provide it.

The quality of the U.S. workforce in increasingly white-collar jobs, requiring more and higher quality participant education, will determine America's competitiveness, standard of living, military strength, and future as a world economic leader. But America's educational system is more and more seen as lagging behind the educational systems of other industrial democracies. Current and former CEO's of leading companies such as Xerox, Johnson & Johnson, and Procter & Gamble have been sounding the alarm that the nation might be headed for a crisis in education and employment. This could lead to America becoming a nation of haves and have-nots — employment haves and have-nots, a polarization that often follows racial lines.

Efforts Being Made

Both large and small firms are becoming involved with schools and colleges in order to link workforce requirements with the education being received and to underscore the link between scholastic achievement and employment opportunities. The Business Roundtable has noted major support by member companies for educational policies such as those recommended in their April 1988 publication, *The Role of Business in Education Reform*. In addition, a June 1989 Roundtable publication, *Business Means Business About Education*, lists almost 200 member companies' educational activities.

"How well we educate all of our children will determine our competitiveness globally, our economic health domestically and our communities' character and vitality .... When our young people cannot compete as individuals, we cannot compete as a nation," the publication warned.

In September 1989, at the University of Virginia in Charlottesville, President Bush convened an educational summit attended by state governors and other officials. It was only the third time in U.S. history that such a summit has occurred. The participants said the summit's purpose was to focus national resolve, discuss and set national educational goals, and to begin to plan and shape more effective educational programs.

The next stage in these discussions was planned for the National Governors' Association meeting in February 1990. Among the topics slated for that gathering are specific plans for improving the readiness of students — particularly the disadvantaged — to start school. Other issues included boosting performance on achievement tests in math and science, lowering dropout rates, establishing drug-free schools, and improving "federal measurement" of accomplishment.[1]

ORIGINAL OBJECTIVES OF EEO LAW

To reflect upon what individual organizations and the nation must accomplish, it is helpful to remember how and why efforts to achieve equal opportunity began.

In 1963, when the U.S. Department of Justice counted more than 1400 racial conflicts in America, the nation was experiencing a racial crisis. The nation watched and read daily accounts of marches, sit-ins, freedom rides, and riots. Fire hoses, tear gas, bombings, and police dogs also were familiar images.

On June 11, 1963, President Kennedy called for civil rights legislation. Seven hours later, civil rights leader Medgar Evars was shot and killed in Jackson, Miss.

On Aug. 28, 1963, 210,000 people marched on Washington, calling for the passage of civil rights legislation. The impetus for the Civil Rights Act of 1964 was the desire to mend the nation's racial divisions and to calm social turmoil that arose from discrimination against and segregation of black Americans.

President John F. Kennedy, in a speech calling for the legislation, said:

> This nation was founded by men of many nations and backgrounds. It was founded on the principle that all men are created equal, and that the rights of every man are diminished when the rights of one man are threatened ....

> One hundred years of delay have passed since President Lincoln freed the slaves, yet their heirs, their grandsons, are not fully free. They are not freed from the bonds of injustice; they are not yet freed from social and economic oppression ....

> It is time to act in the Congress, in state and local legislatures, and above all, in our daily lives. This ... has become one country because all the people who came here had an equal chance to develop their talents. We cannot say to 10 percent of the population that ... your children can't have the chance to develop whatever talents they have, that the only way they're going to get their rights is to go in the street and demonstrate .... We owe them and we owe ourselves a better country than that."[3]

Congressional Debate

Sen. Hubert H. Humphrey, (D-Minn), expressed similar views during the Senate debate on the civil rights laws:

> At present Negroes and members of other minority groups do not have an equal chance to be hired, to be promoted, and to be given the most desirable assignments. Fair treatment in employment is as important as any other area of civil rights. What good does it do a Negro to be able to eat in a fine restaurant if he cannot afford the bill? What good does it do him to be accepted in a hotel that is too expensive for his modest income?

> How can a Negro child be motivated to take advantage of integrated educational facilities if he has no hope of getting a job where he can use that education? Negro men and women with dis-

tinguished records in our best universities have been unable to find a job that will make use of their training and skills.

...It is a depressing fact that a Negro with four years of college can expect to earn less in his lifetime than a white man who quit school in the eighth grade.[4]

In an effort to defeat the civil rights bill, an amendment prohibiting sex discrimination was added by Rep. Howard W. Smith (D-Va). Even if Congress was prepared to pass a bill granting equal rights to black Americans, surely they would not be willing to grant women equal employment rights, Smith believed.

But most in Congress apparently recognized that while white women had not suffered from the all-consuming prejudice and social discrimination that blacks had experienced, their individuality and freedom to achieve had been imprisoned within gender roles deeply entrenched in the workplace.

The civil rights bill passed, and on July 2, 1964, President Lyndon B. Johnson signed it, saying: "The purpose of this law is simple .... It say(s) the only limit to a man's hope for happiness and for the future of his children shall be his own ability."

OPPORTUNITY FOR THE HIGHLY EDUCATED

In the years since the enactment of the Civil Rights Act, education has played a major role in the employment progress of minorities and women.

The Rand Corporation in a February 1986 report titled *Closing the Gap: Forty Years of Economic Progress for Blacks*, reported that, "The 'black elite' have now joined the game. There is substantial evidence that salary increases and promotions for the 'black elite' will be at least as rapid as their white competitors. The principal reason is that the increase in the economic benefits of black schooling began long before affirmative action pressures."

While this view points to more and better education for minorities and women as vital to success, research data also indicates that education by itself without organizational opportunity has become problematic.

The House Committee on Education and Labor examined eight major federal contractors in Los Angeles in January 1987 to assess their progress toward equal opportunity. This review, a matter of public record, is informative because these shortcomings can be found in many, if not most, companies.

Some companies argued that the pool of qualified minorities for senior management positions was small, and they pointed to the sparse numbers of black and Hispanic engineers. The congressional staffs found, however, that the companies' detailed affirmative action plans indicated that many of the professionals and managers in these companies were not engineers but people with a broad array of business and professional talents. Therefore, justifying inadequate progress in minority upward mobility on the limited availability of black and Hispanic engineers was specious.

The committee staff also found that increases in minority employment were not evenly distributed among minority groups but were concentrated among Asians. Not only were the gains made by blacks and Hispanics limited, the kinds of jobs they obtained were also less desirable. Blacks and Hispanics continued to be concentrated among semi-skilled craft workers, office workers, and operatives.

The congressional review concluded:

> The laudable progress made by Asians should not be used to obscure the fact that since the early 1980's blacks and Hispanics have not notably advanced in these companies .... The data indicate that with regard to the proportions of black and Hispanic managers and professionals, the 1980's have been stagnant in these companies.

To assess the impact of increases in minority employment on the position of minorities in the companies, the subcommittee decided to go beyond the occupational categories on the EEO-1 reports and to examine management salary distributions by race. They concluded that, "The income profile of minority managers has not improved relative to white men—salaries have increased but black and Hispanic managers continue to have much lower salaries than whites .... Furthermore, among those blacks, Hispanics, and Asians hired as managers, few achieve top positions; most remain in relatively low paying jobs with limited influence on operations." Moreover, according to the subcommittee, "the success of Asians does not obscure their lack of advancement in the managerial ranks."

It is highly significant that the data for women showed a different trend than for blacks and Hispanics. The number of women employed rose 26 percent, accounting for 47 percent of the net growth in these eight companies. Only Asian/Pacific Islander employment grew at a faster rate. Moreover, the percentage of women officials and managers went from 8.1 percent in 1980 to 11.2 percent in 1986. Of all new officials and managers, 19.2 percent were women.

Contractors argued that any problems were because of the dearth of available, qualified women and minorities, and that additional education and training was the answer to under-representation. "Companies touted their programs and efforts to move women and minorities into upper-management positions. But there was strong rebuttal testimony to indicate that the commitment of these contractors to affirmative action and EEO was grossly inadequate and there had been even less emphasis on fair treatment and full participation since 1980."

One former OFCCP administrator said the problems lie with company human resources offices. He said: "I do not believe that even one large facility could demonstrate that its human resources office has made sufficient efforts to identify, recruit, and hire qualified minorities and females where major underutilization exists." He continued: "You will find that selecting managers express no interest in highly qualified minorities and females and select less qualified non-minority males."

The owner of a placement firm testified that "despite data banks of qualified minorities, there has been no demand for qualified minorities for employment from these companies." He testified that his company recruited blacks with nearly unimpeachable credentials, whom these clients did not hire, while white males with less academic training worked in comparable positions. He said that compared to their white counterparts, blacks were overqualified for the positions they held or were required to comply with higher academic standards to obtain comparable positions.

Progress of the Highly Educated

The difficulties faced by well-trained minority and female employees also have been described in research on companies and careers.

The INROADS experience underscores how education without opportunity is problematic. INROADS has more than 1,000 sponsoring corporations and more than 1,400 minority graduates pursuing professional and managerial careers. Four-year college internships combine summer work experiences at sponsoring companies with year-round college studies. Sponsoring companies pledge to develop career opportunities for each intern, and after graduation an average of more than two-thirds of each year's graduates accept full-time positions with sponsoring companies.

But upon graduating from college, work success and upward mobility for INROADS minority graduates has been elusive. In 1988, a conference was convened, including representatives of sponsoring companies, minority graduates of the program, and INROADS staff to explore "possible reasons for the lack of progress by minority professionals."

A study published in 1988 in association with Rutgers Business School reported: "Top level white managers, although often not admitting it in public," state they cannot find "qualified" minority candidates. They argue that black managers have not received the same degrees or educations that lead to top corporate jobs. White managers feel minority managers are less well-educated, have lower technical and writing skills and, because they are more dissatisfied, are less loyal and more difficult to manage.

"There is a tendency for most white managers to talk as if their companies are colorblind and there is even impatience in talking about this issue which they see as part of history not the present," according to the study.

In contrast, minority managers have a strongly differing view of corporate commitment. Minority managers reject white corporate manager views that insufficient qualified minorities explain the lack of progress. The minority managers see this explanation as a smokescreen that hides discriminatory and biased evaluations of minority performance. They feel that this is a matter of policy and practices, not just time. They felt that minorities face an invisible ceiling and had done their part in preparing themselves, and the responsibility now rests with companies. Without clear commitment by top management, nothing would happen, they said. The study found minority managers were particularly concerned about the limited accountability of middle managers for equal opportunity.

A study of graduates of the Sloan School of Massachusetts Institute of Technology compared career developments of women, minorities, and white males. The study of the business school graduates, published in 1989, found that "five years after graduation, Sloan women MBAs received the same pay as their male peers although the psychic costs to these women in stress and longer hours of work, was higher."

In contrast, after two years, the status of minorities started to differ from their white peers. More minorities were in staff jobs, fewer had mentors, more were dissatisfied by bureaucracy and red tape, and more felt constrained by discrimination. More minorities were only moderately satisfied with their jobs, and more were dissatisfied with their performance appraisals. Nearly all of the minority MBAs reported that they had not been promoted on time along with their work peers. After five years, minorities also tended to work longer hours per week then their Sloan peers. By the end of five years, the average salary of minority Sloan MBAs had only increased 29 percent compared to 41 percent for their white MBA classmates.

Nearly three-fifths of minority Sloan MBAs reported that they had to modify their behavior in order to fit into their organizations. The author of the study, Phyllis A. Wallace, professor of management emerita at the Sloan School, describes it as "overwhelming" for minority Sloan MBAs to face negative expectations of their success by peers, subordinates, and particularly their supervisors.

"In conclusion, minority Sloan MBAs were not as successful as their white Sloan counterparts." Some "realize that labor markets reflect the social norms of the larger society and that pioneers rarely benefit fully," Wallace wrote. "But discussions with Sloan minority graduates make it clear that employment, even for elite minority managers, is more difficult than for white managers. Race is still a powerful factor affecting upward mobility in corporate America."[5]

FAVORING SOME PROTECTED GROUPS

In 1986, this chapter's author addressed the issue of "substituting" in the Harvard Business Review:

> (B)lack managers are talking about "substituting the lesser evil." In their evident push to demonstrate progress toward equal opportunity some companies are promoting white women in lieu of black men and women. Many of the black managers I interviewed mentioned this phenomenon. At higher levels of organizations, white women have problems in achieving acceptance that in some ways are like those of blacks. Even so, race poses the bigger barrier. Since white women comprise 40 percent of the U.S. population, compared with blacks' 12 percent, they naturally should move into positions of power in greater numbers than blacks. What seems to be happening, however, is the movement upward of white women at the expense of blacks—men and women. Black managers are concluding that senior executives who are uncomfortable promoting blacks into positions of trust and confidence—those positions that lead to the top jobs—feel less reluctant to promote white females to these posts. "It's as if there is a mind-set that says, 'We have a couple of women near the executive suite—we've done our job,' and they dismiss competent blacks," one black executive said. "It's corporate apartheid," said another. "If the comfort level is a factor to enter the executive suite, white women will get there before blacks. After all, the mothers, wives, and daughters of top offi-

cers are white women, and they deal with white women all their lives—but only rarely with black men and women."[6]

Subsequent congressional testimony also has identified this substitution of one protected group in place of another. In October 1987, George Sape, a lawyer and former consultant testified: "What might be fair to characterize ... in the last few years with some confusion and some confusing signals sent by this administration to the business community, is that we might have a climate of indifference which stifles progress and creates a climate for inaction." Sape is a member of the steering committee of the Study Group on Affirmative Action and formerly with Organizational Resource Counselors, management counsultants. He also is a partner with the law firm of Epstein, Becker & Green.

Today, "managers believe they are fulfilling all of the mandates and requirements of affirmative action merely by counting the total number of non-white or non-male managers which means they are not really focusing on the specifics of what affirmative action was designed to address.... So, managers cite the number of women that they have in senior management, because in their mind they have satisfied the requirement because one of the groups protected and identified under the law is there in sufficient numbers, so therefore, the entire process must be working well. We know that that's not true."[7]

CONCLUSIONS AND RECOMMENDATIONS

America has made significant progress for groups such as European immigrants in opening doors of opportunity that had previously been closed. For example, the October 1986 Civil Rights Commission study, "The Economic Status of Americans of Southern and Eastern European Ancestry," found that "successive generations of European ethnic groups have made impressive gains in educational achievement and income and, in fact, are now on a par with, or surpass, the economic status of other white Americans even ... of British descent."

Unfortunately, for minorities of color and women, increasing research data on the experiences of the highly educated shows that America is at a critical economic and social juncture. The employment of highly educated, diverse Americans based on competence rather than comfort is the challenge facing the nation in the decades to come.

Success at large companies is particularly important because these international contenders, with immense financial, technological, and human resources, determine the outcome of economic competition with other countries.

More education is the solution only if the most highly educated are succeeding. The motivation for continuing and increasing education is the realization of greater expected payoffs. Unless all highly motivated, educated, and otherwise prepared Americans receive rewards and opportunities that make their educational efforts worthwhile, the motivation to continue these efforts is lost. Education and competence without opportunity creates frustration, crushed hopes, corrupted expectations, and conflict.

Moreover, if the best-educated Americans, representative of all groups, cannot make the nation's most valued ideals work, there is little motivation for those trapped in poverty and despair to attempt self help.

Black Americans, the group that was the primary motivation for employment legislation in 1964, appear to be still experiencing the least relative progress in 1989. America's most basic ideals are violated if members of some groups are more highly valued or deemed more worthy than members of other groups because of color, race, gender, or other features.

Functioning of a Diverse Workforce

People work together interdependently; they do not live within organizational vacuums. Cooperation with, and support of, others—peers, subordinates, bosses, and top-level executives—is critical to effectiveness and success. Regardless of intentions, no one can manage what is neither recognized nor understood. Organizational leaders must understand what happens when diverse people work together. They must understand how to create, develop, and manage diverse organizations. CEO's and other leaders need knowledge to successfully manage workforce diversity.

Behaviors that exclude certain groups are learned. Education on inclusive organizational behaviors must also be learned. Education is a critical prerequisite to progress. Progress in realizing equitable and inclusive American organizations, based on competence rather than comfort, habit, and tradition, is not adequately researched, theorized, written about, or taught. Equal employment opportunity involves human behavior, relationships, and social and behavioral science issues rooted in culture and history. In order to understand and evaluate the realities of equal employment opportunity and the individual in the workplace, companies must first understand the organization, the nature of management, and the nature of managerial work.

It is increasingly a matter of business success for companies to select executive leaders who have demonstrated their ability to build and to lead diverse, productive organizations as we enter the 21st century.

Specific instruction on these issues is not in books and is not included in executive education and training curriculums even in the leading schools and businesses. But increasingly, firms are seeking help. In corporations, in executive education programs, and in schools of business, managers must be taught how to handle these issues. Companies must make it a prerequisite selection criteria for future executive leaders to have demonstrated their ability to build and to manage the diverse and productive organizations required in the 21st century.

Too few firms identify equal opportunity as the strategic leadership, managerial, and productivity issue that it is today. Companies have accepted equal opportunity as a social, legal, and administrative matter. But too many companies focus on the process of equal opportunity, of learning to comply with formal rules and regulations, rather than on progress. The result of these approaches is that many companies have not gotten the best out of highly qualified minorities and women. Also, too many companies have failed to manage resentments and backlash by educating their entire workforce regarding the issues of diversity and equal opportunity.

America's litmus test on equal opportunity will not occur in menial, entry, or middle-level jobs, but within the high-prestige ranks of major corporations involving the best-prepared employees. Economic progress will be determined by the ability to succeed simultaneously and despite diversity, as individuals and as group members, within high-prestige positions.

Objectives

Some of the objectives that must be reached by organizations in order to achieve equal employment progress are:

- Recognizing the complex nature of managing diversity.
- Recognizing the differing experiences of minorities and women.
- Recognizing individuality and overcoming perceptions based in stereotypes, expectations, and assumptions.
- Consistency in applying judgment and avoiding the use of personal choices in place of professional organizational judgments.
- Consistent, long-term, leadership, resolve, and commitment.
- Selection of future executive leaders who have successfully created and managed effective diverse organizations.
- Education of managers and executives from the top down, alongside education of minorities and women.
- Acceptance of shared responsibility for limitations in progress. Success lies in selecting qualified employees

and then providing the climate and other conditions that make their full utilization and success possible.

ENDNOTES

[1] *The Wall Street Journal*, Sept. 29, 1989, p. A16, "Bush, Governors Agree at Summit to Set Performance Goals to Improve Education."

[2] William Brink and Lois Harris, *In The Negro Revolution In America* (Simon And Shuster, 1964), pp. 44-47.

[3] Carl Brauer, *John F. Kennedy and the Second Reconstruction* (New York: Columbia University Press, 1977).

[4] *Congressional Record*, March 30, 1964, pp. 6528-6547.

[5] Phyllis A. Wallace, *MBA's On The Fast Track* (New York: Ballenger Press, 1989).

[6] Edward W. Jones Jr., "Black Managers: The Dream Deferred," *Harvard Business Review* (May-June 1986), pp. 84-93.

[7] "Affirmative Action In The Work Force," Joint Hearing before the Subcommittee on Civil and Constitutional Rights of the Committee On The Judiciary, House of Representatives, One Hundredth Congress. Hearings held in Washington, D.C., Oct. 8, 1987. Pages 24-26, Document Serial No. 100-49, Committee On the Judiciary.

* * *

New Enforcement Initiatives
at the OFCCP

by Edmund D. Cooke Jr.*

The current corporate initiative of the Office of Federal Contract Compliance Programs (OFCCP) had its genesis in the spring of 1988 when the OFCCP's director and deputy director met with officials of a large corporation regarding restructure of that corporation's affirmative action plan. The corporation was asking whether the agency would be receptive to a reorganization of its plan so that all those positions subject to local hiring decision-making would be placed in the affirmative action plan of the local institution and those positions under the control of the corporation's headquarters would be placed in the headquarters' affirmative action plan.

The corporation's position was that it made no sense for managers to include in an affirmative action plan positions over which a particular establishment had no control. At the same time it made perfect sense for the entity with control over the position to be held accountable for the degree to which it complied with Executive Order 11246 in filling those and comparable positions.

The OFCCP officials attending the meeting responded that their sense was that the proposal was probably lawful and indeed desirable, but they suggested that the agency would have to subject the proposal to closer scrutiny and review before officially endorsing it.

---

*Edmund D. Cooke Jr. is a partner in the Washington, D.C., office of the law firm of Epstein, Becker & Green and served formerly as counsel to the House Education and Labor Committee.

PROCEDURAL CONCERNS

One early concern that grew out of the agency's preliminary internal discussions of the advisability of the matter was the solicitor's sense that the modification proposed might require a lengthy "notice and comment" procedure under the Administrative Procedures Act (5 U.S.C. ___). Officials also were concerned that the new procedure might generate additional paperwork burdens for employers in contravention of the Paperwork Reduction Act.

With respect to the rule-making issue raised by the solicitor's office, staff believed, and persuaded the solicitor, that the proposal constituted in most respects a refinement or refocusing of a policy the OFCCP already had been implementing under its current regulations. After assessing the modifications of affirmative action plans that might be required by the proposal, the OFFCP next determined that any additional burden on employers by virtue of the proposed policy would be minor and, moreover, would be more than offset by the program efficiency gains that would occur as a result of the more rational reporting format.

DIRECTIVE ISSUED

By late April 1988, the OFCCP had prepared a draft directive on "Corporate Level Selection Decisions," which was intended to provide OFCCP staff with policy guidance regarding corporate level affirmative action plans and the disposition of positions located at subordinate establishments where the selection decisions relating to such positions are made at the corporate level.

The document was circulated for comment in the early spring of 1988 and was issued as OFCCP Directive 830a1 and published for information purposes in the *Federal Register* on June 14, 1988. In response to employer comments, the directive in its final form accommodated employer concerns and made several changes. First, it permits greater flexibility where more than one level of a corporation participates in employment-related decisions or where that decision fluctuates between levels of the corporation.

Second, it provides guidance with respect to positions that are filled pursuant to a process involving multiple levels within the corporation. Finally, it provides corporations with more time and greater flexibility in coming into compliance with the requirements of the directive.

According to OFCCP senior staff, Directive 830a1 is essentially clarification of existing regulations codified at 41 CFR Part 60-2. Specifically, the notice cites as authority for the directive the requirement in those regulations that contractors prepare affirmative action plans for each of their establishments.[1] The explanatory material in the *Federal Register* notice indicates that most contractors, in preparing their affirmative action plan, must "place each job title into a job group, compare the race and sex composition of the incumbents of the job group against the availability for the job group, and when there is underutilization, establish goals, timetables and action-oriented programs for improving the level of employment of minorities and women."[2]

The explanatory material goes on to point out that "under existing practice, most contractors include all jobs in the affirmative action plan of the establishment in which the job is located."[3] Multi-establishment facilities have long faced a dilemma where high-level and technical jobs are concerned. Not infrequently, the recruitment and selection processes for such positions occur either at the corporate level, or in the case of centralized recruitment and hiring, jointly at the establishment and the corporate office level.

Where the selection for a given position occurs at the establishment level, it makes sense to place the affirmative action requirement there. Thus, it is logical to include that position in the establishment's affirmative action plan and, where appropriate, to create a goal regarding positions for which the establishment is responsible. But as the OFCCP argues in the explanatory statement issued in conjunction with the Directive, where the selection of a given position is made by the corporate office, it is "ineffective to establish in each plant's affirmative action plan a goal for the [position] ... at that plant because that plant has no control over the attainment of the goal."[4]

Specific Requirements

Directive 830a1 simply requires that equal employment opportunity specialists ensure that executive and highly technical positions of multi-establishment employers are included in affirmative action plans at the level where the actual employment decision-making occurs, whether at the corporate headquarters or at a particular facility involved. As the directive explains:

> ...equal opportunity specialists conducting a compliance review of a multi-establishment contractor's corporate office or intermediate level office must investigate and otherwise ensure that the affirmative action program of that office includes in its work force analysis, utilization analysis and goal setting ... all those positions located in subordinate and/or lower-level establishments for which these selection decisions are made at the establishment under review.

Lower-level establishments are directed to exclude from their utilization analysis and goal-setting those positions "for which the selection decisions are made at a higher corporate level."[5] In response to questions regarding corporations that have vague, indefinite, or fluctuating managerial and technical appointment schemes, the department instructs that "managerial and other appropriate titles should be placed in the affirmative action plan of the highest organizational level where ultimate approval authority may reside."[6] The directive stresses that management should be given "substantial discretion in determining proper organizational level for job placement," consistent with the general purposes of the directive.

Senior OFCCP officials have stressed that it is not their intent that OFCCP staff substitute their judgment regarding corporate organization for that of a corporation's management.

Indeed, one senior OFCCP official told BNA that "it's not our job to reorganize American industry" and that the agency's new corporate initiative will not become "a tool of unreasonable enforcement."[7] The agency also has stressed that it is not attempting to establish a national availability pool of corporate-level positions.

EQUAL OPPORTUNITY, UPWARD MOBILITY

As noted above, OFCCP Directive 830a1 was, according to senior OFCCP staff, a derivative of existing regulatory requirements governing how the OFCCP analyzes the affirmative action activity of federal contractors. Thus, it is in one sense not new, but in another sense quite new. It will enable the agency, for the first time, to focus and assist corporations in responding to the requirement that federal contractors ensure all employees equal opportunity with respect to promotion and upward mobility related employment decisions, much as it has in the past with respect to hiring and termination decisions.

Barriers to upward mobility, the so-called "glass ceiling," have significantly impeded the progress of qualified minorities and women. These barriers are what this newly articulated tool may over time begin to impact. As the OFCCP *Federal Register* notice regarding its corporate-level selection decisions directive notes, "the purpose of No. 830a1 is to foster affirmative action in high-level managerial, professional and technical jobs." And as noted above, the corporate policy achieves this objective by focusing affirmative action and related enforcement activities "where the authority and responsibility for filling positions is located, rather than arbitrarily ... at each position site of employment."[8]

Changing Workforce Demographics

The *Workforce 2000* study, prepared by the Hudson Institute for the Labor Department's Employment Standards Administration, reports that by the year 2000, workforce demographics will be dramatically different from those of the 1980's. The number of available workers will decrease, and the proportion of women and minority workers will increase significantly, constituting the vast majority of new job entrants by the year 2000.[9] Indeed, by the year 2000, roughly 47 percent of the U.S. workforce will be female, and nearly a third of all new entrants into the workforce will be minorities.[10]

Notwithstanding this inevitable surge of minorities and women into the workforce, not enough has been or is currently being done to recruit, hire, and retain minorities and women at all levels of the corporate environment. Discussing this "glass ceiling" phenomenon, the Department of Labor's *Opportunity 2000* report noted:

> Women with their eye on top management positions in larger corporations often find their male colleagues have more credibility with the established leadership team, especially if that team consists of men aged 50 and older whose wives have remained at home throughout their marriage. The data suggest that such barriers may be more real than individual success stories would indicate: Fewer than two percent of officers in the Fortune 500 companies are women. Nor do trends appear to be improving.

Corporations, to successfully meet the challenges that the workforce demographics of the year 2000 and beyond appear certain to present, must, as the *Opportunity 2000* report observes, "recognize the emergence of a multi-cultural workforce and take steps to deal with the challenges and opportunities which it represents." In this regard the report is instructive:[11]

> Companies must take steps not only to recruit minorities and the economically disadvantaged, but to ensure their meaningful participation in the workplace. Again, this is no longer solely a matter of law or morality but of competitive necessity. For a company's failure to retain such employees or to provide opportunities for upward mobility is a waste of increasingly scarce human capital. And in a tight labor market in which minorities and the economically disadvantaged make up a growing portion of new labor entrants, companies must view such individuals — indeed all individuals — not only as entry-level employees but as prospective professionals, supervisors, managers, and officers. And they must take steps to

make sure minorities and the economically disadvantaged have access to those opportunities.

THE POLICY—HOW IT OPERATES

According to the Department of Labor, its principal objective in adopting Directive 830a1 was to adapt its current affirmative action compliance procedures to the realities of the workforce regarding how employers, particularly large employers, are organized as well as regarding how they manage hiring and promotions. As the department observes in the summary information portion of the notice published in the *Federal Register*, the selection of candidates for certain jobs at one or more of its several establishments may be made at the corporate, rather than at the establishment, level.

In the past, such positions were typically included in the affirmative action plan of the establishment where they were located. Thus, the plant manager, while selected by the corporate office, would be listed as a position in the affirmative action plan of the establishment for which he is responsible. While it is obvious that managers may be selected in this manner, it is less apparent but equally likely that there would be centralized recruitment and hiring by corporations for a variety of other skilled and technical kinds of positions.

As implemented, the directive requires that positions filled pursuant to decisions made at the establishment level be included in the affirmative action plan of the establishment. Positions filled pursuant to the decisions made at the lower level establishment, but which are subject to approval or other action at the corporate level should "be placed in the affirmative action plan of the highest organizational level where ultimate approval authority resides." Notwithstanding these general guidelines, the directive instructs that "management should be given substantial discretion in determining proper authorization levels for job title placement provided such placement is not inconsistent with the purpose of this directive."[12]

The department has recognized that it is often unclear precisely who makes the selection decision with respect to high-level and technical positions. With respect to such positions, it has informally instructed its equal opportunity specialists and advised contractors that when in doubt about which level makes the decision, "roll [the position] up to the corporate level." If a given decision is made at both the establishment level and at the corporate level from time to time but the ultimate decision is usually made at the corporate level, then include it in the corporate level affirmative action plan. In the latter circumstance, "control" over the personnel action is usually at headquarters. Thus, it is more appropriate that the position be included in the headquarter's affirmative action plan than in the affirmative action plan of a facility with no real control over the hiring decision.

OFCCP CORPORATE INITIATIVE

As has been noted several times, one principal purpose of Directive 830a1 is "to foster affirmative action in high level managerial, professional and technical jobs." To accomplish this objective, the directive appears, as an initial matter, to be attempting to foster greater management accountability for personnel actions. The directive also will have the effect, however, of increasing the size of high-level managerial and technical job groups, making underutilization in those groups more susceptible to statistical significance analyses and to goals.

In the past a single establishment's affirmative action program (AAP) may have listed a plant manager as in a job group consisting of one employee, multi-establishment employers may have a number of plant managers or individuals in comparable positions. Under the new Directive 830a1, these jobs collectively will constitute a job category for which affirmative action analyses can be conducted and with respect to which goals and timetables, where appropriate, can realistically be set. A similar result will occur with respect to other managerial and technical positions for which an extremely small number of positions at a corporation's individual establishments typically made affirmative action goals and timetables unrealistic.

The department is attempting to make its imposition of these new requirements as painless as possible. Contractors were not required to amend their affirmative action plans until the expiration of their current plans or until 90 days from June 14, 1988, whichever is later. The department has stressed repeatedly that it is not attempting to tell corporations how they should organize themselves, but rather, is attempting to require that their affirmative action plans "reflect the actual decision making process" of the particular corporation.

Jobs located at one establishment but required by operation of the directive to be listed in another establishment's affirmative action plan need only be listed in the affirmative action plan of the facility that makes the selection for the job for purposes of utilization analysis, goals, timetables, and other action-oriented programs. The position is merely listed in the workforce analysis section of both affirmative action plans to enable the OFCCP to keep track of all jobs—to know where the position functions in the corporate scheme.

The directive leaves unchanged the procedure for determining availability. Each job group, including any new job groups that emerge by operation of the directive, must still be analyzed on the basis of the eight-factor availability analysis set forth in the Department of Labor's affirmative action regulations.[13] Similarly, the directive does not change in any significant way how the department will conduct affirmative action compliance reviews. The data it reviews, however, will often be slightly different since it may include heretofore unrecognized positions for which selections are made at the headquarters facility level but which do not exist at the corporate level.

The department's senior staff stressed that affirmative action is no longer merely a compliance requirement or a matter of social responsibility, it is "a fundamental management tool" that businesses must learn to use in order to cope with changing workforce demographics that the nation will face by the year 2000.[14] Women and minorities are expected to make up nearly 80 percent of the workers entering the workforce by the year 2000, making their prompt and total integration into the workforce a national priority and a matter of critical concern.[15] For this reason, the department's training for equal opportunity specialists and its redrafted compliance manual target those aspects of the employment scheme critical to successful recruitment and retention of minorities and women.

Training in Investigation and Compliance

During July 1988, the OFCCP conducted a three-week training session for its equal opportunity specialists. The principal objective of the training was to standardize the application of the agency's policies to employers. However, the training emphasized investigation techniques that facilitate and complement the agency's new interest in assisting employers in attracting and promoting women and minorities into technical, administrative, and executive positions. Thus, in many respects, the impact of the new corporate initiative will go beyond merely redefining how various upper- and middle-management positions are included in a corporation's affirmative action plan.

Desk audits, outlined in Chapter 2 of the *OFCCP Compliance Manual*, constitute a major component of the agency's compliance activity. The agency regards the desk audit as an efficient way of reviewing a contractor's compliance with its affirmative action obligations, permitting the agency to know, without going to the work site, the employer's basic structure, personnel policies and procedures. Desk audits also enable the agency to initially assess an employer's good-faith effort to comply with its equal employment obligations and to identify areas of potential discrimination that may require further investigation.[16]

In conjunction with desk audits, equal opportunity specialists are instructed to ensure that "the workforce analysis, utilization analysis and goals in the corporate headquarters AAP include all positions filled or concurred in at the headquarters-level, regardless of where those jobs are physically located."[17] The specialists will therefore be expected to determine that every position in the corporation is included in the affirmative action plan at the corporate level except for those positions where the hiring, firing, and promotion decisions are made at an establishment other than the corporate headquarters. In other words, as the manual explains "the managerial and other appropriate titles should be placed in the AAP of the highest organizational level where ultimate approval [or, presumably, related decision-making] authority may reside."[18]

This assessment occurs in the context of the agency's standard operating procedures for conducting desk audits and compliance reviews. Other compliance manual instructions will contribute to the effectiveness of the agency's implementation of the corporate initiative. For example, information provided relating to the employer's workforce is to be by job title. Each job title "must show the total number of persons in the job title, the total number of men and of women and the total number of men and of women in each of the following groups: Blacks, Hispanics, Asians/Pacific Islanders, and American Indians/Alaska Natives. All job titles, including managerial job titles must be listed."

The manual also instructs that "[t]he wage rate or salary range for each job title must be given ..." and "... [that] [t]itles must be listed in wage rate or range order within department or other similar organizational units."[19] Such data viewed collectively also enables the agency to assess where minorities and women are in the organization and to determine whether job titles assigned to women and minorities correspond to the wages paid to others holding comparable titles. The agency instructs that it will scrutinize more closely job groups that combine jobs in which women and minorities are heavily concentrated with job groups in which they are not, so as to ensure that underutilization is not obscured.

The availability analysis is also sensitive to the issue of up-ward mobility for women and minorities, providing for, in one of its "factors," an assessment of the availability of promotable and transferable minorities and women within the contractor's organization. This factor requires the employer to look at so-called "feeder" job groups from which individuals can reason-ably be expected to be promoted or transferred into higher job categories. Equal opportunity specialists are instructed to iden-tify such feeder job groups by determining where people who were previously promoted or transferred into a given job group came from. The number or percentage of minorities or women found to be in a feeder group then constitutes a base from which an employer assesses his utilization as well as on which he sets goals, if necessary.[20]

Underutilization

Underutilization is defined as "having fewer minorities or women in a particular job group than would reasonably be ex-pected by their availability."[21] The greater concentration on non-entry level positions, on promotion and on internal trans-fers by OFCCP will intensify the employer's awareness of the utilization rates for women and minorities in these upper-level technical, middle-management, and administrative positions. Thus, Directive 830a1 articulates a shift in focus of the agency's compliance activity from a monitoring of entry level positions to a critical assessment of an employer's promotion and upward mobility policies and practices.

The OFCCP regulations require the development and exe-cution of "action oriented programs" that must be designed to correct problem areas.[22] In this regard, the regulations require the establishment of goals and affirmative action objectives to "correct identifiable deficiencies."[23] When those requirements are considered in conjunction with the requirements of Direc-tive 830a1 the result can be action-oriented and "result ori-ented programs required by the compliance manual but focus-ing on the technical, administrative, and middle- and upper-level management positions that many believe have been neglected by prior OFCCP compliance activity."

The basic requirements of the regulations are the same whether the equal opportunity specialist is conducting a desk audit or an on-site compliance review. The compliance manual suggests that the analysis that occurs in conjunction with an on-site compliance review will not differ radically from the analysis that occurs with a desk audit. The basic job group, availability, and utilization analyses conducted on-site should be the same as the desk audit and will be influenced by Directive 830a1. The regulations, and indeed the compliance manual, have long required analyses directed at both the availability and the utilization of minorities throughout the employer's workforce. What has changed is the agency's policy, which now requires its specialists to focus on positions largely neglected in the past.

Requirements for Employers

Portions of the revised compliance manual that discuss new construction industry compliance contain provisions dealing with employers.

The policy requires contractors to inventory and evaluate minority and female employees for promotional opportunities and encourage them to seek the kind of training and preparation necessary for anticipated promotional opportunities. In this regard, equal opportunity specialists are instructed to review the contractor's policies and personnel procedures regarding upgrading and promotion and its recent promotions for the purpose of determining whether minority and/or female employees were or should have been considered for any of the positions that were filled. Again, the requirement that employers engage in non-discrimination with respect to promotion has always been a part of the regulations and indeed has been a part of the compliance process. It is the OFCCP's recently adopted policy focusing on upward mobility for women and minorities as a way of ensuring growth and diversity of the workplace that is different.[24]

The agency's effectiveness in implementing its corporate initiative and achieving its stated upward mobility objective will turn heavily on its capacity to analyze employers' personnel processes effectively, assessing both the objective criteria and the subjective criteria relied on in making personnel decisions. The compliance manual instructs specialists to determine first, whether the criteria as applied have a significantly adverse impact on a minority group or women and thereafter, whether the imposition of objective and subjective criteria result in differential or "disparate" treatment of minorities or women in the selection process.

Objective criteria are typically easier to assess because they can generally be applied to and by different people with the same results. Subjective criteria depend, however, on the application of judgment and, as a consequence, can differ from individual to individual. Equal opportunity specialists are instructed to look first at objective criteria and where disparities continue to exist, to look at subjective criteria. Directive 830a1 creates no new considerations in regard to the assessment of objective and subjective promotion decisions. It merely creates the possibility that upper-level hiring and promotion disparities will be more apparent and that these compliance criteria will now be applied to issues relating to promotion and upward mobility of women and minorities.

Procedures Largely Retained

The agency's basic approach to conducting desk audits and compliance reviews and for computing availability, utilization, and goal-setting remains unchanged. The difference is that now under Directive 830a1, certain positions will appear in a single job group at the corporate level rather than appearing in several affirmative action plans nationwide. Thus, the actual availability figure for the corporate entity will likely vary from where those jobs were previously listed.

Moreover, the new Directive actually does not impose additional requirements on contractors except insofar as it requires that jobs for which selections are not made locally be listed in the workforce analyses of both the corporate and the establishment entities. As noted previously, the directive does not tell a contractor how to make its staffing decisions or who within the corporation's organization should make them. It simply requires that the affirmative action plan reflect who is actually making the employment decisions. Beyond that, the directive states that "[m]anagement should be given substantial discretion in determining proper organizational levels for job title placement ...."[25]

Corporations should review the process by which their personnel decisions are made and have a clear, and defensible, statement regarding where such decisions are made. This assessment should be made with due consideration for the corporation's administrative needs and for the affirmative action goals and action-oriented programs it may be required to undertake. Such a requirement would be a consequence of newly determined underutilization resulting from the reformatting of job groups that occurs in compliance with Directive 830a1.

Careful planning in advance of compliance activity will be critical. Careful assessment should be made of the consequences to the corporation of determining that hiring and termination authority for a given position will be retained at a "higher" level. The corporation will thereafter be held responsible by the OFCCP for the implementation of goals and timetables for such positions. Thus, the determination of personnel authority in many respects will now constitute an assignment responsibility for personnel compliance with the requirements of Executive Order 11246.

EEOC POLICY

While the Equal Employment Opportunity Commission has for some time had an interest in the issue of upward mobility and promotional opportunities for women and minorities, it has no formalized program of the sort initiated at the OFCCP. In early 1988, the commission announced hearings on the advancement of minorities and women in corporate America. But, apparently due to budget constraints, those hearings never occurred.

In the process of planning the hearings, the EEOC accumulated a good deal of information regarding attitudes and perceptions on the part of corporate decision-makers affecting the employment opportunities of women and minorities. Little else has occurred at the commission respecting the issue of promotion and upward mobility of women from a policy perspective. The commission senior staff indicates that the commission has continued to attempt to ensure non-discrimination in corporate upward mobility for women and minorities by including it in its oversight activities as well as in its enforcement activities.

The commission does not routinely require corporations to maintain affirmative action plans. It does, however, routinely request such plans when investigating individual and systemic charges of discrimination.

Role of the Agency

The EEOC was established by the Civil Rights Act of 1964 to administer Title VII of that act. The agency was given no direct enforcement power, authority to adjudicate claims or to impose administrative sanctions. It was, however, given the authority to investigate charges of discrimination, and where it had reasonable cause to believe that a violation of Title VII had occurred, to "endeavor to eliminate any such alleged unlawful employment practice by informal methods of conference, conciliation and persuasion."[26]

The EEOC has been designated by Congress as the lead agency with respect to enunciation and interpretation of equal opportunity employment policy and law and is principally charged with interpreting Title VII. In this regard, it has promulgated procedural regulations and substantive guidelines, codified at 29 CFR Part 1600.

Relationship with OFCCP

The courts and other agencies with responsibility for employment discrimination law enforcement typically accord the EEOC interpretations and guidelines substantial deference. The OFCCP, for example, attempts to define its jurisdiction and authority in terms of and consistent with Title VII and interpreted by the EEOC and the courts. In the OFCCP chapter of its compliance manual, it sets forth policies on proving and remedying employment discrimination and explains the techniques its staff are to use in analyzing whether employment discrimination exists. It states that "it is OFCCP's policy to interpret the non-discrimination requirements of Executive Order 11246, as amended, in a manner consistent with Title VII principles."[27]

The OFCCP and the EEOC have a letter of understanding detailing how the agencies will share information relating to charges of discrimination. Under the letter, the EEOC is responsibile principally for procesing individual charges of discrimination, and the OFCCP's responsibility involves addressing class-action discrimination charges. In general, compliance with EEOC charge-processing procedures will satisfy comparable kinds of requirements under the OFCCP procedures. Similarly, the evidence necessary to prove a charge of discrimination under Title VII is sufficient to prove discrimination under Executive Order 11246. That is, the factual evidence necessary to show that discrimination has occurred under a particular theory of discrimination is typically the same whether based on Executive Order 11246 or on Title VII of the Civil Rights Act of 1964. The remedial relief generally available is, for the most part, identical under the two laws. For example, the Department of Labor has adopted Title VII's two-year restriction on recovery of back pay and, like Title VII, requires mitigation of damages and offset of earnings received by a victim during that period.

The EEOC may issue subpoenas pursuant to its investigative function[28] and obtain enforcement of such subpoenas against an employer where the employer does not voluntarily comply with the request for information. The agency may request specific information concerning alleged discriminatory practices even where there has been no prior showing of any evidentiary foundation for the allegations of discrimination. Moreover, the EEOC subpoena power is not limited to the production of existing documents. It has broad authority to require "the production of any evidence," including evidence that does not exist in written or documentary form.[29]

The EEOC may file and litigate civil actions in federal court against employers that it believes to have violated Title VII. In a recent EEOC directive on enforcement policy, the commission asserts its intent to litigate each case in which it finds reasonable cause to believe that discrimination has occurred and where conciliation has failed. The objective of this policy, according to EEOC, is to strengthen its enforcement program by ensuring the predictability and certainty of EEOC enforcement where the agency believes that a law over which it has jurisdiction has been violated.

Individuals believing they have been discriminated against in violation of Title VII must file a written, sworn statement alleging the nature of the violation and setting forth a factual basis for their charge. The charge must be filed within 180 days of the alleged act of discrimination. In states or other defined localities that have fair employment practice commissions (deferral states and deferral agencies)—to which EEOC must defer for a statutory 180-day period—the change must be filed within 300 days of the alleged discriminatory act.

Title VII provides for a 60-day period of exclusive state jurisdiction over discrimination complaints. Charges filed with EEOC prior to filing with a state's fair employment practice commissions will be deferred to the state agency prior to EEOC asserting jurisdiction over the charge.

This EEOC process can potentially be paired with OFCCP policy on upward mobility at several stages. The new information and formatting of information relating to job groups and the placement of such jobs in affirmative action plans can be of extreme value to the EEOC at the investigation stage of its charge processing. Similarly, it is clear the conciliations will take account of numerical changes in the constituencies of job groups that result from corporate compliance with OFCCP Directive 830a1. Similarly, the newly formulated data may have an impact on the results of the EEOC's fact-finding activities as well as on its enforcement activity and remedial relief formulated as a consequence of that enforcement activity.

The existence of the EEOC's "right-to-sue" letter creates a sort of dual enforcement scheme, which presents the possibility that private litigants may, through the discovery process, obtain employer's AAPs and enforce the OFCCP upward mobility policy indirectly through their litigation activities. That is, to the extent that the OFCCP corporate initiative facilitates that agency's oversight, enforcement and remedial activity, it will also facilitate EEOC's oversight (compliance) and enforcement activities as well as that of private Title VII plaintiffs.

By redefining job groups and clarifying corporate personnel organizational schemes (notwithstanding that the form of such schemes remain the sole discretion of the corporation), it also expands potential affirmative action remedial schemes and, in any event, will generate a clearer assignment of personnel and equal employment opportunity compliance responsibilities. This redefinition and clarification of corporate personnel-related activity benefits not only the OFCCP, which is requiring it, but also the EEOC, which has largely identical concerns, a comparable enforcement scheme, and parallel non-discrimination objectives.

There also exists a strong potential that state and local fair employment practice agencies will adopt similar kinds of requirements for contractors with respect to whom they do business and over private-sector employers operating under their laws. Or they may incorporate in their employment practices a review of the data that employers now will maintain by virtue of Executive Order 11246. Thus, it seems clear that Directive 830a1 will have ramifications beyond those that flow from the OFCCP and compliance activity.

SUMMARY

In some respects, the OFCCP's new corporate initiative is only a small component of the agency's attempt to encourage corporations to ensure the access of women and minorities to the corporation's technical, administrative, and mid- and upper-level management positions. The agency's concern is clearly generated by information and data that has been provided to it in the *Workforce 2000* report completed by the Hudson Institute pursuant to contract with the department. These reports indicate with alarming clarity the consequence of the nation's failure to ensure the integration of women and minorities into the workforce and at all levels. The corporate initiative assists the agency to foster a more positive result by requiring a more rational reporting of data. As reorganized AAP's become an enforcement tool, closer attention to corporate personnel-related activity becomes imperative. Management must assess the ramifications of disclosing the level of actual decision-making because it subsequently will be held accountable for the decision and the resulting staffing demographics.

Implementation of the directive may generate the necessity for goals respecting positions for which such affirmative action was previously unnecessary. As a consequence, it may be necessary to develop and implement new kinds of "action-oriented" affirmative action techniques. Availability calculations may need to be accomplished for the first time or with more precision for positions previously regarded and protected from obligation analyses because of the small number of positions in a given job category.

Corporations will be well advised to determine carefully where personnel decision-making authority resides because those responsible must be aware of and prepared to demonstrate their responsiveness to the affirmative action requirements now attached to upper-tier (non-entry level) positions. Recall that on-site compliance reviews conducted by both the OFCCP and the EEOC can involve interviews with such individuals regarding their understanding of the corporation's affirmative action obligations.

The agency will focus reviews on upper-tier positions. An effort should be made to familiarize and involve selecting officials (managers) in the recruitment process, because given serious underutilization, such efforts constitute the corporation's principal "good-faith effort" defense. The credibility of such a defense may well turn on the thoroughness of such managers' knowledge of not only corporate recruitment policy, but, more importantly, corporate recruitment practices over the relevant time period.

In that regard, evidence that the corporation has aggressively extended hiring or promotion opportunity respecting upper-tier positions to women and minorities (irrespective of whether such offers are accepted) will constitute significant effort of "good faith effort" where underutilization persists. Similar benefits can be derived from other "action-oriented" practices such as aggressive recruitment policies and practices as well as from ensuring the availability and equality of access of training and educational programs that will enable minorities and women to qualify for and succeed in the positions on which the directive will enable the OFCCP to focus.

The new directive also creates an opportunity for corporations to identify and target for affirmative action the positions respecting which they must do better. The long-term benefit of such action is now clear. Indeed, many corporations understand that workforce integration, which the directive seeks to foster, is essential to creating the productive workforce critical to our national competitiveness now, in the year 2000, and beyond.

ENDNOTES

[1] 41 CFR 60–2.1(a).

[2] 41 CFR 60–2.11, 60–2.12, 60–2.13.

[3] Ibid.

[4] Ibid.

[5] Ibid. and *See* 60–2.11(a), (b) and 60–2.12.

[6] Ibid.

[7] *See* 1988 DLR152:A–3

[8] *See Federal Register*, volume 53, sub 123, June 28, 1988.

[9] *See*, for example, *Opportunity 2000*, supra, and *Workforce 2000*, supra.

[10] Ibid.

[11] *Opportunity 2000*, supra, page 89.

[12] OFCCP Order 830a1 June 14, 1988.

[13] *See* 41 CFR 60–2.11.

[14] Statement of Secretary of Labor, Ann McLaughlin, before sixth National Conference of Industry Liaison Groups as reported in BNA, Affirmative Action Compliance Manual, "News and Developments," No. 116 (Oct. 31, 1988) p.7.

[15] Dept. of Labor, *Workforce 2000*.

[16] *OFCCP Compliance Manual*, Chapter 2, Page 2–1.

[17] *See* Chapter 2, *OFCCP Compliance Manual* sub–paragraph 2 C05, page 2–9. The manual explains further regarding corporate level selection decisions that "[f]or example, mid and upper–level management jobs in establishments other than headquarters must be included in the corporate AAP if the selection decisions for those jobs are made at the corporate level."

[18] *OFCCP Compliance Manual* Chapter 2, sub–paragraph 2C05(b).

[19] *OFCCP Compliance Manual,* Chapter 2, Section 2G01 (b)(1).

[20] *See OFCCP Compliance Manual* 2G05(f), page 2–24.

[21] *See* "OFCCP Affirmative Action Regulations," 41 CFR 60–2.11(b).

[22] *See* 41 CFR 60–2.13(f) and 41 CFR 60–2.24.

[23] *See* 41 CFR 60–2.13(e).

[24] *See Compliance Manual* or I03(d) *Promotion Policies* page 4–17.

[25] *See* Directive 830A1.

[26] 42 USC §2000e–5(b).

[27] *OFCCP Compliance Manual,* Chapter 7, subsection 7A06 Applicable Law, p. 7–3.

[28] 42 USC §200e–9.

[29] *See EEOC v. Maryland Cup Corporation,* 785F sec. 471 (4th Cir.), Cert denied, 107 S.Ct. 68(1986). *See,* also, *EEOC v. Shell Oil Co.,* 466 US.54 (1984).

* * *

Legal Standards for Subjective Criteria and Promotions

By William J. Kilberg and Stephen E. Tallent*

Many promotion decisions are based on the employer's observations and judgments about the employee's previous job performance. Hiring decisions necessarily often are based on job candidates' credentials and their scores on objective tests, but decisions to promote properly involve subjective factors, and they serve to help evaluate the original decision to hire the employee. Relying on the large amount of information the company has obtained about employees since they were hired is a helpful and effective method of deciding which employee to promote.

Although information based on personal observation may be plentiful and useful, it also is necessarily subjective — it reflects judgments by employers regarding the accuracy and relevancy of their observations. The complexity of the data considerably increases as its volume and subjectivity increases, often making it impossible to determine what motivated conclusions such as "too aggressive," "disloyal," "unoriginal," "tactless," or "not partnership material." At management and professional levels, subjective evaluations of characteristics such as loyalty, skills in dealing with people, and general attitude become the essential criteria for advancement.

---

*William J. Kilberg is a partner in the Washington, D.C., office of Gibson, Dunn & Crutcher. He has served as solicitor for the U.S. Department of Labor and as special assistant to the secretary of labor. Stephen E. Tallent is a senior partner with Gibson, Dunn & Crutcher. He specializes in labor and employment law and has written and lectured extensively on those topics.

As part of the social changes of the past 30 years, an impulse to consider affirmative action has emerged among the subjective criteria in promotion decisions. The United States is not free from discrimination, and many employers have programs to increase minority representation in labor and management. These programs coincide with an increase in minority and female representation in the workforce.[1] As the U.S. economy requires workers to have increasingly higher education and skill levels, the growing numbers of non-whites and women in the workforce who lack the necessary education and skills must receive more education and training. In a competitive market, economic need and demographics encourage employers to hire and advance disadvantaged workers and others traditionally excluded from employment and promotions if they are willing and able to master the jobs for which they are needed.

The complexity of the promotion decision—including affirmative action concerns—makes it a difficult subject to analyze under employment discrimination laws.[2] Recent U.S. Supreme Court decisions on employment discrimination have addressed several important issues regarding the decision to promote an employee. These issues include:

- Proof of intent to discriminate, especially in the affirmative action context;
- The application of statistical proof to subjective criteria;
- The level of specificity required to prove causation; and
- Allocating the burden of proving or disproving the job-relatedness of promotion criteria.[3]

EMPLOYMENT DISCRIMINATION DICHOTOMY

Since 1971, the principal dichotomy in employment discrimination suits brought under Title VII of the Civil Rights Act of 1964 has been between disparate treatment—in which plaintiffs must prove that the defendant intended to discriminate against them—and disparate impact—where the defendant's intent need not be proven and defendants can be required to prove that they did not discriminate against the plaintiff.

Disparate Treatment

Disparate treatment analysis flows directly from the language of Title VII; that is, the employer has failed to promote the plaintiff or plaintiffs because of an impermissible fact such as race or gender. The hallmark of the disparate treatment case, therefore, is proof that the employer held the impermissible motive, and that this motive caused the failure to promote. Proof may be direct or circumstantial. The latter may include statistical proof of a disparity between the numbers of minority and non-minority members in the workforce. Courts have applied this analysis to individual plaintiffs and to classes of employees.

The Supreme Court established the framework of disparate treatment analysis where direct evidence of intent is absent in *McDonnell Douglas Corp. v. Green*, 411 U.S. 792, 93 S. Ct. 1817, 36 L.Ed.2d 668 (1973), and refined it in *Texas Department of Community Affairs v. Burdine*, 450 U.S. 248, 101 S. Ct. 1089, 67 L.Ed.2d 207 (1981). The *McDonnell Douglas/Burdine* framework balances the competing goals of preserving the employer's discretion and safeguarding the employee's civil rights by manipulating a series of burdens at trial. Plaintiffs bear the primary burden of proving intent and causation throughout the litigation. *Burdine*, 450 U.S. at 253. Consequently, the first step is theirs: "the plaintiff's initial burden, which is 'not onerous,' is to ... create a presumption of unlawful discrimination by 'eliminate[ing] the most common non-discriminatory reasons for the plaintiff's rejection.'" *Wards Cove Packing Co. v. Atonio*, 57 LW 4583, 4590 (1989) (Stevens dissenting) (*Citing Burdine*, 450 U.S. at 253, 254).

If the plaintiff establishes this prima facie case, the employer must meet it by "articulate[ing] some legitimate, nondiscriminatory reason for the employee's rejection." *Wards Cove*, 57 LW at 4590 (Stevens dissenting) (*Citing, McDonnell Douglas*, 411 U.S. at 802, *see Burdine*, 450 U.S. at 254). This requires only the production of evidence; defendants need not persuade the fact-finder that their motives were legitimate.

If defendants meet their burden of production, the plaintiff is then accorded an opportunity to rebut the purported reason for the failure to promote by showing it to be a pretext for discrimination. *Wards Cove*, 57 LW at 4590 (Stevens, J., dissenting) (*Citing, McDonnell Douglas*, 411 U.S. at 804-805, *Burdine*, 450 U.S. at 256).

Disparate Impact

In disparate impact situations, first addressed by the Supreme Court in *Griggs v. Duke Power Co.*, 401 U.S. 424, 91 S. Ct. 849, 28 L.Ed.2d 158 (1971), job candidate selection criteria that are neutral on their face cause racial minorities or women to be rejected for jobs at rates greater than those at which they are represented in the otherwise qualified workforce. In *Griggs*, Duke Power Co. used largely irrelevant criteria to screen out blacks. The company had responded to Title VII by requiring job candidates to have a high school diploma and to pass a written intelligence test, both of which harmed blacks' chances to get a job. Because the requirements were adopted shortly after the Civil Rights Act of 1964 was passed, the plaintiffs probably could have proven under disparate treatment that the company adopted them at least in part to enable it to reject black job candidates. The court, however, chose not to require plaintiffs to prove that defendants' intent in this type of case is to discriminate. In *Griggs*, the court focused instead on the "*consequences* of employment practices, not simply the motivation." *Griggs*, 401 U.S. at 432 (emphasis in original). "The objective of Congress in the enactment of Title VII," Chief Justice Warren Burger declared, "...was to achieve equality of employment opportunities...." *Griggs*, 401 U.S. at 429.

To help achieve this broad goal, the court held that selection devices that the plaintiff had shown "operated to render ineligible a markedly disproportionate number of Negroes" must be justified by a "business necessity." *Griggs* 401 U.S. 429-430, 431. This shifted a very serious burden onto the employer because "business necessity" (that is, the fact that if this device were not used, the employer could not find enough qualified people to fill job openings) has been extremely difficult to prove. Except for attacking the plaintiff's prima facie showing of disparate impact, however, "business necessity" was the only defense to a disparate impact claim contemplated in *Griggs*.

In impact cases, the employer also must prove the job-relatedness or non-disparate impact of each selection device. Use of affirmative action to redress the disparate impact of a particular selection device on a group of applicants will not save that test from condemnation, because Title VII protects "employment opportunities" for the individual, not racial balance between or among groups. Consequently, "[a] racially balanced work force cannot immunize an employer from liability for specific acts of discrimination". *Connecticut v. Teal*, 457 U.S. 440, 448, 454, 102 S. Ct. 2525, 2531, 2534 (1982).

The court's reasoning in *Griggs'* resulted in the doctrine that disparate impact represents a type of Title VII case restricted to a peculiar factual situation. It was considered limited to the type of objective selection devices (written tests and educational requirements) that had been used by Duke Power. Personal judgments, commonly used by managers to help decide who gets promoted, were considered too complex and difficult to be subjected to the broad presumptions inherent in *Griggs*.

THE COLLAPSING DICHOTOMY

The Supreme Court affirmed the applicability of traditional disparate treatment analysis to reverse discrimination claims while upholding an affirmative action plan in *Johnson v. Trans-*

portation Agency, 480 U.S. 616, 626 (1987).[4] The court found that the plaintiff had shown a prima facie case of disparate treatment because gender was a motivating factor in the employer's decision. The employer, however, met its burden of articulating a non-discriminatory rationale for its decision by citing its affirmative action program. Applying the *McDonnell Douglas* framework, the court concluded that the employer had sufficiently justified its plan to show that it was not a pretext for discriminating against men. The court found that the plan was tailored so as not to trammel the rights of the majority because it was designed to be temporary; it did not bar all white males from advancement, nor did it involve discharge of whites, and the employer was able to point to a "conspicuous ... imbalance in traditionally segregated job categories," which its plan was designed to redress. *Johnson*, 480 U.S. at 630. These factors led the court to conclude that the plan was not a mere mask for a discriminatory intent.[5]

In *Price Waterhouse v. Hopkins*, 57 LW 4469 (1989), the court addressed the sufficiency of evidence necessary to establish a prima facie case of disparate treatment where the employer's motives were mixed. The case arose when the employer, a prominent accounting firm, held over for reconsideration and then denied for partnership a female senior manager. The firm's national admissions committee made the decision on the recommendation of partners in the office where the woman worked and after consideration of written comments by partners who had come into contact with her.

Hopkins was widely praised in the comments for her "character as well as her accomplishments," the trial record discloses. "On too many occasions, however, Hopkins' aggressiveness apparently spilled over into abrasiveness." *Hopkins*, 57 LW at 4471. It was in relation to this characteristic that partners submitted written comments, some unidentified and few of which were described by the plaintiff's expert witness as tainted subconsciously with sex-based stereotypes.

As a consequence of the inclusion of these comments among the material used to reject Hopkins as a partner, a U.S. district court found that the employer's motives for denying her a partnership were influenced to an uncertain degree by impermissible sexual stereotyping. Thus, gender was deemed to be one criteria that entered into the employer's decision-making process. The Supreme Court agreed with this assessment. *Hopkins*, 57 LW at 4477. The case, therefore, came to include a "mixed motive" element.

Evidence of Mixed Motive

In considering the weight to be given to evidence of mixed motive in proving causation, the court balanced the employer's "freedom of choice" in choosing partners against the plaintiff's interest in being considered without reference to gender or race. The court found that to "obligate a plaintiff to identify the precise causal role played by legitimate and illegitimate motivations" would strike a balance at odds with the language and interests of Title VII. *Hopkins*, 57 LW 4473. The burden, consequently, should be shifted to the employer to unscramble the motivations.

The court borrowed from other remedial statutes and the law of torts to discuss the rationale behind rejecting the *McDonnell Douglas* "articulation of a legitimate interest" standard in mixed motive cases. The court reasoned that where the employer "has acted out of a motive that is declared illegitimate by the statute, [i]t is fair that he bear the risk that the influence of legal and illegal motives cannot be separated." Thus, the court formulated a rule that puts the risk of non-persuasion on an employer proven by direct evidence to have "knowingly created the risk ... by his own wrongdoing." *Hopkins*, 57 LW at 4475 (citing, *NLRB v. Transp. Management Corp.*, 462 U.S. 393, 403 (1983)).

Even more important than where the court placed the burden in mixed motive cases is the court's reversal of both the district court and the court of appeals regarding the employer's burden. The court declined to apply the stringent clear and convincing standard to the employer, finding instead "conventional rules of civil litigation" mandate no more than that the employer prove its case by a preponderance of the evidence. To require the employer to show by clear and convincing evidence that the same decision would have been reached based on the non-discriminatory motive alone would have confronted the employer with an almost impossible burden.

In addition to adding a codicil to the framework for resolving mixed motive cases, *Hopkins* involves judicial consideration of stereotypical thoughts or evidence of gender discrimination. In *Hopkins*, the concern was that people who had submitted evaluations of the plaintiff had subconsciously reacted negatively because the plaintiff's personality was inconsistent with commonly held stereotypes regarding the appropriate behavior of women. In venturing into this area, the trial judge in *Hopkins* recognized the difficulties inherent in having judicial evaluation of the "inner motive" of subjective judgments: "[I]t is impossible to accept the view that Congress intended to have courts police every instance where subjective judgments may be tainted by unarticulated, unconscious assumptions related to sex." 618 F. Supp. 1109 (D.C.D.C. 1985) at 1118.

Intent Standard

In *Hopkins*, the court found the necessary intent for a disparate treatment case in the employer's failure to eliminate subconscious sexual stereotyping from its promotion process. During its previous term, the court, in *Watson v. Fort Worth Bank and Trust*, 108 S. Ct. 2777 (1988), found that intent could be proven by showing statistically the disparate impact of subjective employment criteria. The doctrinal gloss that many lower courts had read into *Griggs* limited the scope of disparate impact analysis to the sort of objective tests and credentials at issue in that case. *See Watson*, 108 S. Ct. at 2783. Thus, when the plaintiff in *Watson* challenged her supervisors' subjective evaluation of her capabilities with a showing of numerical disparity in promotions, the U.S. Court of Appeals for the Fifth Circuit refused to apply the *Griggs* framework. The Supreme Court, however, had never drawn such a limitation on *Griggs*. In *Watson*, a unanimous court explicitly declined to exclude subjective criteria from disparate impact, reasoning that "if disparate impact analysis is confined to objective tests, employers will be able to substitute subjective criteria having substantially identical effects, and *Griggs* will become a dead letter." *Watson*, 108 S. Ct. at 2786. This decision, therefore, offers plaintiffs the opportunity to avoid, where statistical disparity is high, the often impossible task of proving intent from a subjective decisional process.

Conversely, it also puts on employers the nearly impossible task of validating subjective criteria for job-relatedness under the business necessity defense. This creates a potential Hobson's choice for employers whereby they will face liability even for innocent disparities unless they take the illegal counter-measure of establishing a quota. *Watson*, 108 S.Ct. at 2788.

Protections for the Employer

This dilemma concerned a plurality of the court, which, while agreeing with the judgment, suggested modifications to protect the employer. The plurality suggested that the plaintiff should be required to isolate and identify the "specific employment practices that are allegedly responsible for any observed statistical disparities." *Watson*, 108 S. Ct. at 2788. This development with regard to causation would limit the effect of the extension of disparate impact analysis to subjective promotion decisions because by their nature such decisions are difficult to disentangle in order to trace causation to specific practices. In conjunction with this requirement, the plurality would modify the business necessity defense so that only articulation of a legitimate business reason would be required. Plaintiffs would then be required to show pretext or feasible alternative criteria. Thus, although under the plurality's view the subjective criteria would be encompassed under the rubric of "disparate impact," the ultimate burden of proving the difficult and often decisive issues of causation and pretext would lie with the plaintiff, as in disparate treatment.

The plurality also noted that often the employer can defeat the plaintiff's showing of disparity by attacking the appropriateness of the group of applicants or would-be applicants that comprises the overall pool against which the employer's workforce is measured. The court addressed this issue and the others raised by the *Watson* plurality in *Wards Cove Packing Co. v. Atonio*, 57 LW 4583 (1989). The *Watson* plurality became the *Wards Cove* majority.

The Ward's Cove Packing Co. operates salmon canning facilities during the summer in Alaska. The workforce is divided into two groups. "Cannery workers" are unskilled and low-paid and such jobs are filled "predominantly by nonwhites, filipinos, and Alaska Natives hired locally through a Teamsters hiring hall." "Non-cannery" positions usually are skilled jobs with higher pay and they are filled by white workers "hired during the winter months from the companies' offices in Washington and Oregon." Cannery workers and non-cannery workers are housed and fed separately. *Wards Cove*, 57 LW at 4585.

The U.S. Court of Appeals for the Ninth Circuit held that the plaintiffs had made a prima facie showing of disparate impact by demonstrating that non-whites comprised a high percentage of cannery workers but a low percentage of non-cannery workers. The Supreme Court reversed on this issue, ruling that although statistical proof can still constitute a prima facie showing, it must reflect the proper comparison of the relevant labor pool and at-issue jobs.

In the specific circumstances, the court rejected the contention that the cannery workers represented the qualified applicant pool for skilled non-cannery positions. The court noted that many cannery workers were not qualified to become non-cannery workers and that the labor force in Washington and Oregon contained many qualified workers. The court also declined to infer discrimination from statistical disparity – the fact that statistics showed that most unskilled non-cannery workers were white. It stated instead that if the percentage of selected non-whites in those positions approximated the percentage of non-white applicants, no discriminatory impact should be inferred.

The claim was that deterring practices – such as separate hiring channels, nepotism, and failure to post notices of job openings – reduced the non-white pool of applicants for non-cannery jobs. Those practices were considered irrelevant unless their negative effect could be demonstrated when the case was remanded to a U.S. district court.

Although the error regarding the proper labor pool justified remand to the district court, the Supreme Court addressed several other issues. The guidance presented commands a majority of the court and thus presumably indicates the future of the law.

First, a majority of the court took up Justice Sandra Day O'Connor's conception of the causation requirement in disparate impact cases as expressed in *Watson*: "the plaintiff is in our view responsible for isolating and identifying with specificity the employment practices that are allegedly responsible for any observed statistical disparities." *Wards Cove*, 57 LW at 4587 (*citing Watson*, 108 S. Ct. at 2788). Merely pointing to disparities and then to practices that might have caused them does not suffice.[6] This reasoning echoes the court's dissenters in *Teal*, where they emphasized that Title VII concerns itself not with fairness to groups, but to the effects of specific practices on individuals. *See Watson*, 57 LW at 4587 (citing *Teal*, 457 U.S. 445 (1982)).

Second, the court redefined the "business necessity" defense that originated in *Griggs*. The burden that shifts on the plaintiff's prima facie showing is now merely one of production, as in the *McDonnell Douglas* framework – calling for a reasoned review by the court – not one of persuasion subject to a higher standard of review, as in *Griggs* and *Hopkins*. The employer must show that the "challenged practice serves, in a significant way, the legitimate employment goals of the employer." Regarding the standard of review, the court declared that "the touchstone of this inquiry is a reasoned review of the employer's justification .... A mere insubstantial justification will not suffice .... At the same time, though, there is no requirement that the challenged practice be 'essential' or 'indispensable'...." *Wards Cove*, 57 LW at 4588. The court said the standard is not impossible to meet or so difficult to meet that it encourages illicit, hidden quotas. *Wards Cove*, 57 LW at 4586.

This change in the employer's burden, the court emphasized, will not force plaintiffs to prove events about which they have no information because liberal discovery rules and access to the employer's Equal Employment Opportunity Commission (EEOC) filings relevant to job candidate selection devices provide adequate information to prove pretext without undue burden. Moreover, a plaintiff can try to prove that an employer's legitimate criteria are a pretext for discrimination by showing that alternative techniques with less disparate impact exist. *Wards Cove*, 57 LW at 4587-4588.

IMPACT/TREATMENT

Although the employment discrimination decisions handed down by the Supreme Court in 1989 have spawned much rhetoric, the practical effect of the court's shifts remains unclear. *Wards Cove* illustrates this uncertainty. The majority on the court appears to have looked beyond whether the situation regarding the cannery was subject to redress, and focused instead on broad doctrinal questions. The court did not change theories of discrimination; it changed the ways by which discrimination may be proven. Therefore, whereas the court is reshaping the doctrine surrounding the disparate impact/disparate treatment dichotomy through *Wards* and the other cases, the effect on plaintiffs' ability to gain redress under the new framework has yet to emerge.

The doctrinal changes, nonetheless, have been notable. *Watson* and *Wards Cove* have largely dismantled the procedural and substantive dichotomy of disparate impact and treatment analyses. Procedurally, the previously heavy burden of persuasion necessary to the business-necessity defense in disparate impact cases has been reduced to that of the burden of production common in civil cases. The risk of not being able to persuade the court—so often decisive in disparate impact cases where solid proof is scarce for both sides—now resides with the plaintiff, as it does in disparate treatment analysis.

Substantively, *Watson* destroys the doctrine that where subjective criteria are at issue, disparate treatment must be shown. Moreover, the changes in the substance of the causation requirements and business necessity/justification burden announced in *Wards Cove* diminish the practical substantive effect of a statistical showing of disparate impact. If such a showing can be met by a merely substantial reason reasonably reviewed, then plaintiffs often will be required to prove pretext, which is circumstantial evidence of discriminatory intent. In many cases, practices that show a gross disparity of effect will be condemned only if buttressed with further circumstantial evidence of intent. The focus of the entire inquiry will have shifted from "consequences" to intent.

The *Hopkins* decision must alert employers to the dangers of subjective decision making that may involve subconscious stereotyping. Despite the trial court's reservations, it is now clear that a showing of gender or racial stereotyping may be a sufficient showing of intent for a disparate treatment case. At a minimum, a mixed-motive analysis will shift the burden of proof to the employer, albeit with a preponderance of the evidence standard.

These developments also may make objective promotion criteria desirable. Whereas under the *Griggs/McDonnell Douglas* dichotomy it was clearly worthwhile to avoid objective standards, after *Watson* and *Wards Cove* this disincentive is gone. *Hopkins* provides an incentive to avoid reliance on subjective decision making. As the U.S. workforce becomes increasingly diverse, employers will need hiring, training, and promotion techniques that include subjective criteria without stereotyping by gender or race, so they can hire and promote the candidates whom they feel are the best-qualified for the open jobs. If the result is a workplace chosen more on the basis of relevant criteria evenly applied, Title VII may have been well served by the decisions rendered in 1989, its 25th anniversary.

ENDNOTES

[1] Data compiled by the Hudson Institute suggests that:

- Non-whites, women, and immigrants will comprise more than 83 percent of the net additions to the workforce between now and the year 2000. These groups now comprise about 50 percent of the workforce.
- The fastest-growing jobs will be in the professional, technical, and sales fields that require greater skills and advanced education.

Workforce 2000, Work and Workers for the Twenty-First Century, xx-xxi (W. Johnson & A. Packer, project directors, 1987).

[2] In *Patterson v. McLean Credit Union*, the U.S. Supreme court addressed the question of whether Section 1981 (42 USC 1981), which prohibits interference with the making or enforcement of contracts on the basis of race, covers racial harassment in the workplace and failure to train for promotion. The court held that neither of these activities, although actionable under Title VII, affected the formation or enforcement of the employment contract. 57 LW 4705 (1989). Justice Anthony Kennedy's standard as to whether a promotion claim is actionable under Section 1981 is unclear: "Only where the promotion rises to the level of an opportunity for a new and distinct relation between the employee and the employer is such a claim actionable under 1981."

[3] The cases discussed in this chapter were chosen because they are relevant to Title VII and the promotion decision. However, two other recent Supreme court decisions bear on Title VII developments. In *Lorance v. AT&T Technologies*, the court addressed the issue of when to begin running the statute of limitations under Title VII (42 USC 2000(e)-5(e), 706(e)), where the effects of an allegedly discriminatory seniority system were felt

only much later (57 LW 4654 (1989)). The court declined to adopt the time of discovery of the harm as the proper starting point, because the earlier discriminatory act is the proper focus under Title VII. *Lorance*, 57 LW at 4655. In *Martin v. Wilks*, the court held that white male employees must be individually joined to be precluded from fully re-litigating issues settled by a consent decree between black plaintiffs and the employer. *Martin v. Wilks*, 57 LW 4616, 4618 (1989).

[4] Although this case could have been brought under the aegis of the Equal Protection Clause of the 14th Amendment, "No Constitutional issue was either raised or addressed in the litigation below." The only issue certified to the Supreme court, therefore, was "the prohibitory scope of Title VII." Thus, the decision is relevant to private employers. The court also stated, however, that "where the issue is properly raised, public employers must justify the adoption and implementation of a voluntary affirmative action plan under the Equal Protection clause." *Johnson*, 480 U.S. at 620, note 2. Among the more difficult hurdles unique to affirmative action by government entities is the requirement that the government unit establish (a) the fact of past discrimination in its province, and (b) tailor the plan to remedy only that harm. *City of Richmond v. J.A. Croson, Co.* established that the findings required of a municipality under this strict scrutiny did not encompass national or industry-wide discrimination (even if relying on congressional findings), nor could it include minority groups not found in its locality. *City of Richmond*, 57 LW 4132, 4140-4143 (1989).

[5] The dissent took a stricter reading of Title VII's language and sounded the theme of color-blindness. The law, the dissenters contended, was intended only to remedy identifiable discrimination against individuals, not to promote integration directly where non-intentional factors had created an imbalance in the workforce. *Johnson*, 480 US 667-668 (Scalia, J., dissenting). The dissent called for *Steelworkers v. Weber* (443 US 193 (1979)), which allowed private affirmative action programs under limited circumstances to be overruled. *Johnson*, 480 US at 670.

[6] The dissenters argued that the evidence of barriers inherent in the employer's hiring techniques as presented at trial demonstrated the requisite specific causation. They considered the segregation of cannery and non-cannery workers in housing and at meals combined with word-of-mouth hiring to be a major barrier tending to link the statistical disparity to particular practices. *Wards Cove*, 57 LW at 4593 (Stevens, J. dissenting).

* * *

Predictability in EEO Litigation

by Richard T. Seymour*

The U.S. Supreme Court's first-term 1989 civil rights decisions sharply reinterpreted civil rights laws and redefined how they are to be enforced. For example:

(a) *Wards Cove Packing Co. v. Atonio*, 490 U.S. ___, 104 L.Ed.2d 733, 109 S.Ct. 2115, 49 FEP Cases 1519 (1989) set forth guidelines for plaintiffs' showings of disparate impact for facially neutral selection practices under Title VII of the Civil Rights Act of 1964. The court also held that:

- Plaintiffs should bear the burden of isolating the parts of an employer's selection procedures that have disparate impact, and should bear the burden of showing the extent of the disparate impact attributable to each such part;

- All of the court's decisions over a period of 18 years on the nature of the employer's burden after a showing of disparate impact had been "misconstrued"; and

- Employers responding to a showing of disparate impact need only to meet an undefined burden of production.

The court spoke broadly on each of these issues, indicating that the details will be filled in later. The decision stated that these changes would reduce employers' incentives to adopt affirmative action plans for women and minorities.

---

*Richard T. Seymour is director of the employment discrimination project of the Lawyers' Committee for Civil Rights Under Law, in Washington, D.C. He has extensive experience in handling plaintiffs' class actions alleging racial and sexual discrimination in employment.

(b) *Patterson v. McLean Credit Union*, 491 U.S. ___, 105 L.Ed.2d 132, 109 S.Ct. 2363, 49 FEP Cases 1814 (1989), re-affirmed prior holdings that Section 1981 of the *U.S. Code* applies to private conduct, but held that 42 USC 1981 does not cover racial harassment or racial discrimination in the terms and conditions of employment. Rather, it is limited to discrimination in hiring, some promotions, and in the enforcement of contracts. Again, the details are to be filled in later.

(c) *Jett v. Dallas Independent School District*, 491 U.S. ___, 105 L.Ed.2d 598, 109 S.Ct. 2702, 50 FEP Cases 27 (1989), held that the damage remedy against local government entities under Section 1981 was repealed by implication when Congress enacted 42 USC 1983, and that the exclusive remedy for damages against local government employers was under Section 1983 and subject to Section 1983's limitation that plaintiffs prove the discrimination resulted from the "official policy" of the local government body. Section 1983 forbids all intentional actions under color of law that deprive people of rights guaranteed by the U.S. Constitution and by federal laws. It was enacted in 1871, and it is one of the primary means by which the deprivation of constitutional rights is redressed.

(d) *Will v. Michigan Dept. of State Police*, 491 U.S. ___, 105 L.Ed.2d 45, 109 S.Ct. 2304, 49 FEP Cases 1664 (1989), held that Section 1983 could not be used to sue states or state officials for damages when they are acting in their official capacities. Section 1983 suits for injunctive relief against state officials in their official capacities are still allowed.

(e) *Lorance v. AT&T Technologies*, 490 U.S. ___, 104 L.Ed.2d 961, 109 S.Ct. 2261, 49 FEP Cases 1656 (1989), held that the time for filing with the Equal Employment Opportunity Commission (EEOC) a charge of intentionally discriminatory but facially neutral changes in a seniority system began to run when the changes were adopted, even though no one suffered a loss of job status at that time, and that a charge filed after the loss of job status was untimely.

(f) *Price Waterhouse v. Hopkins*, 490 U.S. ___, 104 L.Ed.2d 268, 109 S.Ct. 1775, 49 FEP Cases 954 (1989), held that, when plaintiffs showed that an employer acted with a mixture of discriminatory motives and legitimate motives, the employer had to show, by a preponderance of the evidence, that it would have made the same decision in the absence of the unlawful motives. The nature of the proof necessary to make that showing was hotly disputed. Four justices supported the view that employers must bear the same burden in justifying their affirmative action plans, a position that would comprise a substantial upgrading of the employer's burden as declared by the court over the past few years. Four justices disagreed, and one justice did not comment on the issue.

(g) *Martin v. Wilks*, 490 U.S. ___, 104 L.Ed.2d 835, 109 S.Ct. 2180, 49 FEP Cases 1641 (1989), allows people who were not parties or class members in a fair employment case to file subsequent lawsuits collaterally attacking the relief obtained, when they are affected by that relief. Such people do not have a duty to intervene in the enforcement action even after notice. If the parties want to bind non-parties by a decree, they must join the non-parties.

(h) *City of Richmond v. J.A. Croson Co.*, 488 U.S. ___, 102 L.Ed.2d 854, 109 S.Ct. 706 (1989), struck down Richmond's minority contractor set-aside plan and imposed requirements for such plans that substantially exceed the requirements for affirmative action plans designed to eliminate employment discrimination based on race and gender.

While the changes brought by these cases are extremely important, the loss of predictability in equal employment opportunity (EEO) litigation is just as important to employers and to groups protected by Title VII. Critics charged that in these rulings the court dismissed 20 years of settled jurisprudence almost casually, and that decisions handed down in recent years by most of the same justices were re-examined at will, making any sense of certainty in the law's demands illusory.

As Justice Owen J. Roberts observed in his dissent in *Smith v. Allwright*, 321 U.S. 649, 669, 88 L.Ed. 987, 1000 (1944):

> The reason for my concern is that the instant decision, overruling that announced about nine years ago, tends to bring adjudications of this tribunal into the same class as a restricted railroad ticket, good for this day and train only.

Roberts was wrong about the case before him: he was dissenting from a decision striking down a rule of the Texas State Democratic Convention that limited participation in Democratic primary elections to white voters. The broader concern he raised is valid, however, even if bad precedents do need to be overruled from time to time.

The Value of Predictability

During the more than 24 years that Title VII has been in effect, the courts and the litigants in thousands of lawsuits have worked out effective sets of principles for applying the commands of the act. It has not been easy or cheap to develop that body of law. Virtually all lawyers active in the field of EEO litigation have proposals for further development of the law, but most of these are within the framework of the established standards. For two reasons, virtually no one outside the Justice Department during the Reagan administration wanted the court to make the sweeping changes that it made in these decisions.

First, strong practical considerations underlie predictability. When the law is stable, employers and unions can make a reasonable assessment of the benefits and risks of a particular course of action. If a particular practice is of doubtful legality, they can change it before they are sued, and improve the employment prospects of minorities and women without risking any back-pay liability. Employers and unions thus can minimize the risk of being sued, and can maximize their prospects of prevailing if they are sued. If the law is stable, both sides in litigation can assess the benefits of settling, and they should be able to find common ground. If litigants fail to settle, the trial court usually can resolve the case quickly, and neither side needs to appeal every issue. Litigation costs are lower.

Second, the dangers of uncertainty are great. Attorneys cannot plan cases if liability standards change sharply from time to time in unpredictable ways. Companies will try to tailor their employment practices to match prevailing court rulings, and they will change these practices each time the court's opinion changes rather than adopt stable practices that may one day result in a ruling that forces them to provide a large amount of back pay. Such frequent changes in employment practices would spur worker unrest and make collective bargaining more difficult. In litigation, the uncertainty would lead to a lack of common understanding of the law that would reduce the chances of settling, and would spawn a gambler's mentality on both sides. Although some cases could be settled, it would be advantageous for many litigants to litigate every conceivable issue, and to appeal every adverse ruling because case law regarding the issues involved might change suddenly.

A new set of standards will emerge and predictability will again be possible if no new major rulings are handed down over time. However, the slow accretion of precedent in numerous cases, based on the complexities of numerous factual situations, is time-consuming and expensive. It could easily take hundreds of district court cases, scores of cases in the courts of appeals, and a handful of cases in the Supreme Court, over a period of at least five or six years to arrive again at predictable standards.

The process would require a lot of work for the attorneys on both sides of all of these cases. In practical terms, it would likely cost many millions of dollars in legal fees. If plaintiffs ultimately prevail in those cases, the defendants would wind up paying the attorneys' fees and expenses for both sides in this litigation.

The court's 1989 decisions give little weight to the practical need for clarity and certainty. Future decisions may follow the same course, leaving employers and workers to face possible sweeping but unclear changes with many issues left unresolved.

Who Benefits from the Changes?

Plaintiffs are harmed by having to meet stricter burdens and standards of proof and the additional time and costs they require. If they can meet the increased burdens, however, employers will have to pay for huge increases in fees and expenses.

Plaintiffs and employers are harmed by threats to the finality of settlements, and by the prospect of repetitive litigation over the propriety of the same relief.

Employers are harmed by possible increases in their burdens to justify voluntary affirmative action.

These decisions probably benefit reverse-discrimination plaintiffs more than anyone, largely because the court expanded their procedural rights in *Martin*. Moreover, if the court follows through on some of the justices' suggestions for increasing employers' burdens in justifying affirmative-action plans, reverse-discrimination plaintiffs will win more cases.

The benefits to employers are harder to identify. *Wards Cove* may result in fewer disparate impact cases being brought because of plaintiffs' added burdens and expense, and it may result in employers winning cases they would have lost under previous law. However, employers that adopt or maintain selection practices with substantial disparate impact might be liable under state or local fair employment practice (FEP) laws if they take advantage of their supposedly greater freedoms under *Wards Cove*. Apart from legal considerations, the Hudson Institute's *Workforce 2000* study for the Labor Department concluded that the percentages of whites and males in the workforce was declining and that most new entrants into the workforce will be women or members of minority groups. Employers may not be able to fill their job openings if they adopt or continue selection practices with substantial disparate impact. While *Wards Cove* reduces the burdens on employers, it also reduces their ability to engage in justifiable voluntary affirmative action.

Women and minorities generally did not fare well by the court's 1989 decisions, although in addition to the main holding of *Price Waterhouse v. Hopkins*, six justices held that making employment decisions on the basis of stereotypes is intentional discrimination. 104 L.Ed.2d at 287-88 and 291-93 (Justice William Brennan's plurality opinion, joined by Justices Thurgood Marshall, Harry Blackmun, and John Paul Stevens); 104 L.Ed.2d at 293-94 (Justice Byron White); and 104 L.Ed.2d at 302-04 (Justice Sandra Day O'Connor). Several courts had been reluctant to find intentional discrimination based on possibly unconscious stereotypes, and had insisted on evidence of more deliberate acts. Other courts, confronted with subjective systems of personnel selection that reduced the chances of black or female applicants being hired or promoted, had accepted the existence of disparate impact but had insisted on much greater levels of proof before finding disparate treatment. E.g., *Lewis v. Bloomsburg Mills*, 773 F.2d 561, 569 note 14 (4th Cir., 1985). *Price Waterhouse* has superseded such rulings. *Patterson* held that proof sufficient to show disparate treatment under Title VII also is sufficient to make out a case of purposeful discrimination under Section 1981. 105 L.Ed.2d at 156-57. Thus, *Price Waterhouse* and *Patterson* make it easier for plaintiffs to prove intentional discrimination, and it makes compensatory damages available for decisions based on racial stereotypes.

With regard to Congress, Brennan referred in his concurring and dissenting opinion in *Wards Cove* to "the frequency with which Congress has in recent years acted to overturn this Court's mistaken interpretations of civil rights statutes." 105 L.Ed.2d at 166 and note 9. The more sweeping the change made by the Supreme Court, the more likely Congress is to take corrective action. Such actions frequently expand further the rights that the court had restricted, so that in the end the statutory protections for civil rights become much stronger than they were before the court tried to limit them. See, e.g., the Voting Rights Act Amendments of 1982, PL 97-205, 96 Stat. 131. The court's 1989 decisions may produce a similar reaction by Congress. A bipartisan bill, S 1261, to override *Wards Cove* was introduced by Sen. Howard Metzenbaum (D-Ohio) and co-sponsored by nine Democrats and two Republicans.

STRATEGY QUESTIONS

Disparate Impact

What is the Practical Significance of the Requirement that Plaintiffs Show the Specific Disparate Impact Arising from the Specific Practice Challenged?

In some cases, this requirement will present no difficulty. Many employers often reduce the number of applicants they consider by administering a written test at the start of the hiring process, and then rejecting all candidates except the top 5 percent or 10 percent of test-takers. It usually is easy to determine the adverse impact of a test or other requirement if it is administered early in the hiring process, but if it is administered in the middle or at the end of the process, the difficulty of showing adverse impact depends on whether the employer's records show who took the test or was subjected to the requirement, and who passed at a high enough level to be considered further. If the challenged requirement is a written test, records often are available. If another objective requirement is challenged, such as educational level or amount of experience, records often are harder to obtain.

The most difficult showing to make from records involves situations where multiple standards are used for selection, with different standards administered at different times in the process. The Lawyers' Committee for Civil Rights Under Law has handled cases like this, and has made the kinds of separate showings contemplated by *Wards Cove*. The best example involved the Houston, Texas, police department, where the committee showed disparate treatment in the administration of the different standards as well as several instances of disparate impact. Both kinds of showings enabled the committee (1) to persuade the defendant to settle, and (2) to craft a consent decree that standardized the considerations used by the defendant and refined them to reduce or eliminate adverse impact. The decree did not contain racially-based goals and timetables; with the changes that were made affirmative action was not needed. This is the solution the Supreme Court majority favored in *Wards Cove*.

However, making the showings required an extremely long, complex, and costly effort. The "liberal discovery rules" mentioned in *Wards Cove* allowed the committee to send staff to Houston to microfilm or duplicate more than 200,000 pages of documents, an effort that took several months. At its headquarters in Washington, D.C., the committee employed 17 undergraduates and law students, under the supervision of a team of paralegals, for several more months to organize this information. All of this work would cost between $100,000 and $200,000 today. The committee's fee submission at commercial rates, for just the additional proof required by *Wards Cove*, easily would be twice this amount.

Does Wards Cove *Require a Perfect Showing of Causation?*

No. Title VII plaintiffs were not previously required to introduce perfect evidence, covering every possible combination, permutation, and speculation the defendant could cite, and they are not required to do so now. In *Dothard v. Rawlinson*, 433 U.S. 321, 329-31, 53 L.Ed.2d 786, 797-98, 97 S.Ct. 2720 (1977), the sex discrimination that the plaintiffs challenged were minimum height and weight requirements for the position of correctional counselor. Their showing of disparate impact was based on nationwide U.S. Census Bureau statistics, and the employer challenged this showing as insufficient, on the ground that the statistics for actual applicants in Alabama might be different. After discussing the problem of female applicants who could have been discouraged from applying by knowledge that they would fail the challenged requirement, the court said:

> Moreover, reliance on general population demographic data was not misplaced where there was no reason to suppose that physical height and weight characteristics of Alabama men and women differ markedly from those of the national population.
>
> For these reasons, we cannot say that the District Court was wrong in holding that the statutory height and weight standards had a discriminatory impact on women applicants. The plaintiffs in a case such as this are not required to exhaust every possible source of evidence, if the evidence actually presented on its face conspicuously demonstrates a job requirement's grossly discriminatory impact. If the employer discerns fallacies or deficiencies in the data offered by the plaintiff, he is free to adduce countervailing evidence of his own. In this case no such effort was made. (Footnote omitted.)

This holding of *Dothard* was quoted and approved in O'Connor's plurality opinion in *Watson v. Fort Worth Bank & Trust Co.*, 487 U.S. ___, 101 L.Ed.2d 827, 846, 108 S.Ct. 2777, 47 FEP Cases 102 (1988). Moreover, the statistical discussion in *Dothard* was cited with approval in *Wards Cove*. 104 L.Ed.2d at 747 note 6.

The U.S. Court of Appeals for the Seventh Circuit recently held that *Wards Cove* does not require the kind of perfect statistical showing for which the defendant argues herein. In *Allen v. Seidman*, ___ F.2d ___, 50 FEP Cases 607 (7th Cir., July 27, 1989), the court described *Wards Cove* as involving "a shoddy showing of disparate impact" and held that it "would raise the threshold of proof too high" to require a plaintiff to eliminate all alternative hypotheses. 50 FEP Cases at 609, 611. The court suggested, however, that in a case in which the applicants differ markedly in important characteristics such as education, plaintiffs might have to conduct a regression analysis to control for such characteristics. In effect, plaintiffs might have to show separately failure rates among applicants with a high school degree, failure rates among applicants with one to two years of college, and rates for all other levels of education. As other variables are added, issues can become quite complicated. The *Allen* court also held that the importance of differences in education can decline over time as a result of on-the-job training and experience, making it unnecessary to control for education in some cases.

This is a fertile field for litigation: What are the important characteristics? How should the dividing points be established? At what rate does the importance of a factor decline? How should one account for a factor's diminution in importance?

If racial or gender differences in a factor such as education or experience explain enough of the disparate impact to undermine the original showing, the factor itself has been identified as having a specific degree of disparate impact and is subject to challenge. *Lewis v. Bloomsburg Mills*, 773 F.2d at 571 note 16. The employer is no better off than before, except that the amount of its exposure to fees and costs is much larger and it now has more practices to defend.

What if No Records Showing the Reasons for Rejection Are Available?

Nothing in the Supreme Court's opinion in *Wards Cove* or in the plurality opinion in *Watson* suggests that the court wants to destroy disparate impact litigation by requiring what is impossible. The court denied that it intended the causation requirement to be "unduly burdensome," and pointed out that the Uniform Guidelines on Employee Selection Procedures, 29 CFR 1607.1 et seq. (1988), require employers to maintain records showing the adverse impact of each component of their selection systems, and that liberal discovery rules provide broad access to all of an employer's records. 104 L.Ed.2d at 752. It is implied that, where the employer is under a legal obligation to make and keep records making a showing of causation possible, and fails to do so, the employer may not have the benefit of the causation requirement.

What About Subjective Systems of Selection?

The safest course of action for plaintiffs is to show that racial or gender differences in specific subjectively considered qualifications do not explain the overall disparate impact, or to show in other ways that the defendant pays little attention to the asserted qualification and that the subjectivity is thus the cause of the disparate impact. Before *Wards Cove,* many plaintiffs' lawyers challenging subjective systems of selection went to great lengths to show that they worked in anomalous fashions, in an effort to prove that the system being challenged worked erratically and irrationally.

For example, the Lawyers' Committee has prepared lists of numerous white employees who were rehired after having been discharged from an earlier period of employment for coming to work drunk or for other misbehavior; the committee has contrasted the fact that many whites hired had little or no experience with the good experience records of numerous blacks who were rejected for jobs at the same time the whites were hired. The committee has listed promotions to supervisory and other highly paid positions of white employees who had recently been disciplined for excessive absenteeism.

Where the committee sees substantial disparate impact arising from the use of subjective selection procedures, it often finds these patterns. When subjectivity is basically all that is left, plaintiffs should not be required to identify criteria that exist only in the mind of the selecting official. The defendant in an important case recently moved to vacate findings of liability on the grounds that it had a large number of selecting officials making decisions on subjective grounds; that their selections were completely without standards; and that each selecting official used his or her own criteria that may not have been the same as those of anyone else. No records show which official rejected which applicant, or why the person was rejected, and the defendant filed an affidavit swearing that no one remembered anything. The employer then made the following argument:

> To satisfy *Atonio* [*Wards Cove*] plaintiffs must instead isolate the individual subjective criteria allegedly used by *each* of the more than 200 officials and managers at [defendant's] facilities who made employment decisions during the 1968-72 period ... and then demonstrate that *each* of these subjective factors "ha[d] a significantly disparate impact on employment opportunities for whites and [blacks]." (Emphasis in original).

Thus, if each official used, for example, 10 criteria, the company would have plaintiffs make separate showings of which people were harmed by which of 2,000 separate criteria and then perform tests of statistical significance on each of them.

Such showings would require something akin to computerized axial tomography (CAT scans) of each company official's brain to obtain the evidence the company says is the minimum acceptable showing.

Wards Cove requires no such evidence. Its requirement of showings of causation, the court said, flowed directly from respondents' challenges to:

> ...several "objective" employment practices (e.g., nepotism, separate hiring channels, rehire preferences), as well as the use of "subjective decision making" ....

104 L.Ed.2d at 751.

The court continued:

> Respondents will also have to demonstrate that the disparity they complain of is the result of one or more of the employment practices that they are attacking here, specifically showing that each challenged practice has a significantly disparate impact on employment opportunities for whites and nonwhites.

Ibid.

Within the context of the causation requirement, subjective decision making is a practice similar to objective practices, requiring a showing of disparate impact as objective practices require. This reading of *Wards Cove* is confirmed by the court's observation that the plurality opinion in *Watson* "correctly stated" the causation requirement, 104 L.Ed.2d at 750, and by its quotation of the *Watson* plurality's statement that the causation requirement applied especially "where an employer combines subjective criteria with the use of more rigid standardized rules or tests." 104 L.Ed.2d at 751. If every subjective criterion of every separate decision maker were subject to separate causation showings, no reason would have existed to refer to the combination of "more rigid standardized rules" and subjective criteria. The quoted passage makes sense only if the use of subjectivity were itself a practice not requiring further subdivision.

This reading of *Wards Cove* is supported by other language in *Watson*. The majority characterized the court's holding as approving the application of disparate impact analysis "to a subjective or discretionary promotion system," 101 L.Ed.2d at 848, a formulation at odds with the belief that plaintiffs must determine which part of the adverse impact comes from which of the unnumbered and unrecorded factors giving rise to subjective decisions.

Are Applicant-Flow Statistics Still Generally Permissible Evidence to Show Disparate Impact?

Yes. *Wards Cove* involved no applicant-flow statistics, and no untainted applicant-flow statistics would have existed there because one of the challenged practices was the existence of two separate recruiting and hiring channels.

The court emphasized the importance of applicant/hire ratios as evidence of discrimination. The court suggested comparing the proportion of new hires in medical and office worker jobs who were non-white to the proportion of applicants for those jobs who were non-white, 104 L.Ed.2d at 748; referred to the possibility that discrimination might produce a dearth of qualified non-white applicants as undermining the conclusions to be drawn from applicant/hire ratios, 104 L.Ed.2d at 748 note 7; referred to the question of whether "the percentage of selected applicants who are nonwhite is not significantly less than the percentage of qualified applicants who are nonwhite," 104 L.Ed.2d at 749; and referred to the same kind of comparison again at 104 L.Ed.2d at 749 note 8.

Wards Cove does not limit disparate impact showings to comparisons of the external labor force to the employer's workforce.

What About Wards Cove's *Emphasis on the "Qualified" Labor Force?*

Wards Cove involved a nonsensical comparison of the percentage of unqualified and unskilled cannery workers who were members of minority groups and the percentage of skilled and highly qualified "accountants, managers, boat captains, electricians, doctors, and engineers" who were minorities. 104 L.Ed.2d at 748. The insufficiency of such a comparison is obvious. A solid statistical showing should take legitimate qualifications into account to the greatest possible extent. In filling entry-level blue collar jobs, for example, the "qualified labor force" is likely to be the blue collar labor force. White managers, professionals, and salespeople seldom are available for hire in blue collar positions.

Taking qualifications into account also requires an examination to determine that the qualifications were applied on a fairly uniform basis. Qualifications that never were observed, that were observed on some occasions and not on others, or that are fabricated, cannot defeat a showing of discrimination. *Cf. Payne v. Travenol Laboratories*, 673 F.2d 798, 827 (5th Cir.), cert. den., 459 U.S. 1038, 74 L.Ed.2d 605, 103 S.Ct. 451, 452 (1982): "Travenol's informal and erratic reliance on length of service falls far short of being a bona fide seniority system under the statute and under *Teamsters*."

Validity

How Great is the Employer's Burden of Production Under Wards Cove?

Wards Cove emphasized that the employer's burden was substantial: the employer must produce evidence that "a challenged practices serves, in a significant way, the legitimate employment goals of the employer." The employer's showing must allow "reasoned review." 104 L.Ed.2d at 752. The court held that the language of its prior cases was misinterpreted as requiring the employer to bear the burden of persuasion, but it did not overrule those cases or disapprove their results. Instead, it cited those cases with approval. *Wards Cove* provides no reason to believe that the standards it clarifies would have led to decisions for the employer in *Griggs v. Duke Power Co.,* 401 U.S. 424, 28 L.Ed.2d 158, 91 S.Ct. 849 (1971), in *Albemarle Paper Co. v. Moody,* 422 U.S. 405, 45 L.Ed.2d 280, 95 S.Ct. 2362 (1975), or in *Dothard v. Rawlinson,* 433 U.S. 321, 53 L.Ed.2d 786, 97 S.Ct. 2720 (1977).

This is significant. *Griggs* rejected the explanation of a company vice president that the challenged requirements "generally would improve the overall quality of the workforce," because the explanation did not meet the standards of the EEOC guidelines. 401 U.S. at 431, 433-36, 28 L.Ed.2d at 164, 165-67. *Albemarle Paper* rejected the validation study of a psychologist because it did not meet the standards of the EEOC guidelines. 422 U.S. at 426-36, 45 L.Ed.2d at 301-07. *Dothard* rejected a showing that the height and weight requirement for correctional counselors was correlated with strength, because it was not specific enough to show that the correlation was with the specific amount of strength required, and thus it did not meet the requirements of the guidelines. 433 U.S. at 331-32, 53 L.Ed.2d at 798-99.

Therefore, a showing by an employer that fails to meet the requirements of the guidelines is inadequate to meet the employer's burden of production under *Wards Cove.*

It is important to distinguish between an employer's heavy burden of production in a disparate impact case under *Wards Cove* and the much lighter burden of producing an "articulation" under *Texas Dept. of Community Affairs v. Burdine*, 450 U.S. 248, 67 L.Ed.2d 207, 101 S.Ct. 1089 (1981).

Evans v. City of Evanston, ___ F.2d ___, 50 FEP Cases 612 (7th Cir., 1989), supports this view. The case involved a sex discrimination challenge to the setting of the cutoff score on the Evanston Fire Department's physical agility test. The U.S. Court of Appeals for the Seventh Circuit held that:

> ... the city was obliged to produce evidence that the method of determining who passed the test in 1983 was related to the city's need for a physically capable firefighting force.

50 FEP Cases at 614.

This is far more than the weak burden of production under *Burdine*.

The plaintiffs in a disparate impact case cannot perform their own validation studies. The plaintiffs do not have access to the workforce, cannot commandeer the cooperation of plant officials in obtaining ratings or other measures of work performance, and cannot administer the test or other selection devices to the employees. Only the employer can do these things.

What Effect Will Wards Cove *Have on Plaintiffs' Review of Validation Studies?*

Even before *Watson* and *Wards Cove*, government agencies and private plaintiffs were delving more and more deeply into the raw data contained in validation studies. It is now commonplace for plaintiffs to obtain computer tapes showing the raw data and to perform their own computer analysis of the data. As validation studies have become more complete, plaintiffs have had to rely less on finding large errors in defendants' analyses and have had to rely increasingly on making their own empirical showings that the defendant's analysis is incorrect, or that it omits important factors which show that selection devices are not related to the job. Because major problems are often found in such validation studies, these projects will continue. *Wards Cove* will accelerate this trend.

What if the Employer Advances No Proof of Justification for a Subjective System of Personnel Selection?

The characterization of the defendant's burden does not matter in a case in which the defendant produces no evidence that how it makes decisions on hiring, initial assignment, and promotion "serves, in a significant way, the legitimate employment goals of the employer." 104 L.Ed.2d at 752. While "[t]he touchstone of this inquiry is a reasoned review of the employer's justification," *id.*, no review at all is possible where no justification has been advanced.

The need to justify the degree of subjectivity and the lack of monitoring in question often is overlooked by employers in reviewing their exposure in the absence of any litigation and in preparing their defenses in litigation. It is common for employers to forget the subject or to rely on the assertion of a management official that some degree of subjectivity is inescapable. While this is probably true for every job, it does not explain why the employer needed as much subjectivity as was shown, or why the employer could not have conducted any more monitoring of the process to ensure that the managers who selected and rejected job candidates made their decisions on valid grounds and did not consciously discriminate or were not influenced by racial or gender stereotypes.

Questions of validity will be a fertile field for litigation.

Will Wards Cove Be Limited?

To the extent that *Wards Cove* is construed to make a substantial difference in the outcome of a particular case already litigated under different standards, *Wards Cove* may not be given retrospective effect under the standards of *Chevron Oil Co. v. Huson*, 404 U.S. 97, 30 L.Ed.2d 296, 92 S.Ct. 349 (1971).

In 1987, the Supreme Court refused to apply retroactively a decision that substantially changed the principles governing the choice of state statutes of limitation for claims under 42 USC Sections 1981 and 1983, because retroactive application would eliminate many claims and would be "manifestly inequitable." *Saint Francis College v. Al-Khazraji*, 481 U.S. 604, 608-09, 95 L.Ed.2d 582, 588-89, 107 S.Ct. 2022 (1987).

Wards Cove and State FEP Laws

While *Wards Cove* is controlling as to the employment practices of federal agencies, other employers need to take into account the provisions of state and local FEP legislation. Twenty-six states and the District of Columbia have laws providing immunity only for professionally developed ability tests, and/or have adopted as their own the 1970 EEOC guidelines or the 1978 uniform guidelines, and/or have adopted their own testing guidelines modelled on the 1970 EEOC guidelines. Some of these incorporate and add to the provisions of the American Psychological Association's (APA) "Standards for Educational and Psychological Tests." The following list illustrates these state provisions. Some city FEP agencies have taken similar action. Local FEP agencies should be contacted for the most timely information.

State	*Discussion*
Arizona:	Section 1403(I)(2) of the Arizona Civil Rights Act, 41 Ariz. *Rev.Stat.*, is similar to Section 703(h) of Title VII, and the Arizona Civil Rights Commission has adopted testing guidelines similar to the 1970 EEOC Guidelines.
California:	The California Fair Employment and Housing Commission has adopted the EEOC uniform guidelines, and has expressly placed the

burden of showing job-relatedness on the employer. 2 Calif. *Admin. Code* § 7287.4(a) -(e).

Colorado: The Colorado Civil Rights Commission has adopted the EEOC uniform guidelines, which are to be applied in conformity with the Colorado Anti-discrimination Act, not with Title VII. 3 *Code of Colorado Regulations* 708-1, § 90.0.

Delaware: Section 711(f) of the Delaware Fair Employment Practices Act, 19 Del. *Code Ann.*, contains provisions similar to those in Section 703(h) of Title VII.

District of Columbia: The D.C. Commission on Human Rights has adopted the 1970 EEOC guidelines. "Employment Guidelines," § 504.1, published in the D.C. *Register* for Aug. 1, 1986.

Hawaii: The Hawaii Department of Labor and Industrial Relations has prohibited tests of physical agility or strength, and has prohibited height and weight standards that have disparate impact on either gender unless the tests and standards comprise a bona fide occupational qualification. 12 Hawaii *Rev. Stat.* § 12-23-54.

Illinois: Section 2-104(4) of the Illinois Human Rights Act contains provisions similar to those in Section 703(h) of Title VII. Ill. *Rev. Stat.*, Chapter 68.

Iowa: The Iowa Civil Rights Commission has adopted employee selection procedures that require the test user to demonstrate the validity and "high degree of utility" of any test or educational or experience requirement, scored interview, or biodata form that has disparate impact on a protected class. Evidence of validity must conform to the APA standards as well as meeting the express requirements of the Iowa procedures (including a study of test fairness or a demonstration that such a study is not feasible). Chapter 8 of the Rules of the Commission, §§ 161-8.1(601A) et seq.

Kansas: The Kansas Commission on Civil Rights has adopted "Guidelines on Employee Selection Procedures" that are similar to those of Iowa, and that also rely on, and add to, the APA standards. Article 30 of the Kansas Commission's Rules, §§ 21-30-2 et seq.

Kentucky: The Kentucky Commission on Human Rights has adopted the 1970 EEOC guidelines. 104 Kentucky Administrative Regulations 1:050, § 3.

Maine: The Maine Human Rights Commission has construed the Maine Human Rights Act, 5 Maine *Rev. Stat. Ann.* §§ 4551 et seq., to prohibit disparate impact discrimination, and its regulations require the test user to demonstrate business necessity for a test with disparate impact under the standards of *Griggs* and of *Robinson v. P. Lorillard & Co.*, 444 F.2d 791 (4th Cir., 1971). Where a test user is subject to the EEOC uniform guidelines, the commission "will look favorably upon evidence presented which meets those standards." Employment Regulations, §§ 3.02 and 3.05.

Maryland: The Maryland Commission on Human Relations has adopted "Guidelines on Employee Selection Procedures" similar to those of Iowa, and that also rely on, and add to, the APA standards.

Michigan: The Michigan Civil Rights Commission has issued "Interpretive Guidelines on Civil Rights Laws" that adopt the 1970 EEOC guidelines. Guidelines, § 5.

Minnesota: Section 363.02(1)(7)(ii) of the Minnesota Human Rights Act contains provisions similar to those in Section 703(h) of Title VII. Minn. *Stat.*, Chapter 363, § 363.02(1)(7)(ii).

Missouri: The Missouri Commission on Human Rights, in the Missouri Department of Labor and Industrial Relations, has adopted "Guidelines on Employee Selection Procedures" that are similar to those of Iowa, and that also rely on, and add to, the APA standards. 8 *Code of State Regulations* 60-3.030 (1986).

Montana: The Montana Commission on Human Rights has adopted the EEOC uniform guidelines as originally published in 1978. The 1978 guidelines are to be construed in accordance with the policies and rules of the Montana Commission. 24 *Administrative Code*, Chapter 9, Rules 24.9.1410, -24.9.1411.

Nebraska: Section 48-1111(1) of the Nebraska Fair Employment Practices Act contains provisions similar to those in Section 703(h) of Title VII. Neb. *Rev. Stat.* (1943), Chapter 48.

Nevada:	Section 613.380 of the Nevada Fair Employment Practices Act contains provisions similar to those in Section 703(h) of Title VII. Nev. *Rev. Stat.*, Chapter 613.
North Dakota:	Section 14-02.4-09 of the North Dakota Fair Employment Practices Act contains provisions similar to those in Section 703(h) of Title VII. 14 N.Dak. *Century Code*, Chapter 14-02.4.
Ohio:	The Ohio Civil Rights Commission has adopted rules and regulations that require test users to demonstrate the validity and "high degree of utility" of any test, educational or experience requirement, scored interview, or biodata form that has disparate impact on a protected class. Evidence of validity must be empirical. The standards are similar to those of the 1970 EEOC guidelines, but make no reference to them. Rules and Regulations, § 4112-5-03.
Oklahoma:	The Oklahoma Human Rights Commission has issued "Guidelines on Discrimination," Part XI of which comprises "Interpretative Guidelines on Employee Selection Procedures." Part XI is similar to the testing guidelines of Iowa, and also relies on, and adds to, the APA standards.
Oregon:	The Civil Rights Division of the Oregon Bureau of Labor and Industries has adopted Rule 839-05-020. The rule makes practices with disparate impact unlawful unless the respondent shows business necessity for the practice. After such a showing, the division

still may show the availability of a less discriminatory alternative.

Pennsylvania: The Pennsylvania Human Relations Commission has adopted "Employee Selection Procedure Guidelines" similar to those of Iowa, and that also rely on, and add to, the APA standards. 1 *Pa. Bulletin* 2005 (1971).

South Carolina: Section 1-13-80(h)(3) of the South Carolina Human Affairs Law contains provisions similar to those in Section 703(h) of Title VII.

South Dakota: The South Dakota Commission on Human Rights has adopted the 1970 EEOC guidelines. "Rules of Practice and Procedure," § 20:03:08.

Tennessee: The Tennessee Human Rights Commission has adopted the 1970 EEOC guidelines. "Official Compilation, Rules and Regulations of the State of Tennessee," § 1500-1-.11(3).

Texas: Section 5.07(a)(7) of the Texas Commission on Human Rights Act provides that it is not unlawful for an employer to engage in any practice "that has a discriminatory effect and that would otherwise be prohibited by this Act" if the employer shows the absence of intentional discrimination and that the practice "is justified by business necessity."

Federal law does not pre-empt state law in these fields, e.g., *California Federal Savings and Loan Association v. Guerra*, 479 U.S. 272, 93 L.Ed.2d 613, 107 S.Ct. 683, 42 FEP Cases 1073 (1987), and these state agencies are not required to follow any substantial relaxation of federal standards. It is unlikely that they would do so.

Employers in areas covered by such laws should follow the EEOC uniform guidelines, and in their personnel practices they should treat *Wards Cove* as if it had never occurred. This would help protect them from liability if Congress passes S 1261, the bill that would reverse *Wards Cove*, or similar legislation. Plaintiffs in such areas should add pendent state and local FEP claims to their Title VII causes of action, or they should bring suit in state courts under state law.

Open Questions Under *Patterson*

What Promotions are Covered by Section 1981?

The Supreme Court held that Section 1981 covers only those promotions that "involve the opportunity to enter into a new contract with the employer" and "where the promotion rises to the level of an opportunity for a new and distinct relation between the employee and the employer." 105 L.Ed.2d at 156. The example given by the court was *Hishon v. King & Spalding*, 467 U.S. 69, 81 L.Ed.2d 59, 104 S.Ct. 2229 (1984), involving the rejection of a female associate seeking promotion to partner.

While the exact types of promotions covered by Section 1981 will have to be addressed in several cases, being promoted from clerical or production worker to foreman or other supervisor probably would involve a "new and distinct relation between the employee and the employer." *Mallory v. Booth Refrigeration Supply Co.*, ___ F.2d ___, 50 FEP Cases 1066 (4th Cir. 1989).

A change from a job with hourly pay to a job with incentive-based pay would seem to involve a new contract because the employee would be going from a position where the employer sets the pay into one in which the employee determines the pay rate by performance, within the range established for the job. The reverse is also true. Such changes involve one of the most important elements of the employment relationship and they create new and distinct employer-employee relationships.

This area also offers fertile ground for litigation.

Does Section 1981 Cover Discharges in Retaliation for Filing EEOC Charges or Title VII Complaints?

Retaliation against employees who take action to ensure their Title VII rights would seem to limit the ability of employees to enforce their employment contracts. The U.S. Court of Appeals for the Fifth Circuit had so held, for example, prior to *Patterson. Irby v. Sullivan*, 737 F.2d 1418, 1430 (5th Cir., 1984); *Goff v. Continental Oil Co.*, 678 F.2d 593, 598 (5th Cir., 1982). After *Patterson*, however, the circuit court raised, but did not decide, the question of whether these precedents should be reconsidered. *Rathjen v. Litchfield*, 878 F.2d 836, 842 (5th Cir., 1989). The U.S. Court of Appeals for the Sixth Circuit recently held that such claims can no longer be brought under Section 1981. *Risinger v. Ohio Bureau of Workers' Compensation*, ___ F.2d___, 1989 U.S.App. LEXIS 12597 (6th Cir., No. 88-3387, August 24, 1989).

Patterson and State Law

In many states, some of the gaps in Section 1981 coverage can be filled by common law tort claims. Claims of racial harassment can be pursued as claims for the intentional infliction of mental distress; claims as to the terms and conditions of employment—depending on the facts of the case—might be prosecuted as claims for breach of contract or for tortious interference with contract rights. Breach of contract claims usually do not allow the recovery of punitive damages.

Martin and the Reopening of Old Decrees

Martin is not limited to decrees containing race-conscious and gender-conscious relief. In theory, every active decree providing any kind of relief that could be considered to be a disadvantage to anyone who is not a party to the case is now subject to collateral attack under *Martin*. Even a decree enjoining the use of an old-boy network disadvantages the people who previously benefited from such a network.

In practice, most challenges will involve affirmative action. More affirmative action challenges probably will occur in the public sector than in the private sector because ranking job applicants and candidates for promotion according to how well they do on tests and other criteria occurs most often in the public sector. The greater the sense of individual injury, the greater the likelihood of challenge.

Whether a wave of challenges to existing decrees will occur, and whether such a wave will continue, is uncertain. As long as the affirmative action decisions since 1984 remain good law, the person launching a collateral attack must be able to show that a sufficient basis did not exist on which a conclusion could be based as to the need for race-conscious or gender-conscious relief. If the first several challenges are unsuccessful, few additional challenges probably will be filed.

In cases still in litigation in late 1989, the parties have relatively few options. An opportunity to appear at a fairness hearing was provided in *Martin*, but this was not enough to bar the objectors from making a collateral attack. Using Rule 23 to sue a third-party class, or white or male applicants, or employees presents major problems, such as selecting the person to be sued and choosing the person to represent the class of people allegedly benefiting from the employer's practices. The person selected to represent the class might not be able to afford counsel, and probably will not be eager to assume the burden of representing all other whites or males. If the class representative has only a small personal stake in the outcome of the suit, is unwilling to represent the class, and cannot afford counsel, he or she probably is presumptively an inadequate class representative, in which event no one would be bound by the outcome of the trial.

Alternatives to responding to attacks if they occur are lacking.

Croson and Affirmative Action Plans

Croson requires state and local governments to inquire into their past discrimination and that of their contractors before implementing a minority contractor set-aside plan. It also limits the plan according to what would be a reasonable remedy for the amount of the discrimination identified, and requires that race-conscious and gender-conscious measures be used only as a last resort, after a thorough exploration of the feasibility of other measures.

Many of the facts in *Croson* have little application in the field of employment. These include the individualized determinations on other questions that the city must make anyway for each of its contractors, the number of contractors affected by a set-aside that is far smaller than the number of applicants and employees affected by an affirmative action plan, and the possibility that assistance other than set-asides would help minority contractors succeed in the marketplace. Nevertheless, plaintiffs and employers should watch closely the developments in this area.

SUMMARY AND CONCLUSION

The unanswered questions in 1989 Supreme Court decisions and the apparent desire of four justices to revisit the affirmative action decisions of a few years ago have spawned confusion in what had been a relatively settled area of the law. The outlook is for much more litigation and for greatly increased costs in resolving that litigation, without anyone receiving a sufficiently clear and deserved benefit to justify the added burdens and expense.

* * *

Case Studies

GANNETT CO.

The presence of high-ranking minorities and women at Gannett Co. Inc. is a vital part of the company's recruitment and promotion efforts.

"They're role models," said Vaughn Clarke, an assistant treasurer at Gannett. "You know that if you get the job, and you're better than someone else, you can get promoted."

Gannett is the nation's largest newspaper group, operating 84 dailies, 35 non-dailies and *USA Weekend*, a weekly magazine. The company also owns and operates 10 television stations and 16 radio stations. Gannett Outdoor, the largest outdoor advertising group in North America, has operations in 11 states and much of Canada.

From 1967 to 1988, Gannett's earnings increased for 82 consecutive quarters. In 1988, revenues of $3.3 billion produced earnings of $364 million, according to Gannett's 1988 Annual Report. Revenues were up 7.6 percent compared to 1987, while earnings rose by 14.1 percent.

Clarke told BNA the opportunity to advance was of greatest interest to him when he joined Gannett. He said he told Gannett that he was not interested in taking any position at any company that was interested in him only because he is black.

"I made that very clear," said Clarke, who added that he was then told by the company that it was looking for someone capable of later heading the department he was joining.

"The main thing is to be able to get the job on the basis of what you can do," Clarke said.

Clarke said people such as Ron Townsend, president of Gannett's television group, and Cathleen Black, publisher of

USA Today, prove that no limit exists on how high a black person or woman can go at Gannett.

For his part, Townsend told BNA the responsibility of a role model goes with his position.

"I tend to put extra pressure on myself," Townsend said. "I feel it's important for me to assume that responsibility."

Townsend, who started his television career in the 1960s, said mentors, both white and black, were instrumental in his career development. He added, however, that opportunities such as those he has had in television have seldom existed for blacks.

"There is no other [television] company that has given a minority or black the opportunity I've had here," Townsend said. "I never had any sense that people were restricting my growth."

NEWS ROOM REPRESENTATION

Women comprise 51 percent of the U.S. population but they hold only 35 percent of the jobs in print-media news rooms and 32 percent of the jobs in the electronic news media. According to a 1987 survey by the American Society of Newspaper Editors (ASNE), women held only 13 percent of all news room management positions. At 76 percent of the nation's daily newspapers, no women worked as editors, associate editors, executive editors, managing editors, or editorial page editors, the poll showed.

Minorities comprise more than 25 percent of the U.S. population, but figures compiled by the American Newspaper Publishers Association (ANPA) show that they made up only 16.1 percent of the workforce at newspapers and they hold only 10 percent of news room jobs.

By 1988, minorities accounted for only 7 percent of the 55,300 daily newspaper journalists working in the United States, according to ASNE. Minority representation at dailies was 4 percent in 1978. A survey by the National Association of Black Journalists (NABJ) found that blacks comprised up only 3.6 percent of the nation's daily newspaper journalists.

Also in 1988, more than half of the 1,600 U.S. dailies still had no minority reporters. Minorities held 13.3 percent of television news jobs and 10 percent of radio news positions, according to a survey by *Broadcast News*.

REPRESENTATION AT GANNETT

Gannett's success in hiring and promoting minorities and women has been far greater than that of the news industry overall. In 1988, minorities comprised 21.1 percent of Gannett's workforce, up from 12.3 percent in 1981. Women comprised 40 percent of the Gannett workforce in 1988, up from 34.9 percent in 1981.

Minorities held 16.5 percent of the jobs in the "top four" categories, compared to 8.8 percent in 1981. Women held 40.9 percent of the four positions, compared to 32.8 percent in 1981.

At the company's flagship newspaper, *USA Today*, minorities comprised 23 percent of the workforce—21.6 percent of the news room employees. Women made up 51.6 percent of the workforce—46 percent of news room employees. Women held 39.5 percent of professional and managerial positions, while minorities were represented in 18 percent of those jobs.

Other statistics for the company include:

- Women comprise nearly 40 percent of the Gannett workforce.
- Five of the seven black U.S. daily newspaper publishers work for Gannett.
- Gannett has 21 female publishers, and two of the three largest U.S. newspapers with female executive editors are Gannett newspapers.

- Minorities operate four Gannett broadcasting companies.

- The number of Gannett minority managers more than doubled during the 1980s.

- At Gannett's *USA Today*, women comprise 45 percent of news room employees and minorities 21 percent.

"What Gannett is doing right is implementing their commitment," said Al Fitzpatrick, assistant vice president for minority affairs at Knight-Ridder Inc., which owns 29 daily newspapers including the *Philadelphia Inquirer* and *Miami Herald*. Knight-Ridder also is considered an industry leader in providing opportunities for minorities and women.

But Fitzpatrick said the challenge ahead for Gannett, Knight-Ridder, and other major media companies is the elevation of women and minorities into what he called "key decision-making roles."

"We don't have any black presidents or vice presidents" at major newspapers, he said, adding the issue will "be something worth watching in the next five years or so."

Top-Level Commitment

Gannett's accomplishments in helping women and minorities advance in the company started in the 1970s to "reflect the communities [the company serves] in the makeup of its workforce," Madelyn P. Jennings, the company's senior vice president for personnel, told BNA.

Jennings was among several executives at Gannett who credited former company chairman Allen H. Neuharth with making workforce diversity one of the company's main objectives.

In an interview with BNA, Neuharth emphasized the strong link between workforce diversity and business success.

"It's the smart thing to do from a business standpoint," said Neuharth, now chairman of Gannett Foundation, said. He said media companies need workforce diversity to "appeal to a very diverse audience."

Despite its progress, "Gannett still has a lot of work to do in this area," Neuharth said. Neuharth said that during his 19 years as chairman and president of Gannett he was determined that the company would not be one that "leads the way in preaching equal opportunity but not in practicing it.

"If the CEO of a company does not lead, or drive, or push in this area, very little is likely to happen," he said.

Neuharth spoke to BNA at a time when he was being criticized himself for advocating in a July 28, 1989, *USA Today* column, the return of "sky girls" to commercial air travel. In the Friday "Plain Talk" column, Neuharth wrote that, "Most of the young, attractive, enthusiastic female flight attendants — then called stewardesses — have been replaced by aging women who are tired of their jobs or by flighty young men who have trouble balancing a cup of coffee or tea."

The column was widely condemned. Some of this reaction appeared in *USA Today* the following Monday, in a response from the Association of Flight Attendants and in a letter signed by more than 175 *USA Today* news staffers. The letter called Neuharth's column "bigoted and insulting."

Despite the criticism, Neuharth defended the colume, saying the reaction was to the term "sky girls" in the headline.

"I think it was the quick reaction of people who knee-jerk and shoot from the hip," he said. Neuharth said he received a "heavy volume of reaction" to the column, both pro and con. "People who read it thoughtfully got the message," he said.

He said he did not believe reaction to the column would affect Gannett efforts to create a diverse workforce. But he added that some people inside and outside the communications industry frequently are "waiting to criticize anybody who's made some progress or had a certain amount of success."

AFFIRMATIVE ACTION AND COMPETITIVENESS

Gannett officials believe the company's financial success is closely related to the results of its affirmative action efforts. They say employee diversity is vital to succeeding in an increasingly competitive and increasingly diverse marketplace.

"It gives you a competitive edge," Jose A. Berrios, director of Gannett's personnel and equal employment opportunity programs, told BNA. Diversity is especially important in news room staffs because of the diverse audiences that Gannett newspapers and broadcasting stations cover and serve, Berrios said.

"We want a diverse workplace, so we recruit everybody," he explained.

'PARTNERS IN PROGRESS'

In 1979, Neuharth launched Gannett's "Partners in Progress" (PIP), a program designed to ensure that more minorities and women were hired and promoted.

Placing women and minorities in middle management is one area in which the company needs to make more progress, said James R. Jones, the company's vice president for employee relations.

"Middle management is where we need more help. They're the toughest jobs to fill," Jones told BNA. To meet this need, the company plans to do more to retain and attract a large enough pool of women and minorities to move into middle management positions, Jones said.

Company Reporting Requirements

All Gannett units submit annual PIP reports and departmental employee profiles to the employee relations department. A Gannett written directive to managers calls this information "vehicles for monitoring affirmative action progress and assessing how well units are using available opportunities to improve their EEO status."

Managers are directed to "maintain detailed records of these numbers throughout the year as part of your own monitoring system. The year-end data is the only means we have for effectively evaluating your progress in the area of EEO. Lack of sufficient or correct information will negatively affect your unit's evaluation," the directive said.

Gannett emphasizes hiring and promotion of minorities into what the EEOC refers to as top four positions — officials and managers, professionals, technicians, and salespeople. Gannett tabulates figures on employment in these positions as employers must compile such information for the Employer Information Reports (EEO-1) they are required to submit to the federal EEOC.

When the percentage of minorities or women in top four job categories in any Gannett unit is below half of the percentage they represent in the local area's general population, the company requires that unit to report top four vacancies to Gannett's employee relations department. That department then conducts an applicant search and notifies recruiting sources of available openings.

The company directive describes the unit evaluation process this way:

Each unit's EEO/affirmative action progress is reviewed each year by Gannett's Vice President/Employee Relations as part of the overall management review in December. The procedures used to accomplish this evaluation follow:

A self-rating form is used to calculate an overall rating for your unit. You are asked to complete the form and assign yourself points according to your employment percentages. Your unit's total score determines your rating. In turn, this rating is taken into consideration when determining incentive bonuses for unit executives and department heads. It is also used in selecting winners of our Partners In Progress awards ....

Jennings and Berrios said this system of tying bonuses to affirmative action performance might be the most effective way to get results.

"When it affects their pocketbooks, they'll pay attention," Jennings said.

Units that achieve affirmative action goals for minorities and women in top four jobs and total employment receive a plaque recognizing their performance. The corporate EEO Advisory Committee then selects one "Super Award" winner from among the units that receive plaques. The super award, a silver cup and $2,500 to pay for affirmative action internships, is given to that unit that has made exceptional progress in achieving quality and diversity.

An EEO Advisory Committee was been established in each division to help Gannett management improve its equal employment opportunity effort. Each committee comprises managers who report directly to their division director, analyzing EEO progress and recommending ways to bring more minorities and women into higher levels of management within the division and throughout Gannett. Copies of these reports also are sent to the corporate Advisory Committee, the company's chief executive officer, and the other top-level managers who sit on the Gannett Management Committee.

EMPLOYEES COMMENT

Gannett executives, managers, and other employees told BNA that workforce diversity efforts have been successful largely because emphasis was placed on results.

"We think that it is an absolute necessity, from a business standpoint, for us to be this diverse," said Gracia Martore, an assistant treasurer who has worked at Gannett for four years.

Toni Miller, vice-president for finance at *USA Today*, joined *USA Today* as director of financial reporting and analysis and was promoted to her current job 11 months later when her boss retired.

Miller said she left her previous employer, a magazine, to join Gannett after hearing that it is "top notch in terms of minority and female development." Such a reputation helps the company "attract talented minorities and women," Miller said.

US WEST

In 1987, US West Inc. — the telecommunications giant with 70,000 employees in 14 states — decided to give special attention to minority women, a major segment of its workforce that had been largely forgotten when it came to promotions. The company launched an accelerated development program to help them acquire the skills necessary to move into management positions.

Juanita Cox-Burton, who heads the program, knows that few other black women have been able to reach similar levels of responsibility at the company, and she thinks she knows why. "Because 80 percent of the women-of-color [at US West] work at clerical jobs, when [promotion] decisions are made, their names don't pop-up because nobody knows they exist," she said. "Some of us have gotten through the glass ceiling. We did it on our own, taking a lot of risks, getting lots of exposure and knowing the right people, but we're a small number," she said.

US West is the Denver-based holding company of US West Communications Inc., which comprises the telephone companies formerly known as Pacific Northwest Bell, Mountain Bell and Northwestern Bell. Fifty-four percent of the company's work force is female, while 63 percent of the workers are either members of minority groups or are female. Despite these statistics, minority women were seldom found in management ranks.

ORIGINS OF THE PROGRAM

The accelerated development program for minority women, which is designed to tap the leadership talents of exceptional "women-of-color," evolved from the efforts of a coalition of resource groups, which were formed to present issues pertinent to black, Hispanic, and female employees to US West management. Those resource groups also serve as a link between "communities-of-color" and the company.

The resource groups formed a coalition to research upward mobility and in 1985 discovered that minority women fared worst in the race to the top. While one white man in 21 reached the company's mid-management ranks, and one minority male in 42 reached mid-management, only one white woman in 136 achieved such a position. But minority women fared even worse than did their white counterparts. Only one minority woman in 286 attained a middle- or upper-management post. Thanks to the accelerated development program one minority woman in 180 now reaches a middle- or upper-management post.

"It's not just a US West problem, it exists across the United States," said Cox-Burton. "The only difference is that we're doing something about it." She added that the corporation's officers "were as appalled as we were" when they learned how seldom minority women were employed in middle- and upper-management.

Selection

Recruitment for the accelerated development program entailed surveying the 6,000 minority women employed by the company. A profile was sent to these women asking them to provide information about their work and educational backgrounds, skills, and career objectives. About 2,000 surveys were returned to a team supervised by Cox-Burton, which then rated the surveys according to four categories: leadership, education, job experience and background, and supervisors' input about the employee's suitability for promotion.

Of the 2,000 women who returned surveys, 215 were interviewed and 50 were ultimately chosen for the program.

The program's activities began with an orientation that included speeches by top officers of US West and social events at a Denver hotel. When the social events ended, the women remained for several days for seminars on "efficacy."

These classes focused on the socialization processes to which all women have been subjected, such as "learned helplessness," Cox-Burton said. "All women have learned to be helpless" and have been taught to become wives and mothers, she said. Moreover, when women work, they are usually employed in subservient jobs such as secretarial or administrative assistant posts, she said.

"Someone has always controlled our lives for us," Cox-Burton said.

Competition and Challenges

Program participants were encouraged to think about whether they exert control over their lives and whether they would be comfortable with doing so once they embarked on the "fast-track." Role-playing and team games were also used during these sessions to help women explore these issues.

The manner in which the women played the games provided an "indication of how we play life," she explained. One such game set up adversarial teams that competed to obtain the most money. Had all the teams worked together, each group would have "won." But some women assumed the game required winners and losers and demonstrated "behavior that is very demeaning and destructive," she said. "We do this within [the context of] a game, but it's an indication of how we deal with life."

During sessions held at a mountain community outside of Denver, another game was conducted in which the participants were blindfolded and instructed to walk along ropes that were strung across "a huge area," Cox-Burton said. The women encountered bushes, trees, and hills. Following the rope required the women to make choices about whether to continue along their present path, whether to turn around, whether to pursue a fork in the path, and about how to negotiate around obstacles or return from dead-ends.

"Some women stopped, and didn't go anywhere," she said, while some women pursued a dead-end path, were told so, and continued down it. "The same way they walk the rope is the same way they walk life."

An "assessment process" also occurred in which women were placed in fictional crisis situations and were responsible for managing the company through such crises. "They were all at a disadvantage," Cox-Burton noted, "because none was an officer of a major corporation. But from that process we were able to discern what their level of ability was to be an officer. We gave them lots of feedback, and they gave each other feedback."

Subsequent programs have dealt with helping women hone leadership and survival skills, also through various games and role-playing exercises.

"We intentionally avoided telling them what's right and what's wrong," Cox-Burton said. Women were urged to make those determinations themselves, based on information given to them.

The women selected for the program were already "risk-takers" who were willing to extend themselves in order to advance their careers, she said. Nevertheless, she believes that the participants in the program have been "empowered" by it. Women who have long sought promotions and been stymied in those efforts often come to believe that some personal deficiency prevents their advancement, she said, when, in fact, minority women have long been "invisible" to corporate officials making promotion decisions. Such women didn't lack the experience, education or ability, they simply never were given the opportunity to advance, she said.

While racism and sexism are factors in employment decisions that affect minority women, Cox-Burton believes that more subtle factors also are at work. "People who are at the top are white males; they make the decisions," she commented. "We all have a tendency to hire people who look, act and talk like us." If minority women manage to break through, they are likely to "do the same thing," she said. "It's human behavior. But we just aren't there to compete with them [white males]," she said.

Cox-Burton said she believes the program has helped the participants overcome any lack of self-confidence that might have stemmed from being passed over for promotions, and she believes the women have emerged stronger. Managers who supervise women from the accelerated development program "know these women are different from most of their employees. You can tell that, even if you didn't know that woman a year ago. You can see their personal power, charisma," she said.

The women have all devised five-year "career plans," which they are responsible for implementing. The company does not place them in different jobs but instead urges the women to identify the types of jobs they desire, and to create the opportunity to be employed in such a post.

Participants' Experiences

The program teaches women that if they desire a job that currently doesn't exist at US West that they should do as Alma Alvarez-Smith did, research the possibilities and sell US West managers on the need for the post.

Like other minority women, Alvarez-Smith was all but invisible to the mid- and upper-management of US West, at least when it came to promotions. She found she was unable to advance beyond the non-management, customer service representative post she held for most of her 10 years at US West. While hers is a first-level management job, "for me it's a major promotion," Alvarez-Smith said. She credits the program with providing her with the skills to obtain her present job, and for providing greater self-confidence.

The program "really forces you to look at what you're doing, how you're perceived, and what you could do differently," she said.

The program also has wrought changes in the way she deals with all facets of her life, not just her work life. "I do handle many things differently," she said. "A lot of it has to do with self-confidence. I'm asserting myself more, really reaching out.

I'm an entirely different person today than I was a year and half ago, though the core is the same," she said.

While Alvarez-Smith believes that formerly she was a rather passive and accommodating individual, she believes she's now more assertive. "I'm still a team player," she said. But before, "it was okay to just take the accolades that go with a job well done, and let someone else take the promotion. I'm not willing to do that anymore," she said.

Marilyn Figueroa had been employed by US West for 14 years as a service representative. Her involvement in the accelerated development program led to employment in the construction sector of US West's operations. In June 1988, Figueroa became a project manager on a telecommunications construction project, and in December 1988, she became a construction manager. She assumed responsibility for all underground construction in Arizona, except for the Phoenix area. She also became responsible for buried construction in Tucson.

Figueroa credits the program with providing her with the knowledge of how to reach her career goals. "It hasn't been easy," Figueroa said of meeting the demands of the program, her new job responsibilities, as well as family responsibilities. But she never questioned whether she ought to participate in the program. "I was honored I got selected," she said. "I had no second thoughts."

Nevertheless, "there were some hard times," she said. "When they took place they were not happy experiences," she said, but looking back on those experiences has revealed "how much they did help me." She refers specifically to "evaluation-type" exercises. "They gave you some pretty hardcore feedback," she said. Many of the women weren't "trained to take that kind of feedback. But we've learned that feedback is something positive, something we need and want," Figueroa said.

Expectations of program participants are high, she noted. "I think a lot of people perceived [the program] as a bed of roses.

It hasn't been. People on the program have worked very hard; we're not even allowed to be satisfied. We have to be outstanding," she said. "There's a lot of people watching." If the program isn't a success, "others might not have this kind of opportunity," Figueroa said. "So there is a lot of pressure."

Results

Thus far, the program appears to be working. Forty-six percent of the participants had already received promotions, while 92 percent had changed jobs, according to Juanita Cox-Burton.

The program is expensive, but US West believes the importance of the objective justifies the resources committed to it, she said. The program costs about $50,000 to $75,000 per participant, according to Cox-Burton, but those costs are determined by the design of the program.

"We put a lot of things into it," she noted. "We're not just trying to overcome a problem, we're also trying to develop leaders."

Support of top management for the program, as well as support among the general US West population, is crucial to the success of the effort, Cox-Burton said.

"Without that hierarchy of people saying it's the right thing to do, it won't get done," she said. At first there was some "grumbling" among US West workers about a specialized program directed toward minority women, but that kind of criticism was addressed, Cox-Burton said.

"I think we've mustered [the support of] the majority of the population. They've read the statistics and other information and agree it's the right thing to do, that it makes good business sense," she said.

Business Rationale

US West regards its efforts to promote minority women as a sound strategy to protect its market share. "The market is changing," she said, and "consequently our customers are different. When we target our market, we're really looking at women and people-of-color, a lot more so than white males," she noted.

Women and minority men are leaving corporations to start up new enterprises more frequently than white males, in part because of the "glass ceiling" which has prevented their advancement.

"If the market is changing, it doesn't make sense for white males to make all the decisions," Cox-Burton said.

Other Programs Planned

She expects that the program for minority women will serve as a model for other accelerated development efforts open to people of all races and both sexes. US West hopes that participants in the next program will represent a "pluralistic" mix.

The next program will begin in mid-1990, so details have yet to be finalized, according to Lucila Altamirano, director of accelerated development for US West. "We do want a good mixture of people," she said.

Altamirano said she hopes to design the selection process so that it will identify minorities and women who fit the criteria for participating along with white males. Moreover, "we're going to be going out and talking to people about employee development, about what the company is looking for in terms of leadership, and providing the tools to help them identify their strengths and weaknesses."

'PLURALISM' EMPHASIZED

US West's efforts toward fostering "pluralism," the company's term for a workplace that is multi-racial, multi-cultural, substantially female, and includes gays and lesbians, extends to external recruiting. While its external recruiting efforts aren't designed specifically to attract minorities and women, on occasion the company does recruit for a specific type of employee, according to Steve Wilson, director of accelerated development/external.

Managers are expected to be mindful of the mix of employees within their work groups, and are supposed to seek employees who will provide greater pluralism within those groups, he said. "It's kind of a top-down policy that they need to look at that [the mix of employees]," he said.

Wilson recruits high-potential individuals who will be candidates for leadership roles at US West. He identifies such individuals through their academic experiences, community involvement and employment history, or through their activities at other firms. The barriers that have stymied career improvements for minorities and females also hinder development in other arenas, including academic settings. But minority and female candidates must nevertheless distinguish themselves in some way, Wilson said. They must be risk takers.

"We don't have the time with an external hire to bring somebody in who needs tons and tons of training. There are certain qualities that they [recruits] have got to have," he commented.

High potential individuals who are women or minorities are recruited in part by identifying campuses and other areas where they are likely to be found. And once at US West, such candidates are immersed in the US West corporate values, which include "pluralism," he said.

REACTION TO POLICIES

Does the company's emphasis on pluralism cause discomfort for white male employees? Not for Steve Lang, who is manager of media relations. Lang recently attended a seminar on "white malism," which is required of all US West employees. The workshop was not just about white males, it was "about the way men and women see things" and the problems that might arise in the workplace because of those differences.

The seminar revealed that "generally speaking, men set goals and move toward them with as much dispatch as they can. They concentrate on the end result. Women achieve their goals, but they do it differently. They try to do it in a group process and reach the goal by using a more consensus-oriented approach," which is an approach that "frustrates men." Lang said he believes the participants enjoyed the seminar, which was conducted in a "non-threatening" manner and wasn't confrontational.

Lang also supports the accelerated development program for minority women, and he doesn't believe that this support is a function of his relatively comfortable station at US West. Support for such initiatives depends less on "where you are, than on who you are," he said. Individuals who are highly competitive and insist on comparing their performance with others will probably resent such a program, he said, while persons who seek to "do just as well as they can" for themselves and don't measure their worth by the activities of others will not oppose accelerated development efforts targeted to women and minorities.

Union Assessment

Mary Blue, the president of the Communications Workers of America, Local 7777, which represents about 5,000 workers at US West Communications Inc., believes the company could be doing more to help minorities and women move up. She told BNA that plenty of minority employees and white women are fully qualified for better positions than they currently hold and don't need a special program to equip them for better jobs. Members of these groups don't attain those jobs, though, because the management structure of the company still is largely white, and largely male, she said.

While she applauds the seminars designed to sensitize employees to racism and sexism, she believes the company is sometimes weak in its response to discrimination-related incidents.

"The way I see it, management people are responsible for keeping the work environment free of discrimination," and when they fail to do so, they should be disciplined, she said.

But Blue also acknowledged that the union also has not always been as sensitive to these issues as it should and tends to rely upon contract language as the only vehicle with which it can press claims against the company. Moreover, she estimates that about one-third of her members are minorities, but no minorities are officers of the union.

For these reasons, a complaint by a male black employee may not have been initially handled as it should have, she said. The employee complained that he was prohibited from doing the work of higher job classification because he was black, while a white male with the same job in another work group was given the opportunity to gain additional experience by performing the more difficult tasks.

The contract stipulates that the black employee's job required him to perform only the tasks assigned to that job title and did not entitle him to gain additional experience, Blue noted.

"We said, 'that's your job title, that's what you get paid for doing, and there's nothing we can do about it.'"

But a "committee on equity" formed by the union to address issues of concern to minorities considered the employee's complaint. Ultimately, the work groups were changed so that the black employee was able to gain the experience of doing additional tasks, she said.

EFFECTS OF STEREOTYPES

Stereotypes hinder the advancement of minority employees at all companies, said Colleen Mayer, vice president of the Pacific/Asian-American Network, a recently formed US West resource group. "We would like to see more Pacific/Asian people in top management positions, in leadership roles. We're trying to break the stereotype of being the invisible Americans." The stereotype promotes the image of Pacific/Asian Americans as "quiet, obedient," and "trying to be part of the mainstream," she said. "Part of the stereotype is that Asians aren't leaders."

While a combination of work experience, exposure and risk-taking brought Mayer midway up the corporate ladder, she believes few other Pacific/Asian women will follow because of the Pacific/Asian stereotype. Indeed, Pacific/Asian women often find that roles prescribed by their cultures conflict with their career objectives, and that family and personal conflict often results, Mayer said.

"If my grandparents were still alive, and I went to their house, I'd immediately be in a submissive role." These sorts of cultural conflicts hinder upward mobility and have caused Mayer to resort to living a kind of double life. "One is based on my grandparent's cultural values, and one is based on where I want to go within the company."

Mayer applauds US West's concern for these issues and believes that its sensitivity to pluralism will help its position in the international market place. US West is a "very good place to work. I know some people in other larger corporations and I know I wouldn't want to go there," she said.

AETNA LIFE & CASUALTY

"Minorities and women are still under-represented at Aetna—
particularly in technical and managerial jobs. We must be able to
identify and understand some of the barriers to progress that exist
within big corporations. Then it will be easier to determine how to
knock them down." — John J. Dwyer, senior vice president, Commercial Insurance Division, Aetna Life & Casualty.

At Aetna, the commitment to eliminating the barriers that
prevent women and minorities from being promoted begins
with recruitment and extends throughout the corporate structure. Programs to assure that each employee has an opportunity to advance, job tracking, and extensive training programs
are used in an effort to ensure that each employee has the
same opportunity to succeed.

Ethan Loney, senior administrator for Aetna's equal employment opportunities program, told BNA that the company
is committed to recruiting and maintaining a diverse workforce. Aetna's affirmative action brochure says "if Aetna is to
successfully compete for the best talent available, it must demonstrate its ability to attract, retain and develop an increasingly
diverse workforce. That workforce, by its very nature, includes
a growing percentage of women and minorities."

RECRUITMENT AND PROMOTIONS

Aetna, headquartered in Hartford, Conn., is one of the
nation's largest financial services organizations, with assets of
$81.4 billion. The company employs some 41,000 workers, of
which nearly 70 percent are women and 18 percent are minorities. However, only 16 percent of all company officers are
women, and only 5 percent are minorities, Loney said, adding
that he and his staff are working to increase the number of
women and minorities in the pool of promotable workers.

In 1965, women comprised only 1.6 percent of officer-level
employees, and that declined to only 1.4 percent in 1975. By
1987, however, the figure had grown to 15.8 percent.

The number of minority employees in officer-level jobs increased from 0.2 percent in 1965 to 1.1 percent in 1975 and to 5.1 percent in 1987.

In addition to blacks, Loney said Aetna recruits Asian Americans, Hispanics and American Indians, and the company often seeks employees of a certain ethnic background to fill overseas positions.

At Aetna the equal opportunity and affirmative action programs stress recruitment and developmental training programs. "It's important to emphasize the programs, because anyone can hire or promote," Loney explained. "But if they don't have the training or support, it's not going to work out."

Loney said the company tries to increase its pool of available minority candidates by recruiting heavily at colleges with large minority populations, and by contacting minority student groups at other colleges and universities. Aetna's "Minorities in Corporate America" program is designed to identify top-level minority college students and introduce them to the firm.

These students are brought to Aetna headquarters where they meet the company's top managers and are told about the firm's commitment to equality in the workplace. "We are basically trying to woo these students to come to work for us," Loney explained. Strengthening ties with colleges and universities can ensure continued growth in minority representation throughout the company he added.

In addition, the Aetna Foundation has awarded a grant for scholarships for the master's of business administration component of a Florida A&M University business development program. The program combines three years of undergraduate work with a two-year MBA and includes professional development seminars that expose students to workplace situations and help them make the transition from college to jobs.

Aetna helps finance the program at Florida A&M, an historically black school, to increase the number of minority group members with MBAs and to increase the pool of minority students from which it can draw new employees.

Aetna also recruits at local community organizations, high schools, and community colleges to help fill its field office jobs. Aetna also tries to hire adequate numbers of women and minorities as college interns. This enables them to learn about career opportunities with the company and provides Aetna with word-of-mouth recruitment advertising on college campuses, Loney explained.

WORKFORCE DEMOGRAPHICS

Aetna also is committed to the communities where it operates to hire more women and minorities, Loney stressed. "If you are worried about the workforce of tomorrow, you have to start even earlier than college," he said. The company's three-part "Stepping Up" program helps school-age children develop workplace skills.

For example, in Aetna's "Saturday Academy" junior high school students acquire business and data processing skills and improve their writing abilities.

"Students at Work" provides work/study for potential high school dropouts. Students are guaranteed regular, full-time jobs with Aetna if they complete the program and graduate from high school. Aetna's "Hire and Train" program identifies and assists marginally employed and unemployed adults and young people. Experts assess participants' educational needs and provide training that fulfills these needs and prepares them for jobs at Aetna. For example, Aetna has worked with the Hartford branch of the National Puerto Rican Forum to provide clerical skills training for local residents who were hired by the company after completing the program. Hire and Train, first offered only in Hartford, has been extended to several field offices.

Loney said Aetna also has reviewed its job descriptions to eliminate any requirements that may not be valid and that might discriminate against women and/or minorities. For example, the company tried to determine whether requiring a high school diploma for many jobs was necessary. The company decided that for some jobs, high school dropouts could be hired and subsequently earn their diplomas at the Aetna Institute for Corporate Education.

The Aetna Institute annually provides training to more than 28,000 employees, ranging from basic literacy programs to management education. The curriculum includes training in insurance disciplines such as underwriting, marketing, claims, and systems. Aetna also offers computer-based training and uses direct-broadcast satellite television to bring training from its home office to employees in 94 locations nationwide. Aetna employees can advance by selecting a job and then taking the appropriate classes at the institute to prepare for it.

Loney described the institute programs as an extra benefit that helps the company attract qualified women and minorities because many members of these groups might not otherwise have access to such programs that help prepare them for higher-level positions.

Posted job openings list requirements for the position. Posting jobs allows employees to "self-select" the job track they want to pursue, Loney explained. Employees are allowed to bid on any job and can bid for lateral moves, promotions, or even demotions if they want to switch job tracks.

In addition, all Aetna employees receive an annual review from their immediate supervisor. This is followed by a salary appraisal in which the employee's wage increase is tied to how well the worker met the performance goals outlined by the supervisor the previous year. Employee salary appraisals are reviewed by management and compared to wage increases in other financial services companies.

Some workers complain about this process and its result, Loney admitted, but Aetna has established strict personnel policies that "provide enough checks and balances to rectify errors when they become apparent." This program especially benefits women and minorities because it all but eliminates managers' opportunities to discriminate or show favoritism, Loney said.

The company's affirmative action and equal employment opportunity statements appear in all policy manuals and employee handbooks, and the firm's employee relations counselors are trained to advise employees regarding conflicts with supervisors on matters of race, sex, and age.

In addition, the company has established a grievance resolution procedure that allows employees to report problems to their supervisor's supervisor, and to call an employee relations counselor if the problem is not resolved.

WORKFORCE DIVERSITY STRESSED

Aetna management courses and non-management career development courses include the "message that we live in a diverse society and the better job we can do in operating in a changing society, the better we can do in the long run," Loney explained. The company offers presentations by outside consultants that prepare its managers to work in an environment populated increasingly by women and minorities.

These one-hour to three-day presentations stress the company's belief that the better issues are understood, the better people can deal with them. The courses stress how to manage diverse populations, and some examine participants' feelings about racial issues.

Loney said workforce diversity has been included in all management training to enable supervisors to manage changing workforces effectively. Managers learn know how to deal with all categories of employees.

"They simply must learn not to overvalue or undervalue anyone," Loney explained. If managers "can't say something to a woman because she might cry, then [the manager] shouldn't be a manager," he said.

Employees who do not accept blacks as supervisors, co-workers in wheelchairs, or 55-year-old trainees will not succeed with Aetna, company officials said.

Valeria Howard, a claims manager for the personal and financial security unit of the Rocky Mountain Claims Division, said this emphasis on diversity has been evident through most of her 15 years with the company.

Howard told BNA she was aware of a strong commitment by Aetna to recruit and promote minorities when she was hired. Although she thought the focus on affirmative action declined later, she since has seen a "renewed emphasis" on it during the past two years.

Howard said the company is "putting in a lot of effort to expose people to different opportunities. [Women and minorities] have a chance to move up within the management system if that is what they choose to do." Howard said Aetna also is implementing community programs for women and minorities. "That is where our source of future employees is going to come from," she said. "Aetna is giving them the opportunity to become the best candidates for the job."

Howard said a female minority manager in a "white-male dominated world" must work even harder. "And you have to be so much more cautious about what you do and what you say." As a minority manager, she has experienced the other side of racism. "The minorities accuse me of not listening, so its a complicated situation. But Aetna does have programs in place if people feel they are being treated unfairly and if they use them. If people use the system, nobody can be unfair to anybody.

"But no matter how good the programs in place are, you have to have good survival skills and learn to play the game," Howard added.

CONSULTING PAIRS PROGRAM

Nicholas Aponte, an Hispanic American who is an investment director at the Aetna Investment Management Group, told BNA he thinks Aetna has made a "very good effort" to address workforce diversity issues. Aponte said the company understands the different perspectives minorities and women bring to the workplace.

Aponte is part of a new Aetna program called "Consulting Pairs," which each company division can implement.

In this program, pairs of employees of different racial or ethnic backgrounds—often a woman and a man—address issues of diversity in the workplace. The teams—an Hispanic male and a black female, for example—received three weeks of "intensive" offsite training on issues relating to race and relationships between the sexes, Aponte explained. The pairs now advise other pairs of workers who are experiencing conflict in their work relationship.

The pairs also share new ideas and skills with supervisors to help them manage workers, and they help employees increase their awareness of cultural differences among workers.

"Minorities may have different needs and expectations," Aponte said.

XEROX CORP.

Xerox Corp. has made progress in recruiting minorities and women and now is focusing on "corporate mobility," or ways of assuring that members of these groups are not limited in the kinds of positions they hold, the company's manager of affirmative action told BNA.

Ted Payne stressed that female and minority employees are not promoted to jobs that exceed their skills so Xerox can meet its balanced workforce goals. He said Xerox policies and programs work to make sure all employees are given an opportunity to prepare themselves to rise in the management ranks.

Management training emphasizes the basic principles of how to manage. For example, Payne said, the company gives managers scripts to follow if they feel uncomfortable talking to workers about performance problems. Xerox also assesses managers' competency in the area of affirmative action as part of their annual performance appraisal.

Payne said that since Xerox introduced managerial training programs in the mid-1970s, employee productivity has risen 10 percent to 15 percent.

EARLY COMMITMENT

Xerox Corp.'s commitment to hiring minorities began in response to Executive Order 11246, issued by President Johnson in 1965, requiring employers to adopt affirmative action programs. Xerox responded by implementing programs to hire minorities — primarily black males — at its Stamford, Conn., headquarters and in several field locations.

In 1971, Xerox spent $1 million establishing affirmative action programs throughout the company. The firm identified affirmative action as a business priority and set numerical targets for representation of minorities at various job levels. A key component of the program was to identify jobs that would lead to upper-level management positions and to hire women and minorities to fill them. About $330,000 was budgeted for recruiting women and minorities.

Throughout the 1980s, Xerox has made affirmative action part of its human resources strategic plan and has increased hiring of women, Hispanics, blacks, and Asian-Americans.

STRESSING THE BASICS

Xerox, a business products and financial services company, has been included in *Black Enterprise* magazine's "The 50 Best Places for Blacks to Work." After Xerox was listed in 1986, Payne recalled, David T. Kearns, current chairman and chief executive officer, had reprints of the article distributed to every Xerox employee. "This began a path being beaten to our door," said Payne, who has received requests for information about Xerox's affirmative action program from equal employment opportunity officers at dozens of other companies.

Payne said Xerox has no secret formula for hiring and promoting qualified women and minorities. He attributes the company's success in affirmative action to the fact that it sets goals and meets them. "Just like a football team which practices blocking and tackling. We are just stressing the basics," Payne explained.

"Xerox really doesn't have any minority programs in the classic sense," he said. Instead, the company places people in the jobs, lets them get experience, and then puts them in a pool of employees who are qualified for promotion. "When you get enough women and minorities into the pool, some are going to make it to the upper levels," Payne said.

At Xerox, fairness and affirmative action are part of the business process. The company previously had spent a lot of time planning for investment in facilities and equipment. In the 1980s, it began devoting more of its resources to attracting and retaining well-qualified, motivated employees. A key component of the company's human resources plan is having a workforce with diverse backgrounds, Payne added.

PIVOTAL POSITIONS EMPHASIZED

In 1972, Xerox realized that if it wanted to hire and promote women and minorities into key positions, it had to determine how the people then in those positions got them, Payne said. To learn this, the firm studied the biographies of employees in such jobs to establish career paths that other employees could follow.

Xerox examined the careers of the officials who directed all company functions, including human resources, sales, and finance. At that time, the firm had approximately 500 sales managers, most of them white males. They were given the responsibility of promoting the minorities the company had hired, when they met the qualifications for promotion. Managers initially were given a goal of appointing one or two black sales managers within six months to a year. This goal was increased over the years, Payne said.

Payne also noted that while the initial focus had been on the hiring and advancement of black males, shortly thereafter the company expanded that effort to include women and other minority groups.

A. Barry Rand, a black who has been president of Xerox's U.S. Marketing Group since 1986, is one of only six corporate vice presidents who report directly to the president of Xerox. He directs a sales force of nearly 33,000 employees.

Rand joined Xerox in 1968 as "a bag-carrying salesman," Payne said. Rand quickly became one of the firm's top salespeople and was promoted to regional sales manager. He then moved up to corporate director of major account marketing and became vice president of field operations in 1983. In 1984, he was appointed vice president of eastern operations, before moving up to his current position in 1986.

BLACK CAUCUSES A KEY FACTOR

In 1971, several black employees, including Rand, formed informal networks and challenged Xerox managers to address the lack of advancement of entry-level minority employees. According to Payne, the employees were disturbed that a typical white employee was likely to advance faster than a typical black employee hired at the same time.

Then-President McColough met with members of the black caucuses and found the groups to be a valuable forum. He directed the company to recognize the black support groups and work with them as along as their goals and objectives were similar to those of the company.

Today Xerox has over 100 support groups that hold annual regional conferences to discuss workplace issues. The format has been so successful that women and other minority groups also have established support systems, Payne said.

The caucuses are not official units of Xerox, but the company benefits from their presence, Payne said. He characterized the groups as self-help forums where experienced black employees offer suggestions and advice to new and inexperienced black Xerox workers. The groups meet on their own time rather than during work hours, and black managers often come in on weekends to help new hires get acquainted with the workplace. Payne cited this as another example of how Xerox and its employees stress the basics. The support groups also monitor the company's employment practices to assure fair treatment for minorities.

Payne maintained that Xerox now has the "most diverse workforce in America, bar none. No one has more minorities distributed throughout the workforce." Payne said that although Xerox remains committed to fairness, the same is not true of all of corporate America.

"Affirmative action keeps a hand on your back and keeps pushing you forward," Payne said. Some employers practice affirmative action only because the government requires it. In some companies, the government keeps that hand at your back. "At Xerox, the company keeps that hand in place."

A 'SOUND BUSINESS PRACTICE'

Affirmative action previously meant "get as many blacks as you can," Payne said. Managers now determine the demographics of the local workforce and hire employees roughly in proportion to the extent their race and gender are represented in it.

In a bulletin to all managers, the company stated that: "[b]alancing our workforce is sound business practice. In the short-term it will help us achieve our revenue and profit plans." The bulletin notes that all of the firm's accounts with the federal government and with local and state governments require that Xerox have equal opportunity programs. The bulletin stresses, "the long-term impact [of the changing workforce] may be even more significant" than simply meeting government mandates.

"The U.S. workforce is shrinking .... More and more employers will be vying for fewer and fewer employees. Staying competitive demands being able to take advantage of all our human resources, regardless of race, age or sex, for all positions from entry-level through senior management ... But we would balance our workforce even if we didn't have compelling business reasons. It is absolutely the right thing to do."

Payne said a "balanced workforce" means that all four employee groups—majority males, majority females, minority males and minority females—are represented in all functions and at all levels at Xerox.

To achieve this balance, the company has established goals based on U.S. census data and the composition of the Xerox workforce. A goal has been established for each job category and grade within it. The goals represent the percent each type or group of person is represented in the local population.

Each operating unit sets an annual target designed to change the percent representation of each group in the unit so that the target will be achieved by the mid-1990s. Managers are responsible for meeting goals. When openings occur, managers are encouraged to "seize the opportunity to improve the representation of those groups which are underutilized," he stressed.

The Xerox program works like this: Grade band 15-18 in a particular operating unit may contain four minority females, and they comprise 2 percent of all employees in those grades. If the workforce goal based on internal and U.S. census data indicates that minority women should represent 13 percent of those grades, the company knows that the number of minority females in those grades must increase by 2 percent a year to reach the goal for those grades by the 1995. Annual targets set each year, and they are periodically reassessed based on new data.

The company stresses that a grade-band goal should not be reached with various population groups represented only in a limited number of job categories, such as sales and personnel. "Women and minorities must be represented in all functions, including finance, data processing, engineering and service," a managers' booklet advises.

In 1988, minorities represented 18.5 percent of all Xerox officers and managers, and women comprised 19.8 percent. Twenty percent of the firm's professional workers were minorities, and 29 percent were women. Minorities represented 21 percent of the firm' sales employees and 17 percent of the company's technical workers, while women comprised 40 percent and 9 percent, respectively. These figures were significantly higher than comparative figures for 1978, and in some cases, especially higher level jobs, they had nearly doubled.

AMERICAN TELEPHONE & TELEGRAPH

After spending 22 years designing integrated circuits at Bell Labs in Reading, Pa., Wayne Crigler devoted six years to teaching electrical engineering at a historically black college in Greensboro, N.C.

Crigler's stint as a visiting professor at North Carolina Agriculture & Technical State University is part of a program AT&T started in 1973, involving 10 historically black colleges and universities: Howard University, North Carolina A&T State University, Tuskegee University, Southern University, Tennessee State University, Prairie View A&M University, Jackson State University, Atlanta University Center, Xavier University, and Hampton University.

Scientists and engineers already working for AT&T volunteer for the teaching assignments. AT&T keeps them on the payroll—and picks up other expenses—with the hope "that someone from a small school in Alabama who's been exposed to an AT&T mind will seek out AT&T as an employer," Burke Stinson, district manager of media relations, told BNA.

While most visiting professors stay one year, Crigler extended his assignment each year from the time he began teaching in August 1983. The opportunity to extend signifies AT&T's commitment to the program, Crigler said. "Typically, most management would like you to come back and produce money in regular operations," he noted.

For Crigler, the best part of the program is that "you take a technical person who's been working in industry, and he or she discusses with a student their experiences from the real world. You start bringing that real-world experience in, and the students actually perk up."

Besides pushing AT&T as an employer, the program also gives students—and their non-AT&T professors—an opportunity to spend summers at a Bell Labs facility. While the student gets the advantage of working at a top company during the summer, the faculty member gets the chance to interact with colleagues in the field and make contacts.

Programs Spurred by Consent Decree

The visiting professor program and other affirmative action efforts at AT&T began following a consent decree between the company and the Equal Employment Opportunity Commission in 1973. The company agreed to compensate women and minority male employees alleged to be victims of discrimination in job assignments, pay, and promotions. AT&T also promised a new promotion and wage policy for women and minority employees.

The agreement between AT&T and the EEOC came after the agency filed charges of racial and sex discrimination against the company in December 1970. The EEOC charged that there was "pervasive and systemic" discrimination in the company's hiring and promotion policies under the agreement. AT&T did not acknowledge it had discriminated against any of its employees.

Numbers Grow

In the years following the consent decree, the number of women in middle management and upper management positions at AT&T rose from 300 in 1972 to 12,000 by 1989, Stinson said. About 10,000 blacks were among the ranks of middle managers or above, accounting for 7.7 percent of the 126,000 people holding these positions at the company. Two blacks sit on the company's board of directors, and there are black engineers and scientists who head major divisions.

Stinson said the company is working to improve on these numbers. "AT&T would probably be the first to admit that while progress has been made, we have a mile to go before we can say we are where we could be," Stinson said. He said one major obstacle to greater workforce diversity at AT&T has been the relative scarcity of minorities with training in science and engineering.

"AT&T considers itself a high-tech company and its pools of talent are in science and engineering schools, which are dominated by white men," Stinson said.

According to testimony before the House Subcommittee on Science, Research and Technology, black student enrollment in science and engineering in 1987 was about 1 percent of total enrollment in those fields, while blacks accounted for about 8 percent of total college enrollments. Similarly, blacks accounted for only 2.3 percent of all employed scientists and engineers in 1987, although blacks constituted 10 percent of the overall U.S. workforce.

With such a small pool to draw from, Stinson said, "We have to work twice as hard to move up these percentages a notch or two."

Overall, about 50 percent of the people the company now hires are women, and about 30 percent are minorities, Stinson said. Getting them on the promotion track remains a problem, however.

MENTORING INHERENT IN JOB

Mentoring is one of the approaches AT&T has been using to help women and minorities advance. The chairman of the board, for example, was officially responsible for mentoring a number of people, as were other officers in the firm. The process has evolved into an informal one, in which supervisors are encouraged to seek out promising employees and give them extra guidance, Stinson said.

Yvonne Shepard, a 20-year veteran of AT&T, considers it part of her job to be a mentor. As division manager of new business development at AT&T's headquarters in Basking Ridge, N.J., Shepard told BNA that part of her role "is to help develop the talent in this company—that's what I get paid for."

Shepard, who is Puerto Rican, was herself the beneficiary of mentoring shortly after she began work at AT&T, although she didn't realize it at the time. A math major from a small women's Catholic college in Indiana, Shepard began work doing long-term economic analysis and software development at Bell Laboratories, AT&T's research and development division. She then took advantage of a job opening in Chicago that involved more computer work; she also enrolled at Northwestern University in Evanston, where, at company expense, she earned a master's degree in computer science.

"The decision to go to grad school came from somebody who called me aside and said, 'I want to tell you something, kid. At Bell Labs, you don't get anywhere without a graduate degree and being a member of the technical staff,' " Shepard remembered.

"At the time, I didn't even realize what was going on. I thought, 'Boy, I was fortunate that this person [a department head several management levels up] advised me' .... It's clear to me now that he was mentoring me, that he felt that I had capabilities, that I could offer more than I had.

"He was telling me what the rules of the game were, and at that time not many women got to know what the rules of the game were," she said.

Shepard has since moved several times between research and development positions at various Bell Labs facilities and AT&T's business divisions, primarily at its Basking Ridge headquarters. Each new job brings with it a chance to provide more mentoring. Whom she mentors depends largely on rapport and a sense of affinity.

"What ends up happening is that, because I am a woman and because I am a minority, as I get a new assignment, a lot of women and minorities come to me for career planning. People need to feel comfortable to come and talk to you," she said.

The role of a mentor, Shepard said, is to help find the balance between what's best for the employee and what's best for the company.

"It varies from person to person. Some people need a broader set of experiences; others need more self-assurance," she said. For those in the latter group, Shepard strives to point out their successes, often recommends a public-speaking course, and directs people with questions in the employee's field of expertise to go to that employee for the answers. She also will invite them to make presentations, "but most often they'll decline to do it," she admitted.

The most important quality, Shepard concluded, is to be perceived as accessible and caring. "An open door—that's really the role of a mentor," she said.

BUILDING A LARGER POOL

While Shepard helps women and minorities once they already work for AT&T, the job of Wayne Crigler and others in the visiting professor program is to help women and minorities get into the door. The program also encourages workers to visit their former schools as role models. Jaime Mitchell, for instance, who designs integrated circuits at Bell Labs in Murray Hill, N.J., has gone back to visit in Greensboro, where he earned his master's degree in electrical engineering in 1985 and where Crigler had been one of his professors.

A Panamanian brought up in The Bronx in New York City, Mitchell said Crigler had helped by telling him the "ins and outs" of Bell Labs and by making sure recruiters did not overlook anyone. But Mitchell said he was sold on AT&T almost before he got to college.

"They're always the leading edge of technology," he said. The company's employment record also drew Mitchell to AT&T. "The fact that they were hiring from my school—I didn't assume that they were very prejudiced—and I saw the kind of students they were hiring, so I worked to bring my grades up," he said. "One thing about Bell Labs was, if you had the grades, you got the job."

Mitchell's first glance at the job market, when he was just starting out as an undergraduate at Howard University, was back in the 1970's, however, when "downsizing wasn't even a term," he noted. Today, holding on to one's job may be as hard as getting it in the first place.

"When I talk with the folks who graduated with me, they're all doing something else," Mitchell said. "I'm one of the very few who's doing what he graduated to do. I feel very lucky."

He said part of that "luck" stems from AT&T's work ethic: "They judge you by the quality of work you do." But the work environment also can be harsh. "You've got to be demanding; you've got to demand to get on the project you want to," he said.

COUNTERING THE 'OLD-BOY NETWORK'

Like most corporations, AT&T has yet to lose all vestiges of its "old-boy network," made up primarily of white male managers who place personal preference first in handing out jobs and promotions. Tying into that network thus becomes critical to advancement, particularly in these times of staff reductions. As Mitchell put it, drawing on an analogy to baseball: "You have to be able to read the signs that your team is passing back and forth to each other."

Isolation also can be personally frustrating for minorities.

"You might be the only black among 200 whites at a meeting," an experience quite different from the nearly all-black environment of graduate school at North Carolina A&T, Mitchell said.

In an effort to counter feelings of isolation, a group of black engineers in Mitchell's division started getting together in the late 1980s to talk about their problems, air frustrations, find out what others were working on, and just generally pass along information. Among other accomplishments, the group served to make newly hired black engineers aware that they were not alone in their career concerns. Mitchell, for instance, remembers his excitement at the first meeting: "I thought, 'Wow, so this is where all the black role models are.' It's amazing—you sit there and you realize there are so many black Ph.D.s around."

The director of the lab asked to meet with the group, and some changes followed. New recruits, for instance, no longer are left to fend completely for themselves.

"There had been no formalized process to welcome someone into the company, and that can leave a bad taste in your mouth," Mitchell remembered. Now, a new employee is taken around the lab and meets everyone within the first week.

"We thought maybe they were treating us differently, but that wasn't it; we were just more sensitive," Mitchell said, noting that the group discovered that newly hired white workers felt the same way. "Although the old boys' network helped [ease their transition]," he added.

Now, when the group meets every month, the topic more than likely will be "downsizing," the corporate world's term for cutting staff.

"Forty-to 50-year-olds are feeling a bit panicked," Mitchell admitted. But Mitchell, who is 30, said, "I think everybody's trying to handle that fairly."

FAMILY CONSIDERATIONS

AT&T reduced its workforce substantially in the 1980s. In 1984, the company employed 374,000 people. By 1989, the worldwide workforce consisted of some 303,000. At the same time, however, the number of managers actually increased, with more and more people doing white-collar jobs in computer science and marketing. The competition, then, for the quality workers who can fill these positions remained high.

To attract and retain these workers, the company agreed in its 1989 contract with the Communications Workers of America to foster an environment that recognizes that both men and women have lives outside their employment and that they have children and parents who need care.

According to Stinson, "The major thrust of the '90s will be trying to get the word out that AT&T has family care as part of its culture, that the days of regimentation and conformity are over, and that the days of diversity and creativity are upon us."

Under the new contract, AT&T helps provide both child and elder care and pays part of adoption expenses. It also has established a $5 million fund to encourage existing child and elder care providers to expand their operations. The phone company, after all, has workers busy 24 hours a day, 365 days a year.

"They need odd hours of day care," Stinson said. "Now what it takes for the 1990s is courage, courage for the employee to say, 'I'm going to be late today because I need to take my daughter to the doctor's,' and not 'my car won't start,' etc.

"Now the burden of proof is more or less on the supervisor to say why they can't accommodate that person," he said. Employees also have the right to appeal a supervisor's decision to the employee assistance program or through the supervisor's boss.

"It's in the contract," Stinson said. "You're being treated as an adult."

CHASE MANHATTAN CORP.

As part of its efforts to attract minority employees, Chase Manhattan Corp. sponsors a minority summer internship program that includes six weeks of business training with entry-level, full-time employees. The 13 interns of 1989 received salaries of $325 a week and room and board while learning accounting, corporate taxation, how to explain financial analyses, and how to identify and mitigate risks.

"They truly end up with skills that most internships don't provide in just a summer job," Jim Young, the banking giant's manager of equal opportunity, told BNA.

"They get a realistic view of what it takes to train to be an officer of the bank," Young said.

The interns then spent four weeks working in various areas of the corporation, observing the day-to-day business of the bank, and "getting exposure to the line people involved in hiring," Young explained.

Most interns also have an adviser/mentor, usually a member of a minority group, who gives them the opportunity to observe how employees perform their jobs, Young said.

"I'm not saying that it is or is not different for minorities, but [the interns] are able to gather insight as to how [their mentors] have done well.

"I think that most minorities perceive that it's different and that it's tougher in corporate America. I think they should have access to see for themselves," he said.

Interns' Experiences

Eight of 1988's 12 interns received offers of full-time employment at Chase in 1988, and six accepted, Young said.

Also, many former Chase minority interns have gone to graduate school or accepted jobs with the bank's competitors within a few years after completing Chase's program.

"They certainly have no trouble getting on the interview schedule of any major financial institution in the country," Young told BNA.

The 1989 interns who spoke to BNA said they were generally pleased with their experiences, but they asked that their names not be used.

"In this division, everybody's great," one of the interns said. "More than, 'What can you do to help this division?' it's more, 'What can we show you to help you learn?' "

It is difficult to get into the program, the intern said, adding, "I feel like we are the chosen few, that they want us to stay."

OVERALL PROGRESS

Black Enterprise magazine's February 1989 issue cited Chase Manhattan for its overall commitment to affirmative action, naming it among, "The 50 Best Places for Blacks to Work." Chase also has been praised by that publication and other organizations as a result of the achievements of executives such as Senior Vice President Hughlyn F. Fierce, a black man who heads the corporation's Asia-Pacific region.

In 1989, minorities comprised 15.7 percent of the bank's 7,755 officers and managers based in New York, Young said. Minorities comprised 3.5 percent of Chase executives at the senior vice president level and above; 9.5 percent of vice presidents; 15.8 percent of second vice presidents; 22.6 percent of assistant treasurers; and about 38 percent of lower-level supervisors, Young added.

Women comprised 38.1 percent of all officers and managers, including 7.1 percent of senior vice presidents and above; 23.2 percent of vice presidents; 38 percent of second vice presidents; 54 percent of assistant treasurers; 55.6 percent of those at the first supervisory level; and 70 percent of level-two supervisors.

Chase has been especially aggressive in recruiting women, Young said.

"The financial services industry is no longer the 'old-boy network,' there's been a significant change," he said. When he joined Chase in 1971, the bank had few female assistant treasurers, he said. By the end of the 1980s, women held more than half of those positions, Young noted.

Another company spokesperson, who asked not to be identified, told BNA that most of Chase's minority and female employees believe that their advancement within the firm was due more to their individual efforts than to bank programs designed to help them.

"To a man and a woman, they feel that they've gotten where they've gotten through their own hard work," the spokesperson said.

* * *

APPENDIX A

OFCCP Corporate-Level
Selection Decisions (A-3)

Office of Federal Contract Compliance Programs

Corporate-level Selection Decisions

AGENCY: Office of Federal Contract Compliance Programs (OFCCP), Labor.

ACTION: Notice.

SUMMARY: On June 14, 1988, the OFCCP issued a Policy Directive designated Order No. 830a1. The Directive provides guidance to Government contractors and subcontractors regarding the formatting of workforce and utilization data for purposes of written Affirmative Action Programs (AAPs).

EFFECTIVE DATE: June 14, 1988.

FOR FURTHER INFORMATION CONTACT: Annie A. Blackwell, Director, Division of Policy, Planning and Review, Office of Federal Contract Compliance Programs, Employment Standards Administration, Department of Labor, 200 Constitution Avenue, NW, Washington, DC 20210 (202-523-9430).

SUPPLEMENTARY INFORMATION: On June 14, 1988, the Office of Federal Contract Compliance Programs (OFCCP) issued a new Policy Directive designated as OFCCP Order No. 830a1. The Directive addresses the contents of written affirmative action programs (AAP) for Government contractors and subcontractors subject to Executive Order 11246, as amended. Because the Directive will affect the way in which many contractors prepare their AAPs the Notice and the full text of the Directive are being published in the **Federal Register** to achieve wide dissemination of the new policy.

The regulations at 41 CFR Part 60-2 require nonconstruction contractors to prepare written APPs for each of their establishments. 41 CFR 60-2.1(a). In preparing their AAPs, contractors must place each job title into a job group, compare the race and sex composition of the incumbents of the job group against availability for the job group, and when there is underutilization establish goals and timetables and action oriented programs for improving the employment of minorities and women. 41 CFR 60-2.11, 60-2.12, 60-2.13.

Under existing practice, most contractors include all jobs in the AAP of the establishment in which the job is located.

Among multi-establishment employers selections for some jobs may not be made at the establishment level. For example, plant managers may be selected by the corporate office; likewise, there may be centralized recruitment and hiring for accountants, engineers or other skilled positions. For affirmative action to be most effective, it must be applied at that level in the contractor's organization which has responsibility for the selection at issue. That is, if selections of plant managers are made by the corporate office, it is ineffective to establish in each plant's AAP a goal for the manager of that plant because that plant has no control over attainment of the goal. Instead, it is logical to include all plant managers in one job group at the corporate level, where goals and timetables and other affirmative action measures will relate directly to the actual selections for plant manager positions.

The purpose of Order No. 830a1 is to foster affirmative action in high level managerial, professional and technical jobs. The Directive does this by requiring that corporate office and intermediate level office AAPs include in their "workforce analysis, utilization analysis and goal setting * * * all those positions located in subordinate and/or lower-level establishments for which the selection decisions are made" at the corporate office or intermediate level office. Thus, affirmative action analyses and efforts will be focused where the authority and responsibility for filling positions is located, rather than arbitrarily lodged at each position's site of employment.

During OFCCP's development of this Directive, a number of questions arose as to the scope and effect of the policy. Following are several questions and answers intended to clarify OFCCP's views on this subject.

1. Question: When must contractors update their AAPs to conform to Order No. 830a1?

Answer: Contractors are not required to amend their AAPs until their current corporate headquarters or intermediate level AAPs expire, or until 90 days from June 14, 1988, whichever is later.

2. *Question:* How does this policy affect a contractor's right to make its own personnel decisions?

Answer: This Directive does not tell a contractor how to make its staffing decisions or who within the contractor's organization should make them. The policy simply requires that the contractor's AAPs reflect the actual decisionmaking process. Indeed, the Directive states that "[m]anagement should be given substantial discretion in determining proper organizational levels for job title placement * * *."

3. *Question:* By requiring that jobs located in one establishment be carried in another establishment's AAP, does this policy result in duplicate or additional recordkeeping?

Answer: If a particular job is located in one establishment but selection for the job is made at another establishment, the job will be listed only once for purposes of the utilization analysis, goals and timetables and action oriented programs—in the AAP of this establishment where the selection is made. In order for OFCCP to keep track of all jobs, the Directive requires that such jobs be listed in the workforce analysis sections of both AAPs. Two points bear emphasis. First, this policy applies only to a limited number of jobs, and will therefore have no effect whatsoever on the way most jobs are addressed in local establishment AAPs. Second, with the limited exception of requiring that jobs for which selections are not made locally be listed in two workforce analyses, OFCCP is not imposing additional requirements on contractors. Existing rules and policy require that a contractor's AAPs address all of its job titles—this Directive simply further designates the particular AAP within which certain jobs must be addressed.

4. *Question:* In which AAP should a job be listed if the selection is made at one level of the corporation but concurred in at a higher level? What if

the level at which selection is made fluctuates from time to time?

Answer: The contractor should use its good judgment in determining the best way to treat such situations. As noted in the answer to question 2, OFCCP is not attempting to dictate to contractors how best to conduct their businesses, and OFCCP will accord the contractor substantial discretion in determining the proper organization level.

5. *Question:* What impact will this Directive have on availability computations?

Answer: The basic approach to computing availability remains unchanged—for each job group the contractor must consider at least the eight availability factors set forth in 41 CFR 60–2.11. Of course, because certain positions will now appear in a single job group in the corporate level AAP, rather than being scattered in several AAPs nationwide, the actual availability figure may vary from that previously used.

6. *Question:* How does this Directive affect OFCCP's compliance review procedures? Will OFCCP shift from its emphasis on single establishment reviews to emphasis on simultaneously reviewing an entire corporation?

Answer: OFCCP will continue to conduct nonconstruction compliance reviews as it has in the past, on a single establishment basis. The only deviation from prior practice is that a review of a corporate headquarters or intermediate level establishment will include review of positions for which selections are made at that level but which are located at subordinate level establishments.

7. *Question:* What prompts OFCCP to issue the Directive at this time?

Answer: As the agency charged with administering the nondiscrimination and affirmative action requirements of Executive Order 11246, OFCCP is constantly seeking improved methods and procedures for advancing the employment of minorities and women. Several recent studies, and OFCCP's own experience in reviewing the compliance of Government contractors, have shown that there remains substantial underemployment of minorities and women in managerial, professional and technical occupations. OFCCP believes that one of the reasons for this, although certainly not the only reason, is that the current approach to AAPs does not require contractors to place sufficient scrutiny and emphasis on these jobs. By this Directive, those positions for which the vital staffing decisions are made at a particular corporate level and location will be grouped for analysis and goal setting purposes in the AAP of that same corporate level and location. In this way, the affected positions, which may be scattered in a number of subordinate establishments, will be incorporated into the AAP of the establishment in which the pertinent decision makers are located and where managerial responsibility for action programs to achieve the goals affecting these positions may be assigned.

June 23, 1988.
Washington, DC.
Jerry D. Blakemore,
Director.

The text of the Directive, OFCCP Order No. 830a1, is as follows:

1. *Subject:* Corporate-level Selection Decisions

2. *Purpose:* To provide OFCCP policy/guidance regarding inclusion in corporate or intermediate level affirmative action programs (AAPs) of positions located at individual, subordinate establishments for which selection decisions are made at the corporate or intermediate level

3. *Background:* In the case of multi-establishment contractors, it is not unusual for selection decisions regarding certain positions to be made at the corporate level or at an intermediate level, rather than at the subordinate establishment where the position is located. This is particularly true for example, in the case of plant manager positions, but it also may apply to other positions such as professional and technical jobs. In such cases, it is not appropriate for affirmative action goals for such positions to be established in the subordinate establishment's AAP because the decision to select regarding such positions is not within the control of that establishment. On the other hand, the

inclusion of such positions in the AAP of the contractor's corporate or intermediate level offices would provide for utilization analysis and goal setting for those positions to be accomplished at the same level at which the selection decisions are made. OFCCP's practice of encouraging contractors to treat such positions in this fashion is longstanding.

4. *Policy:* Equal Opportunity Specialists conducting a compliance review of a multi-establishment contractor's corporate office or intermediate level office must investigate and otherwise ensure that the affirmative action program of that office includes in its workforce analysis, utilization analysis and goal setting, as required by 41 CFR 60–2.11(a), 60–2.11(b), and 60–2.12, respectively, all those positions located in subordinate and/or lower-level establishments for which the selection decisions are made at the establishment under review. Similarly, Equal Opportunity Specialists conducting a compliance review of a contractor's establishment which is subordinate to a higher-level establishment in the contractor's organization will ensure that all positions in the work force of this lower-level establishment for which the selection decisions are made at a higher corporate level are excluded from the utilization analysis and goal setting of the establishment under review, although such positions must still be shown in the establishment's work force analysis, as required by 41 CFR 60–2.11(a), in order that the complete work force structure of the establishment under review is readily apparent.

In those cases where because of informal or fluctuating managerial appointment authorities, the appropriate level for job title placement cannot be clearly or consistently defined, managerial and other appropriate titles should be placed in the AAP of the highest organizational level where ultimate approval authority may reside. As a result, there may be instances when the majority of mid- and upper-level management and other titles should appropriately be placed in the corporate headquarters' AAP, notwithstanding personnel responsibility at intermediate organizational levels. Management should be given substantial discretion in determining proper organizational levels for job title placement provided such placement is not inconsistent with the purpose of this directive.

OFCCP will not require contractors to amend affirmative action programs to conform to this directive until their current corporate headquarters' or intermediate level's program plans expire, or until ninety (90) days from the date of this directive, whichever is later. At such time, contractors shall be required to conform such plans to this directive.

Jerry D. Blakemore,
Director.
June 14, 1988.

APPENDIX B

COURT DECISIONS

Martin v. Wilks, 49 FEP 1641 (B-3)

Lorance v. AT&T Technologies, 49 FEP 1656 (B-19)

Wards Cove Packing Co. v. Atonio, 49 FEP 1519 (B-29)

MARTIN v. WILKS

Supreme Court of the United States

MARTIN, et al. v. WILKS, et al.; PERSONNEL BOARD OF JEFFERSON COUNTY, ALABAMA, et al. v. Same; ARRINGTON, et al. v. Same, Nos. 87-1614, 87-1639, and 87-1668, June 12, 1989

CIVIL RIGHTS ACT OF 1964

1. Consent decree ▶108.6962 ▶108.7406 ▶108.7471

White firefighters who were not parties to employment discrimination action that resulted in consent decrees may challenge employment decisions taken pursuant to decrees, even though they did not timely intervene in that action, since a person cannot be deprived of his legal rights in proceeding to which he is not party, and joinder as party, rather than knowledge of lawsuit and opportunity to intervene, is method by which potential parties are subjected to jurisdiction of court and bound by judgment or decree; failure to intervene does not have preclusive effect.

2. Joinder ▶108.7406 ▶108.7471

It makes sense to place on parties to action burden of bringing in additional parties where such a step is indicated, rather than placing on potential additional parties a duty to intervene when they acquire knowledge of action, since parties to action presumably know better than anyone else nature and scope of relief sought and at whose expense such relief might be granted, and difficulties foreseen in identifying those who could be adversely affected by decree granting broad remedial relief arise from nature of relief sought and not because of any choice between mandatory intervention and joinder.

3. Consent decree ▶108.6962 ▶108.7471

"Impermissible collateral attack" doctrine does not bar individuals who failed to intervene in action that resulted in consent decrees from bringing new action challenging decisions made under decrees, despite contention that they were aware that underlying action might affect them and they chose to pass up opportunity to intervene, since attributing preclusive effect to failure to intervene is inconsistent with Rules 19 and 24 of Federal Rules of Civil Procedure.

4. Consent decree ▶108.6962

Voluntary settlement in form of consent decree between one group of employees and their employer cannot settle, voluntarily or otherwise, conflicting claims of another group of employees who do not join in agreement, even if second group is party to litigation.

———

On writ of certiorari to the U.S. Court of Appeals for the Eleventh Circuit (45 FEP Cases 890, 833 F.2d 1492). Affirmed.

See also 28 FEP Cases 1834; 37 FEP Cases 1; and 39 FEP Cases 1431.

James P. Alexander, Birmingham, Ala. (James K. Baker, City Attorney, Birmingham, Ala., and Robert K. Spotswood, Richard H. Walston, Michael R. Pennington, and Bradley, Arant, Rose & White, Birmingham, Ala., with him on brief), for petitioners in No. 87-1668.

Robert D. Joffe, Thomas D. Barr, Robert F. Mullen, Paul C. Saunders, Alden L. Atkins, Mark A. Sirota, and James E. Fleming (Cravath, Swaine & Moore), New York, N.Y., William L. Robinson, Richard T. Seymour, and Stephen L. Spitz, Washington, D.C., and Susan W. Reeves (Reeves & Still), Birmingham, Ala., filed brief for petitioners in No. 87-1614.

Frank M. Young, III, James C. Huckaby, Jr., Charles A. McCallum, III, William T. Carlson, Jr., and Lisa J. Huggins (Haskell, Slaughter & Young), Birmingham, Ala., filed brief for petitioners in No. 87-1639.

Raymond P. Fitzpatrick, Jr. (Courtney H. Mason, Jr., with him on brief), Birmingham, Ala., for respondents.

Thomas W. Merrill, Deputy Solicitor General (Charles Fried, Solicitor General, W. Bradford Reynolds, Assistant Attorney General, Donald B. Ayer, Deputy Solicitor General, Roger Clegg, Deputy Assistant Attorney General, Michael R. Lazerwitz, Assistant to the Solicitor General, and Dennis J. Dimsey, U.S. Department of Justice, on brief), for United States, as amicus curiae, urging affirmance.

Steven R. Shapiro and John A. Powell, New York, N.Y., and Robert L. Hobbins, Michael J. Wahoske, Mark B. Rotenberg, Leslie J. Anderson, David J. Trevor, Frederick A. McNeill, and Creighton R. Magid (Dorsey & Whitney), Minneapolis, Minn., filed brief for American Civil Liberties Union, Alabama Civil Liberties Union, and Women's Equity Action League, as amici curiae, urging reversal.

Robert E. Williams and Douglas S. McDowell (McGuiness & Williams), Washington, D.C., filed brief for Equal Employment Advisory Council, as amicus curiae, urging reversal.

Benna R. Solomon and Beate Bloch, Washington, D.C. (Zachary D. Fasman, Patrick W. Shea, C. Geoffrey Weirich, and Paul, Hastings, Janofsky & Walker, Washington, D.C., of counsel), filed brief for National League of Cities, National Governors' Assn., U.S. Conference of Mayors, Council of State Governments, International City Management Assn., National Conference of State Legislatures, and National Assn. of Counties, as amici curiae, urging reversal.

N. Thompson Powers, Ronald S. Cooper, and Janice Barber (Steptoe & Johnson), Washington, D.C. (Barry L. Goldstein, Washington, D.C., Julius L. Chambers and Ronald L. Ellis, New York, N.Y., Claudia Withers, Washington, D.C., Marcia D. Greenberger and Brenda Smith, Washington, D.C., and William C. McNeill, III, and Eva J. Paterson, San Francisco, Calif., of counsel), filed brief for NAACP Legal Defense & Educational Fund, Inc., Women's Legal Defense Fund, National Women's Law Center, and International Assn. of Black Professional Firefighters, as amici curiae, urging reversal.

James M. Shannon, Attorney General of Massachusetts, Alice Daniel, Deputy Attorney General, Jane S. Schacter and Peter Sacks, Assistant Attorneys General, attorneys general of 31 other states, and chief legal officers of District of Columbia and Virgin Islands filed brief for Massachusetts, 31 other states, District of Columbia, and Virgin Islands, as amici curiae, urging reversal.

Thomas A. Woodley and Michael S. Wolly (Mulholland & Hickey), Washington, D.C., filed brief for International Assn. of Fire Fighters, AFL-CIO, as amicus curiae, urging affirmance.

Ronald A. Zumbrun and Anthony T. Caso (Deborah L. Garlin, of counsel), Sacramento, Calif., filed brief for Pacific Legal Foundation, as amicus curiae, urging reversal.

Before REHNQUIST, Chief Justice, and BRENNAN, WHITE, MARSHALL, BLACKMUN, STEVENS, O'CONNOR, SCALIA, and KENNEDY, Justices.

Full Text of Opinion

CHIEF JUSTICE REHNQUIST delivered the opinion of the court.

[1] A group of white firefighters sued the City of Birmingham, Alabama (City) and the Jefferson County Personnel Board (Board) alleging that they were being denied promotions in favor of less qualified black firefighters. They claimed that the City and the Board were making promotion decisions on the basis of race in reliance on certain consent decrees, and that these decisions constituted impermissible racial discrimination in violation of the Constitution and federal statute. The District Court held that the white firefighters were precluded from challenging employment decisions taken pursuant to the decrees, even though these firefighters had not been parties to the proceedings in which the decrees were entered. We think this holding contravenes the general rule that a person cannot be deprived of his legal rights in a proceeding to which he is not a party.

The litigation in which the consent decrees were entered began in 1974, when the Ensley Branch of the NAACP and seven black individuals filed separate class-action complaints against the City and the Board. They alleged that both had engaged in racially discriminatory hiring and promotion practices in various public service jobs in violation of Title VII of the Civil Rights Act of 1964, 42 U.S.C. §2000e *et seq.,* and other federal law. After a bench trial on some issues, but before judgment, the parties entered into two consent decrees, one between the black individuals and the City and the other between them and the Board. These proposed decrees set forth an extensive remedial scheme, including long-term and interim annual goals for the hiring of blacks as firefighters. The decrees also provided for goals for promotion of blacks within the department.

The District Court entered an order provisionally approving the decrees and directing publication of notice of the upcoming fairness hearings. 3 App. 694–696. Notice of the hearings, with a reference to the general nature of the decrees was published in two local newspapers. At that hearing, the Birmingham Firefighters Association (BFA) appeared and filed objections as *amicus curiae.* After the hearing, but before final approval of the decrees, the BFA and two of its members also moved to intervene on the ground that the decrees would adversely affect their rights. The District Court denied the motions as untimely and approved the decrees. *United States* v. *Jefferson County,* 28 FEP Cases 1834 (ND Ala. 1981). Seven white firefighters, all members of the BFA, then filed a complaint against the City and the Board seeking injunctive relief against the City and the Board seeking injunctive relief against enforcement of the decrees. The seven argued that the decrees would operate to illegally discriminate against them; the District Court denied relief. App. 37.

Both the denial of intervention and the denial of injunctive relief were affirmed on appeal. *United States* v. *Jefferson County*, 720 F.2d 1511 [33 FEP Cases 829] (CA11 1983). The District Court had not abused its discretion in refusing to let the BFA intervene, though the Eleventh Circuit, in part because the firefighters could "institut[e] an independent Title VII suit, asserting specific violations of their rights." *Id.*, at 1518. And, for the same reason, petitioners had not adequately shown the potential for irreparable harm from the operation of the decrees necessary to obtain injunctive relief. *Id.*, at 1520.

A new group of white firefighters, the Wilks respondents, then brought suit against the City and the Board in district court. They too alleged that, because of their race, they were being denied promotions in favor of less qualified blacks in violation of federal law. The Board and the City admitted to making race conscious employment decisions, but argued the decisions were unassailable because they were made pursuant to the consent decrees. A group of black individuals, the *Martin* petitioners, were allowed to intervene in their individual capacities to defend the decrees.

The defendants moved to dismiss the reverse discrimination cases as impermissible collateral attacks on the consent decrees. The District Court denied the motions, ruling that the decrees would provide a defense to claims of discrimination for employment decisions "mandated" by the decrees, leaving the principal issue for trial whether the challenged promotions were indeed required by the decrees. App. 237-239, 250. After trial the District Court granted the motion to dismiss. App. to Pet. for Cert. 67a. The court concluded that "if in fact the City was required to [make promotions of blacks] by the consent decree, then they would not be guilty of [illegal] racial discrimination" and that the defendants had "establish[ed] that the promotions of the black individuals . . . were in fact required by the terms of the consent decree." *Id.*, at 28a.

On appeal, the Eleventh Circuit reversed. It held that "[b]ecause . . . [the *Wilks* respondents] were neither parties nor privies to the consent decrees, . . . their independent claims of unlawful discrimination are not precluded." *In re Birmingham Reverse Discrimination Employment Litigation*, 833 F.2d 1492, 1498 [45 FEP Cases 890, 894] (1987). The court explicitly rejected the doctrine of "impermissible collateral attack" espoused by other courts of appeals to immunize parties to a consent decree from charges of discrimination by nonparties for actions taken pursuant to the decree. *Ibid.* Although it recognized a "strong public policy in favor of voluntary affirmative action plans," the panel acknowledged that this interest "must yield to the policy against requiring third parties to submit to bargains in which their interests were either ignored or sacrificed." *Ibid.* The court remanded the case for trial of the discrimination claims, suggesting that the operative law for judging the consent decrees was that governing voluntary affirmative-action plans. *Id.* at 1497 [45 FEP Cases, at 894].[1]

We granted certiorari, 487 U.S. —— (1988), and now affirm the Eleventh Circuit's judgment. All agree that "[i]t is a principle of general application in anglo-American jurisprudence that one is not bound by a judgment *in personam* in a litigation in which he is not designated as a party or to which he has not been made a party by service of process." *Hansberry* v. *Lee*, 311 U.S. 32, 40 (1940). See, *e.g.*, *Parklane Hosiery Co.* v. *Shore*, 439 U.S. 322, 327, n. 7 (1979). See, *e.g.*, *Blonder-Tongue Laboratories, Inc.* v. *University Foundation*, 402 U.S. 313, 328-329 (1971); *Zenith Radio Corp.* v. *Hazeltine Research, Inc.*, 395 U.S. 100, 110 (1969). This rule is part of our "deep-rooted historic tradition that everyone should have his own day in court." 18 C. Wright, A. Miller, & E. Cooper, Federal Practice and Procedure §4449, p. 417 (1981) (18 Wright). A judgment or decree among parties to a lawsuit resolves issues as among them, but it does not conclude

---

[1] Judge Anderson, dissenting, "agree[d] with the opinion for the court that these plaintiffs [the *Wilks* respondents] were not parties to the prior litigation which resulted in the consent decree, and that the instant plaintiffs are not bound by the consent decree and should be free on remand to challenge the consent decree prospectively and test its validity against the recent Supreme court precedent." *In re Birmingham Reverse Discrimination Employment Litigation*, 833 F.2d 1492, 1503 [45 FEP Cases 890, 899] (CA11 1987). He distinguished, however, between claims for prospective relief and claims for back pay, the latter being barred, in his opinion, by the City's good-faith reliance on the decree. *Id.* at 1502 [45 FEP Cases, at 898].

the rights of strangers to those proceedings.[2]

Petitioners argue that, because respondents failed to timely intervene in the initial proceedings, their current challenge to actions taken under the consent decree constitutes an impermissible "collateral attack." They argue that respondents were aware that the underlying suit might affect them and if they chose to pass up an opportunity to intervene, they should not be permitted to later litigate the issues in a new action. The position has sufficient appeal to have commanded the approval of the great majority of the federal courts of appeals,[3] but we agree with the contrary view expressed by the Court of Appeals for the Eleventh Circuit in this case.

We begin with the words of Justice Brandeis in Chase National Bank v. Norwalk, 291 U.S. 431 (1934):

"The law does not impose upon any person absolutely entitled to a hearing the burden of voluntary intervention in a suit to which he is a stranger.... Unless duly summoned to appear in a legal proceeding, a person not a privy may rest assured that a judgment recovered therein will not affect his legal rights." Id. at 441.

While these words were written before the adoption of the Federal Rules of Civil Procedure, we think the Rules incorporate the same principle; a party seeking a judgment binding on another cannot obligate that person to intervene; he must be joined. See Hazeltine, supra, at 110 (judgment against Hazeltine vacated because it was not named as a party or served, even though as the parent corporation of one of the parties it clearly knew of the claim against it and had made a special appearance to contest jurisdiction). Against the background of permissive intervention set forth in Chase National Bank, the drafters cast Rule 24, governing intervention, in permissive terms. See Fed. Rule Civ. Proc. 24(a) (intervention as of right) "[u]pon timely application anyone shall be permitted to intervene"); Fed. Rule Civ. Proc. 24(b) (permissive intervention) ("[u]pon timely application anyone may be permitted to intervene"). They determined that the concern for finality and completeness of judgments would be "better [served] by mandatory joinder procedures." 18 Wright §4452, p. 453. Accordingly, Rule 19(a) provides for mandatory joinder in circumstances where a judgment rendered in the absence of a person may "leave ... persons already parties subject to a substantial risk of incurring ... inconsistent obligations...."[4] Rule 19(b) sets forth the factors to be considered by a court in deciding whether to allow an action to proceed in the absence of an interested party.[5]

---

[2] We have recognized an exception to the general rule when, in certain limited circumstances, a person, although not a party, has his interests adequately represented by someone with the same interests who is a party. See Hansberry v. Lee, 311 U.S. 32, 41–42 (1940) ("class" or "representative" suits); Fed. Rule Civ. Proc. 23 (same); Montana v. United States, 440 U.S. 147, 154–155 (1979) (control of litigation on behalf of one of the parties in the litigation). Additionally, where a special remedial scheme exists expressly foreclosing successive litigation by nonlitigants, as for example in bankruptcy or probate, legal proceedings may terminate preexisting rights if the scheme is otherwise consistent with due process. See NLRB v. Bildisco & Bildisco, 465 U.S. 513, 529–530, n.10 [115 LRRM 2805] (1984) ("proof of claim must be presented to the Bankruptcy Court ... or be lost"); Tulsa Professional Collection Services, Inc. v. Pope, 485 U.S. 478, (1988) (nonclaim statute terminating unsubmitted claims against the estate). Neither of these exceptions, however, applies in this case.

[3] For a sampling of cases from the Circuits applying the "impermissible collateral attack" rule or its functional equivalent, see, e.g., Striff v. Mason, 849 F.2d 240, 245 [47 FEP Cases 79, 82–83] (CA6 1988); Marino v. Ortiz, 806 F.2d 1144, 1146–1147 [42 FEP Cases 912, 913–914] (CA2 1986) aff'd by an equally divided Court, 484 U.S. 301 [45 FEP Cases 1081] (1988); Thaggard v. City of Jackson, 687 F.2d 66, 68–69 [32 FEP Cases 228, 230] (CA5 1982), cert. denied sub nom. Ashley v. City of Jackson, 464 U.S. 900 [32 FEP Cases 1846] (1983) (Rehnquist, J., joined by Brennan, J., dissenting); Stotts v. Memphis Fire Dept., 679 F.2d 541, 558 [28 FEP Cases 1491, 1504] (CA6 1982), rev'd on other grounds sub nom. Firefighters v. Stotts, 467 U.S. 561 [34 FEP Cases 1702] (1984); Dennison v. City of Los Angeles Dept. of Water & Power, 658 F.2d 694, 696 [26 FEP Cases 1739, 1740] (CA9 1981); Goins v. Bethlehem Steel Corp., 657 F.2d 62, 64 [49 FEP Cases 1812, 1814] (CA4 1981), cert. denied, 455 U.S. 940 [49 FEP Cases 1896] (1982); Society Hill Civic Assn. v. Harris, 632 F.2d 1045, 1052 (CA3 1980). Apart from the instant one, the only Circuit Court decision of which we are aware that would generally allow collateral attacks on consent decrees by nonparties is Dunn v. Carey, 808 F.2d 555, 559–560 (CA7 1986).

[4] Rule 19(a) provides (emphasis added):
"A person who is subject to service of process and whose joinder will not deprive the court of jurisdiction ... shall be joined as a party in the action if (1) in the person's absence complete relief cannot be accorded among those already parties, or (2) the person claims an interest relating to the subject of the action and is so situated that the disposition of the action in the person's absence may (i) as a practical matter impair or impede the person's ability to protect that interest or (ii) leave any of the persons already parties subject to a substantial risk of incurring double, multiple, or otherwise inconsistent obligations by reason of the claimed interest. If the person has not been so joined, the court shall order that the person be made a party. If the person should join as a plaintiff but refuses to do so, the person may be made a defendant, or, in a proper case, an involuntary plaintiff. If the joined party objects to venue and joinder of that party would render the venue of the action improper, that party shall be dismissed from the action."

[5] Rule 19(b) provides that:
"If a person ... cannot be made a party, the court shall determine whether in equity and good conscience the action should proceed among the parties before it, or should be dismissed, the absent person being thus regarded as indispensable. The factors to be considered by the court include: first, to what extent a judgment rendered in the person's absence might be prejudicial to the person or to those already parties; second, the extent to which, by protective provisions in the judgment, by the shaping of relief, or other measures, the prejudice can be lessened or avoided; third, whether a judgment rendered in the person's absence

[2, 3] Joinder as a party, rather than knowledge of a lawsuit and an opportunity to intervene, is the method by which potential parties are subjected to the jurisdiction of the court and bound by a judgment or decree.[6] The parties to a lawsuit presumably know better than anyone else the nature and scope of relief sought in the action, and at whose expense such relief might be granted. It makes sense, therefore, to place on them a burden of bringing in additional parties where such a step is indicated, rather that placing on potential additional parties a duty to intervene when they acquire knowledge of the lawsuit. The linchpin of the "impermissible collateral attack" doctrine — the attribution of preclusive effect to a failure to intervene — is therefore quite inconsistent with Rule 19 and rule 24.

Petitioners argue that our decisions in *Penn-Central Merger & N & W Inclusion Cases*, 389 U.S. 486 (1968) and *Provident Tradesmens Bank & Trust Co.* v. *Patterson*, 390 U.S. 102 (1968) suggest an opposite result. The *Penn-Central* litigation took place in a special statutory framework enacted by Congress to allow reorganization of a huge railway system. Primary jurisdiction was in the Interstate Commerce Commission, with very restricted review in a statutory three-judge district court. Review proceedings were channeled to the District Court for the Southern District of New York, and proceedings in other district courts were stayed. The District Court upheld the decision of the Interstate Commerce Commission in both the merger and the inclusion proceedings, and the parties to that proceeding appealed to this Court. Certain Pennsylvania litigants had sued in the District Court for the Middle District of Pennsylvania to set aside the Commission's order, and this action was stayed pending the decision in the District Court

for the Southern District of New York. We held that the borough of Moosic, one of the Pennsylvania litigants, could not challenge the Commission's approval of the merger and inclusion in the Pennsylvania District Court, pointing out the unusual nationwide character of the action and saying "[i]n these circumstances, it would be senseless to permit parties seeking to challenge the merger and the inclusion orders to bring numerous suits in many different district courts." 389 U.S. 505, n.4.

We do not think that this holding in *Penn Central*, based as it was upon the extraordinary nature of the proceedings challenging the merger of giant railroads and not even mentioning Rule 19 or Rule 24, affords a guide to the interpretation of the rules relating to joinder and intervention in ordinary civil actions in a district court.

Petitioners also rely on our decision in *Provident Bank, supra,* as authority for the view which they espouse. In that case we discussed Rule 19 shortly after parts of it had been substantially revised, but we expressly left open the question of whether preclusive effect might be attributed to a failure to intervene. 390 U.S. 114-115.

Petitioners contend that a different result should be reached because the need to join affected parties will be burdensome and ultimately discouraging to civil rights litigation. Potential adverse claimants may be numerous and difficult to identify; if they are not joined, the possibility for inconsistent judgments exists. Judicial resources will be needlessly consumed in relitigation of the same question.

Even if we were wholly persuaded by these arguments as a matter of policy, acceptance of them would require a rewriting rather than an interpretation of the relevant Rules. But we are not persuaded that their acceptance would lead to a more satisfactory method of handling cases like this one. It must be remembered that the alternatives are a duty to intervene based on knowledge, on the one hand, and some form of joinder, as the Rules presently provide, on the other. No one can seriously contend that an employer might successfully defend against a Title VII claim by one group of employees on the ground that its actions were required by an earlier decree entered in a suit brought against it by another, if the later group did not have adequate notice or knowledge of the earlier suit.

The difficulties petitioners foresee in identifying those who could be adversely affected by a degree granting broad remedial relief are undoubtedly

---

will be adequate; fourth, whether the plaintiff will have an adequate remedy if the action is dismissed for nonjoinder."

[6] The dissent argues on the one hand that respondents have not been "bound" by the decree but rather, that they are only suffering practical adverse affects from the consent decree. *Post,* at 2-5 [49 FEP Cases, at 1647-1648]. On the other hand, the dissent characterizes respondents' suit not as an assertion of their own independent rights, but as a collateral attack on the consent decree which, it is said, can only proceed on very limited grounds. *Post,* at 15-20 [49 FEP Cases, at 1652-1653]. Respondents in their suit have alleged that they are being racially discriminated against by their employer in violation of Title VII: either the fact that the disputed employment decisions are being made pursuant to a consent decree is a defense to respondents' Title VII claims or it is not. If it is a defense to challenges to employment practices which would otherwise violate Title VII, it is very difficult to see why respondents are not being "bound" by the decree.

present, but they arise from the nature of the relief sought and not because of any choice between mandatory intervention and joinder. Rule 19's provisions for joining interested parties are designed to accommodate the sort of complexities that may arise from a decree affecting numerous people in various ways. We doubt that a mandatory intervention rule would be less awkward. As mentioned, plaintiffs who seek the aid of the courts to alter existing employment policies, or the employer who might be subject to conflicting decrees, are best able to bear the burden of designating those who would be adversely affected if plaintiffs prevail; these parties will generally have a better understanding of the scope of likely relief than employees who are not named but might be afforded. Petitioners' alternative does not eliminate the need for, or difficulty of, identifying persons who, because of their interests, should be included in a lawsuit. It merely shifts that responsibility to less able shoulders.

Nor do we think that the system of joinder called for by the Rules is likely to produce more relitigation of issues than the converse rule. The breadth of a lawsuit and concomitant relief may be at least partially shaped in advance through Rule 19 to avoid needless clashes with future litigation. And even under a regime of mandatory intervention, parties who did not have adequate knowledge of the suit would relitigate issues. Additional questions about the adequacy and timeliness of knowledge would inevitably crop up. We think that the system of joinder presently contemplated by the Rules best serves the many interests involved in the run of litigated cases, including cases like the present one.

[4] Petitioners also urge that the congressional policy favoring voluntary settlement of employment discrimination claims, referred to in cases such as *Carson* v. *American Brands, Inc.*, 450 U.S. 79 [25 FEP Cases 1] (1981), also supports the "impermissible collateral attack" doctrine. But once again it is essential to note just what is meant by "voluntary settlement." A voluntary settlement in the form of a consent decree between one group of employees and their employer cannot possibly "settle," voluntarily or otherwise, the conflicting claims of another group of employees who do not join in the agreement. This is true even if the second group of employees is a party to the litigation:

"[P]arties who choose to resolve litigation through settlement may not dispose of the claims of a third party ... without that party's agreement. A court's approval of a consent decree between some of the parties

therefore cannot dispose of the valid claims of nonconsenting intervenors." *Firefighters* v. *Cleveland*, 478 U.S. 501, 529 [41 FEP Cases 139, 151] (1986).

Insofar as the argument is bottomed on the idea that it may be easier to settle claims among a disparate group of affected persons if they are all before the Court, joinder bids fair to accomplish that result as well as a regime of mandatory intervention.

For the foregoing reasons we affirm the decision of the Court of Appeals for the Eleventh Circuit. That court remanded the case for trial of the reverse discrimination claims. *Birmingham Reverse Discrimination*, 833 F.2d, at 1500–1502 [45 FEP Cases, at 896–897]. Petitioners point to language in the District Court's findings of fact and conclusions of law which suggests that respondents will not prevail on the merits. We agree with the view of the Court of Appeals, however, that the proceedings in the District Court may have been affected by the mistaken view that respondents' claims on the merits were barred to the extent they were inconsistent with the consent decree.

Affirmed.

Dissenting Opinion

JUSTICE STEVENS, with whom JUSTICE BRENNAN, JUSTICE MARSHALL, and JUSTICE BLACKMUN join, dissenting.

As a matter of law there is a vast difference between persons who are actual parties to litigation and persons who merely have the kind of interest that may as a practical matter be impaired by the outcome of a case. Persons in the first category have a right to participate in a trial and to appeal from an adverse judgment; depending on whether they win or lose, their legal rights may be enhance or impaired. Persons in the latter category have a right to intervene in the action in a timely fashion,[1] or they may be joined

---

[1] Federal Rule Civ. Proc. 24(a) provides, in part:
"Upon timely application anyone shall be permitted to intervene in an action: ... (2) when the applicant claims an interest relating to the property or transaction which is the subject of the action and the applicant is so situated that the disposition of the action may as a practical matter impair or impede the applicant's ability to protect that interest, unless the applicant's interest is adequately represented by existing parties."

as parties against their will.[2] But if they remain on the sidelines, they may be harmed as a practical matter even though their legal rights are unaffected.[3] One of the disadvantages of sideline-sitting is that the bystander has no right to appeal from a judgment no matter how harmful it may be.

In this case the Court quite rightly concludes that the white firefighters who brought the second series of Title VII cases could not be deprived of their legal rights in the first series of cases because they had neither intervened nor been joined as parties. See *Firefighters* v. *Cleveland*, 478 U.S. 501, 529-530 [41 FEP Cases 139, 151-152] (1986); *Parklane Hosiery Co.* v. *Shore*, 439 U.S. 322, 327, n.7 (1979). The consent decrees obviously could not deprive them of any contractual rights, such as seniority, cf. *W. R. Grace & Co.* v. *Rubber Workers*, 461 U.S. 757 [31 FEP Cases 1409] (1983), or accrued vacation pay, cf. *Massachusetts* v. *Morash*, 490 U.S. —— [29 WH Cases 369] (1989), or of any other legal rights, such as the right to have their employer comply with federal statutes like Title VII, cf. *Firefighters* v. *Cleveland, supra*, at 529 [41 FEP Cases, at 151].[4] There is no reason, however, why the consent decrees might not produce changes in conditions at the white firefighters'

place of employment that, as a practical matter, may have a serious effect on their opportunities for employment or promotion even though they are not bound by the decrees in any legal sense. The fact that one of the effects of a decree is to curtail the job opportunities of nonparties does not mean that the nonparties have been deprived of legal rights or that they have standing to appeal from that decree without becoming parties.

Persons who have no right to appeal from a final judgment — either because the time to appeal has elapsed or because they never became parties to the case — may nevertheless collaterally attack a judgment on certain narrow grounds. If the court had no jurisdiction over the subject matter, or if the judgment is the product of corruption, duress, fraud, collusion, or mistake, under limited circumstances it may be set aside in an appropriate collateral proceeding. See Restatement (Second) of Judgments §§69-72 (1982); *Griffith* v. *Bank of New York*, 147 F.2d 899, 901 (CA2) (Clark, J.), cert. denied, 325 U.S. 874 (1945). This rule not only applies to parties to the original action, but also allows interested third parties collaterally to attack judgments.[5] In both civil and criminal cases, however, the grounds that may be invoked to support a collateral attack are much more limited than

---

[2] Federal Rule Civ. Proc. 19(a) provides, in part:
"A person who is subject to service of process and whose joinder will not deprive the court of jurisdiction over the subject matter of the action shall be joined as a party in the action if . . . (2) the person claims an interest relating to the subject of the action and is so situated that the disposition of the action in the person's absence may (i) as a practical matter impair or impede the person's ability to protect that interest. . . ."

[3] See *Provident Tradesmens Bank & Trust Co.* v. *Patterson* 390 U.S. 102, 110 (1968).

[4] As Chief Justice Rehnquist has observed:
"Suppose, for example, that the Government sues a private corporation for alleged violations of the antitrust laws and then enters a consent decree. Surely, the existence of that decree does not preclude a future suit by another corporation alleging that the defendant company's conduct, even if authorized by the decree, constitutes an antitrust violation. The nonparty has an independent right to bring his own private antitrust action for treble damages or for injunctive relief. See 2 P. Areeda & D. Turner, Antitrust Law ¶330, p. 143 (1978). Similarly, if an action alleging unconstitutional prison conditions results in a consent decree, a prisoner subsequently harmed by prison conditions is not precluded from bringing suit on the mere plea that the conditions are in accordance with the consent decree. Such compliance might be relevant to a defense of good-faith immunity, see Pet. for Cert. in *Bennett* v. *Williams*, O.T. 1982, No. 82-1704, but it would not suffice to block the suit altogether." *Ashley* v. *City of Jackson*, 464 U.S. 900, 902 [32 FEP Cases 1846, 1848] (1983) (opinion dissenting from denial of certiorari).
In suggesting that compliance with a consent decree might be relevant to a defense of good-faith immunity, this passage recognizes that neither due process nor the Rules of Civil Procedure foreclose judicial recognition of judgment that may have a practical effect on the interests of a nonparty.

[5] See F. James & G. Hazard, Civil Procedure §12.15, p. 681 (3d ed. 1985) (hereinafter James & Hazard). Since at least 1874, this court has recognized that a third party may collaterally attack a judgment if the original judgment was obtained through fraud or collusion. In a case brought by an assignee in bankruptcy seeking to recover property allegedly transferred in fraud of the bankrupt's debtors, the Court wrote:
"Judgments of any court, it is sometimes said, may be impeached by strangers to them for fraud or collusion, but the proposition as stated is subject to certain limitations, as it is only those strangers who, if the judgment is given full credit and effect, would be prejudiced in regard to some pre-existing right who are permitted to set up such a defense. Defenses of the kind may be set up by such strangers. Hence the rule that whenever a judgment or decrees is procured through fraud or either of the parties, or by the collusion of both, for the purpose of defrauding some third person, such third person may escape from the injury thus attempted by showing, even in a collateral proceeding, the fraud or collusion by which the judgment was obtained." *Michaels* v. *Post*, 21 Wall. 398, 426-427 (1874) (footnote omitted).
See also *Wells Fargo & Co.* v. *Taylor*, 254 U.S. 175, 184 (1920); 1 A. Freeman, Judgments §318, p. 634 (5th ed. 1925). Similarly, strangers to a decree are sometimes allowed to challenge the decree by showing that the court was without jurisdiction. *Id.*, at p. 633. But cf. *Johnson* v. *Muelberger*, 340 U.S. 581 (1951) (noting that under Florida law, a child, seeking to protect her interest in her father's estate, may not collaterally attack her parents' divorce for want of jurisdiction). Of course, unlike parties to a decree, the question of subject matter jurisdiction is not *res judicanta* as to interested third parties. Cf. *Insurance Corp. of Ireland* v. *Compagnie des Bauxites de Guinee*, 456 U.S. 694, 702, n.9 (1982).

those that may be asserted as error on direct appeal.⁶ Thus, a person who can foresee that a lawsuit is likely to have a practical impact on his interests may pay a heavy price if he elects to sit on the sidelines instead of intervening and taking the risk that his legal rights will be impaired.

In this case there is no dispute about the fact that the respondents are not parties to the consent decrees. It follows as a matter of course that they are not bound by those decrees.⁷ Those judgments could not, and did not, deprive them of any legal rights. The judgments did, however, have a practical impact on respondents' opportunities for advancement in their profession. For that reason, respondents had standing to challenge the validity of the decrees, but the grounds that they may advance in support of a collateral challenge are much more limited than would be allowed if they were parties prosecuting a direct appeal.⁸

---

⁶ We have long held that proceedings brought before a court collaterally "are by no means subject to all the exceptions which might be taken on a direct appeal." *Thompson* v. *Tolmie*, 2 Pet. 157, 162 (1829). See also *Teague* v. *Lane*, 489 U.S. ——, —————— (1989) (petitioner for writ of habeas corpus); *Liljeberg* v. *Health Services Aquisition Corp.*, 486 U.S. ——, —————— (1988) (Rule 60(b) motion); *United States* v. *Frady*, 456 U.S. 152, 165 (1982) (§2255 motion); *Ackermann* v. *United States*, 340 U.S. 193, 197-202 (1950) (Rule 60(b) motion); *Sunal* v. *Large*, 332 U.S. 174, 177-179 (1947) (petition for writ of habeas corpus).

⁷ As we held in *Firefighters* v. *Cleveland*, 478 U.S. 501, 529 [41 FEP Cases 139, 151-152] (1986): "Of course, parties who choose to resolve litigation through settlement may not dispose of the claims of a third party, and *a fortiori*, may not impose duties or obligations on a third party, without that party's agreement. A court's approval of a consent decree between some of the parties therefore cannot dispose of the valid claims of nonconsenting [individuals] .... And, of course, a court may not enter a consent decree that imposes obligations on a party that did not consent to the decree. See, *e.g.*, *United States* v. *Ward Baking Co.*, 376 U.S. 327 (1964); *Hughes* v. *United States*, 342 U.S. 353 (1952); *Ashley* v. *City of Jackson*, 464 U.S., at 902 [32 FEP Cases, at 1847] (Rehnquist, J., dissenting from denial of certiorari); 1B Moore ¶0.409[5], p. 326, n.2. However, the consent decree entered here does not bind Local 93 to do or not to do anything. It imposes no legal duties or obligations on the Union at all; only the parties to the decree can be held in contempt of court for failure to comply with its terms. *See United States* v. *Armour & Co.*, 402 U.S., at 676-677."

⁸ The Eleventh Circuit, in a decision involving a previous attempt by white firefighters to set aside the consent decrees at issue in this litigation, itself observed: "There are ... limitations on the extent to which a nonparty can undermine a prior judgment. A nonparty may not reopen the case and relitigate the merits anew; neither may he destroy the validity of the judgment between the parties." *United States* v. *Jefferson County*, 720 F.2d 1511, 1518 [33 FEP Cases 829, 833] (1983).

Professors James and Hazard describe the rule as follows: "Ordinarily, a nonparty has no legal interest in a judgment in an action between others. Such a judgment does not determine the nonparty's rights and obligations under the rules of res judicata and he may so assert if the judgment is relied upon against him. But in some situations one's interests, particularly in one's own personal legal status

---

The District Court's rulings in this case have been described incorrectly by both the Court of Appeals and this Court. The Court of Appeals repeatedly stated that the District Court had "in effect" held that the white firefighters were "bound" by a decree to which they were not parties.⁹ And this Court's opinion seems to assume that the District Court had interpreted its consent decrees in the earlier litigation as holding "that the white firefighters were precluded from challenging employment decisions taken pursuant to the decrees." *Ante*, at 1 [49 FEP Cases, at 1642].¹⁰ It is important, therefore, to make clear exactly what the District Court did hold and why its judgment should be affirmed.

I

The litigation in which the consent decrees were entered was a genuine adversary proceeding. In 1974 and 1975, two groups of private parties and the United States brought three separate Title VII actions against the City of Birmingham (City), the Personnel Board of Jefferson County (Board), and various officials,¹¹ alleging discrimination in hiring and promotion in several areas of employment, including the fire department. After a full trial in 1976, the District Court found that the defendants had violated Title VII and that a test used to

---

or claims to property, may be placed in practical jeopardy by a judgment between others. In such circumstances one may seek the aid of a court of equity, but *the grounds upon which one may rely are severely limited*. The general rule is that one must show either that the judgment was void for lack of jurisdiction of the subject matter or that it was the product of fraud directed at the petitioner." James & Hazard §12.15, p. 681 (emphasis supplied) (footnotes omitted).

⁹ The Court of Appeals wrote:
— "Both the City and the Board, however, denied that they had violated Title VII or the equal protection clause. Both contended that the plaintiffs were bound by the consent decrees and that the promotions were therefore lawful as a matter of law because they had been made pursuant to those decrees." *In re Birmingham Reverse Discrimination Employment Litigation*, 833 F.2d 1492, 1496 [45 FEP Cases 890, 893] (CA11 1987).
— "Without expressly so stating, the district judge treated the plaintiffs as if they were bound by the consent decrees and as if they were alleging solely that the City had violated the City decree." *Ibid.*
— "The court held that the plaintiffs — both the United States and the individual plaintiffs — were bound by the consent decrees." *Id.*, at 1497 [45 FEP Cases, at 894].
— "In effect, the court treated the plaintiffs as if they were parties to the City decree seeking an order to show cause why the City should not be held in civil contempt for violating the terms of the decree." *Id.*, at 1497, n.16 [45 FEP Cases, at 893].

¹⁰ See also, *ante*, at 5 [49 FEP Cases, at 1643-1644], where the Court suggests that the District Court held that its consent decrees had "conclude[d] the rights of strangers to those proceedings." (Footnote omitted.)

¹¹ These parties, along with six black firefighters who were party-plaintiffs to the 1974-1975 litigation, are petitioners herein.

screen job applicants was biased. App. 553. After a second trial in 1979 that focused on promotion practices—but before the District Court had rendered a decision — the parties negotiated two consent decrees, one with the City defendants and the other with the Board. App. to Pet. for Cert. 122a (City decree), 202a (Board decree). The United States is a party to both decrees. The District Court provisionally approved the proposed decrees and directed that the parties provide notice "to all interested persons informing them of the general provisions of the Consent Decrees . . . and of their right to file objections." App. 695. Approximately two months later, the District Court conducted a fairness hearing, at which a group of black employees objected to the decrees as inadequate and a group of white firefighters—represented in part by the Birmingham Firefighters Association (BFA) — opposed any race-conscious relief. Id., at 727. The District Court overruled both sets of objections and entered the decrees in August of 1981. App. to Pet. for Cert. 236a.

In its decision approving the consent decrees, the District Court first noted "that there is no contention or suggestion that the settlements are fraudulent or collusive." Id., at 238a. The court then explained why it was satisfied that the affirmative action goals and quotas set forth in the decrees were "well within the limits upheld as permissible" in Steel Workers v. Weber, 443 U.S. 193 [20 FEP Cases 1] (1979), and other cases. App. to Pet. for Cert. 240a-241a. It pointed out that the decrees "do not preclude the hiring or promotion of whites and males even for a temporary period of time," id., at 241a, and that the City's commitment to promote blacks and whites to the position of fire lieutenant at the same rate was temporary and was subject both to the availability of qualified candidates and "to the caveat that the decree is not to be interpreted as requiring the hiring or promotion of a person who is not qualified or of a person who is demonstrably less qualified according to a job-related selection procedure." Id., at 242a. It further found that the record provided "more than ample reason" to conclude that the City would eventually be held liable for discrimination against blacks at high-level positions in the fire and police departments.[12] Id., at 244a.

Based on its understanding of the wrong committed, the court concluded that the remedy embodied in the consent decrees was "reasonably commensurate with the nature and extent of the indicated discrimination." Ibid. Cf. Milliken v. Bradley, 418 U.S. 717, 744 (1974). The District Court then rejected other specific objections, pointing out that the decrees would not impinge on any contractual rights of the unions or their members. App. to Pet. for Cert. 245a. Finally, after noting that it had fully considered the white firefighters' objections to the settlement, it denied their motion to intervene as untimely. Id., at 246a.

Several months after the entry of the consent decrees, the Board certified to the City that five black firefighters, as well as eight whites, were qualified to fill six vacancies in the position of lieutenant. See App. 81. A group of white firefighters then filed suit against the City and Board challenging their policy of "certifying candidates and making promotions on the basis of race under the assumed protection of consent settlements." App. to Pet. for Cert. 113a. The complaint alleged, in the alternative, that the consent decrees were illegal and void,

---

[12] In approving the decree, the District Court expressed confidence that the United States and the black firefighters brought suit in good faith and that there was a strong evidentiary basis for their complaints. It observed:

"The objectors treat this case as one in which discrimination on the basis of race or sex has not been established. That is only partially true, at least as it relates to positions in the police and fire departments. This Court at the first trial found — and the Fifth Circuit agreed — that blacks applying for jobs as police officers and firefighters were discriminated against by the tests used by the Personnel Board to screen and rank applicants. The evidence presented at the second trial established, at the .01 level of statistical significance, that blacks were adversely affected by the exam used by the Personnel Board to screen and rank applicants for the position of police sergeant. Since governmental employers such as the City of Birmingham have been limited by state law to selecting candidates from among those certified by the Board, one would hardly be surprised to find that the process as a whole has had an adverse effect upon blacks seeking employment as Birmingham police officers, police sergeants, or firefighters — regardless of whether or not there was any actual bias on the part of selecting officials of the City. A natural consequence of discrimination against blacks at entry-level positions in the police and fire departments would be to limit their opportunities for promotion to higher levels in the departments.

"Employment statistics for Birmingham's police and fire departments as of July 21, 1981, certainly lend support to the claim made in this litigation against the City — that, notwithstanding this court's directions in 1977 with respect to certifications by the Personnel Board for the entry-level police officer and firefighters positions and despite the City's adoption of a 'fair hiring ordinance' and of affirmative action plans, the effects of past discrimination against blacks persist. According to those figures, 79 of the 480 police officers are black, 3 of the 131 police sergeants are black, and none of the 40 police lieutenants and captains are black. In the fire department, 42 of the 453 firefighters are black, and none of the 140 lieutenants, captains, and battalion chiefs are black." App. to Pet. for Cert. 242a-243a.

The evidence of discrimination presented at the 1979 trial is described in greater detail in the United States' 100-page, post-trial brief, which is reprinted in the Joint Appendix. See App. 594-693.

or that the defendants were not properly implementing them. *Id.*, at 113a-114a. The plaintiffs filed motions for a temporary restraining order and a preliminary injunction. After an evidentiary hearing, the District Court found that the plaintiffs' collateral attack on the consent decrees was "without merit" and that four of the black officers were qualified for promotion in accordance with the terms of the decrees. App. 81-83. Accordingly, it denied the motions, *id.*, at 83, 85-86, and, for the first time in its history, the City had a black lieutenant in its fire department.

The plaintiffs' appeal from that order was consolidated with the appeal that had been previously taken from the order denying the motion to intervene filed in the earlier litigation. The Court of Appeals affirmed both orders. See *United States* v. *Jefferson County*, 720 F.2d 1511 [33 FEP Cases 829] (CA11 1983). While that appeal was pending, in September 1983, the *Wilks* respondents filed a separate action against petitioners. The *Wilks* complaint alleged that petitioners were violating Title VII, but it did not contain any challenge to the validity of the consent decrees. App. 130. After various preliminary proceedings, the District Court consolidated these cases, along with four other reverse discrimination actions brought against petitioners, under the caption *In re: Birmingham Reverse Discrimination Litigation. Id.*, at 218. In addition, over the course of the litigation, the court allowed further parties to intervene.[13]

On February 18, 1985, the District Court ruled on the City's motion for partial summary judgment and issued an opinion that, among other things, explained its understanding of the relevance of the consent decrees to the issues raised in the reverse discrimination litigation. *Id.*, at 277. After summarizing the proceedings that led up to the entry of the consent decrees, the District Court expressly "recognized that the consent decrees might not bar all claims of 'reverse discrimination' since [the plaintiffs] had not been par-

ties to the prior suits."[14] *Id.*, at 279. The court then took a position with respect to the relevance of the consent decrees that differed from that advocated by any of the parties. The plaintiffs contended that the consent decrees, even if valid, did not constitute a defense to their action, *cf. W.R. Grace & Co.* v. *Rubber Workers*, 461 U.S. 757 [31 FEP Cases 1409] (1983), and, in the alternative, that the decrees did not authorize the promotion of black applicants ahead of higher scoring white applicants and thus did not justify race-conscious promotions. App. 281-282. The City, on the other hand, contended that the promotions were immunized from challenge if they were either required or permitted by the terms of the decrees. *Id.*, at 282. The District Court took the intermediate position that promotions required by — and made because of — the decrees were justified.[15] However, it denied the City's summary judgment motion because it raised factual issues requiring a trial. *Id.*, at 288-289.

In December 1985, the court conducted a 5-day trial limited to issues concerning promotions in the City's fire and engineering departments.[16] At

---

[14] During an earlier hearing, the District Court informed counsel:
"I do believe that the Court of Appeals said there is no per se prohibition against an attack, an indirect attack, in any event by a person whose rights may be affected during the implementation or claims implementation of the decree. To the extent the motions to dismiss or summary judgment take that position, I think the Court of Appeals said, no, that is not the law of this Circuit." *Id.*, at 237.

[15] The court indicated that if the race-conscious promotions were a product of the City's adherence to pending court orders (*i.e.* the consent decrees), it could not be said that the City acted with the requisite racially discriminatory intent. See *id.*, at 280 ("the court is persuaded that the defendants can.... defend these reverse discrimination claims if they establish that the challenged promotions were made because of the requirements of the consent decree"). See also Tr. (May 14, 1984), reprinted. App. 237. In reaching this conclusion, the District Court was well aware of the Court of Appeals' previous suggestion that such a defense might be available:
"The consent decree would only become an issue if the defendant attempted to justify its conduct by saying that it was mandated by the consent decree. If this were the defense, the trial judge would have to determine whether the defendant's action was mandated by the decree, and, if so, whether that fact alone would relieve the defendant of liability that would otherwise attach. This is, indeed, a difficult question... We should not, however, preclude potentially wronged parties from raising such a question merely because it is perplexing.'" App. 280-281, n. 6, quoting *United States* v. *Jefferson County*, 720 F.2d, at 1518-1519 [33 FEP Cases, at 833-834].

[16] At the close of the plaintiffs' case, the District Court granted the motion of the Board to dismiss the claims against it pursuant to Fed. Civ. Proc. 41(b). The basis for the motion was the fact that even without regard to the consent decrees, the plaintiffs had not proved a prima facie case against the Board, which had done nothing more than provide the City with the names of employees, both white and black, who were qualified for promotion. There was no evidence that the Board's certification process, or its testing procedures, ad-

---

[13] Among those allowed to intervene were seven black firefighters who were parties to the consent decrees and who sought to defend the decrees; the United States, which reversed course in the litigation and aligned itself with the plaintiffs; and additional white firefighters pressing individual reverse discrimination claims.

that trial, respondents challenged the validity of the consent decrees; to meet that challenge, petitioners introduced the records of the 1976 trial, the 1979 trial, and the fairness hearing conducted in 1981. Respondents also tried to prove that they were demonstrably better qualified than the black firefighters who had been promoted ahead of them. At the conclusion of the trial, the District Court entered a partial final judgment dismissing portions of the plaintiffs' complaints. The judge explained his ruling in an oral opinion dictated from the bench, supplemented by the adoption, with some changes, of detailed findings and conclusions drafted by the prevailing parties. See App. to Pet. for Cert 27a, 37a.

In his oral statement, the judge adhered to the legal position he had expressed in his February ruling. He stated:

"The conclusions there expressed either explicitly or implicitly were that under appropriate circumstances, a valid consent decree appropriately limited can be the basis for a defense against a charge of discrimination, even in the situation in which it is clear that the defendant to the litigation did act in a racially conscious manner.

"In that February order, it was my view as expressed then, that if the City of Birmingham made promotions of blacks to positions as fire lieutenant, fire captain and civil engineer, because the City believed it was required to do so by the consent decree, and if in fact the City was required to do so by the Consent Decree, then they would not be guilty of racial discrimination, either under Title 7, Section 1981, 1983 or the 14th Amendment. That remains my conclusion given the state of the law as I understand it." Id., at 77a.

He then found as a matter of fact that petitioners had not promoted any black officers who were not qualified or who were demonstrably less qualified than the whites who were not promoted. He thus rejected respondents' contention that the City could not claim that it simply acted as required by terms of the consent decree:[17]

"In this case, under the evidence as presented here, I find that even if the burden of proof be placed on the defendants, they have carried that proof and that burden of establishing that the promotions of the black individuals in this case were in fact required by the terms of the consent decree." Id., at 78a.

The written conclusions of law that he adopted are less clear than his oral opinion. He began by unequivocally stating: "The City Decree is lawful." [18] Id., at 106a. He explained that "under all the relevant case law of the Eleventh circuit and the Supreme Court, it is a proper remedial device, designed to overcome the effects of prior, illegal discrimination by the City of Birmingham." [19] Id., at 106a-107a. In that same conclusion, however, he did state that "plaintiffs cannot collaterally attack the Decree's validity." Id., at 106a. Yet, when read in context — and particularly in light of the court's finding that the decree was lawful under Eleventh Circuit and Supreme Court precedent — it is readily apparent that, at the extreme, this was intended as an alternative holding. More likely, it was an overstatement of the rule that collateral review is narrower in scope than appellate review. In any event, and regardless of one's reading of this lone sentence, it is absolutely clear that the court did not hold that respondents were bound by the decree. Nowhere in the District Court's lengthy findings of fact and conclusions of law is there a single word suggesting that respondents were bound by the consent decree or that the court intended to treat them as though they had been actual parties to that litigation and not merely as persons whose interests, as a practical matter, had been affected. Indeed, respondents, the Court of Appeals, and the majority opinion all fail to draw attention to any point in this case's long history at which the judge may have given the impression that any nonparty was legally bound by the consent decree.[20]

---

versely affected whites. I am at a loss to understand why the Court of Appeals did not affirm the judgment in favor of the Board.

[17] Paragraph 2 of the city consent decree provides, in pertinent part:
"Nothing herein shall be interpreted as requiring the City to... promote a person who is not qualified... or promote a less qualified person, in preference to a person who is demonstrably better qualified based upon the results of a job related selection procedure." App. to Pet. for Cert. 124a.

[18] The District Court's opinion does not refer to the second consent decree because the claims against the Board had been dismissed at the end of the plaintiffs' case. See n. 16, supra.
[19] In support of this proposition, the court cited, inter alia, our decision in Steelworkers v. Weber, 443 U.S. 193 [20 FEP Cases 1] (1979). We recently reaffirmed the Weber decision in Johnson v. Transportation Agency, 480 U.S. 616 [43 FEP Cases 411] (1987). See also Sheet Metal Workers v. EEOC, 478 U.S. 421 [41 FEP Cases 107] (1986) (plurality opinion); id., at 483 [41 FEP Cases, at 132] (Powell, J., concurring in part and concurring in judgment); id. at 489 [41 FEP Cases, at 134] (O'Connor, J., concurring in part and dissenting in part); id., at 499 [41 FEP Cases, at 138] (White, J., dissenting) (all reaffirming that courts are vested with discretion to award race-conscious relief).
[20] In Provident Tradesmens Bank & Trust Co. v. Patterson, 390 U.S., at 114, we expressly did not decide whether a litigant might "be bound by [a] previous decision because, although technically a nonparty, he had purposely bypassed an adequate opportunity to intervene." See Note, Preclusion of Absent Disputants to Compel Intervention, 79 Column. L. Rev. 1551 (1979) (arguing in favor of such a rule of mandatory intervention); 7 C. Wright, A. Miller, M. Kane, Federal Practice and Procedure §1608, p. 115, n. 33 (2d ed. 1986) (drawing a parallel between the mandatory intervention rule and this Court's decision in Penn-Central Merger and N & W Inclusion Cases, 389 U.S. 486 (1968)). Today, the

II

Regardless of whether the white firefighters were parties to the decrees granting relief to their black co-workers, it would be quite wrong to assume that they could never collaterally attack such a decree. If a litigant has standing, he or she can always collaterally attack a judgment for certain narrowly defined defects. See, *e.g.*, *Klapprott* v. *United States*, 335 U.S. 601 (1949); and cases cited in n. 5, *supra*. See also *Korematsu* v. *United States*, 584 F.Supp. 1406 (ND Cal. 1984) (granting writ of *coram nobis* vacating conviction based on Government concealment of critical contradictory evidence in *Korematsu* v. *United States* 323 U.S. 214 (1944)). On the other hand, a district court is not required to retry a case — or to sit in review of another court's judgment — every time an interested nonparty asserts that *some* error that might have been raised on direct appeal was committed. See nn. 6 and 8, *supra*. Such a broad allowance of collateral review would destroy the integrity of litigated judgments, would lead to an abundance of vexatious litigation, and would subvert the interest in comity between courts.[21] Here, re-

Court answers this question, at least in the limited context of the instant dispute. holding that "[j]oinder as a party [under Fed. Civ. Proc. 19], rather than knowledge of a lawsuit and an opportunity to intervene [under Fed. Rule Civ. Proc. 24], is the method by which potential parties are subject to the jurisdiction of the court and bound by a judgment or decree." *Ante*, at 7-8 [49 FEP Cases, at 1645]. See also *ante*, at 6 [49 FEP Cases, at 1644] ("a party seeking a judgment binding on another cannot obligate that person to intervene: he must be joined"). Because I conclude that the District Court did not hold that respondents were bound by the consent decrees, I do not reach this issue.

[21] One leading commentator relies on the following poignant language employed by the Virginia Supreme Court to explain the significance of the doctrine limiting collateral attacks:

" 'It is one. . . which has been adopted in the interest of the peace of society and the permanent security of titles. If, after the rendition of a judgment by a court of competent jurisdiction, and after the period has elapsed when it becomes irreversible for error, another court may in another suit inquire into the irregularities or errors in such judgment, there would be no end to litigation and no fixed established rights. A judgment, though unreversed and irreversible, would no longer be a final adjudication of the rights of the litigants, but the starting point from which a new litigation would spring up; acts of limitation would become useless and nugatory; purchasers on the faith of judicial process would find no protection; every right established by a judgment would be insecure and uncertain; and a cloud would rest upon every title." 1 H. Black, Law of Judgments §245, pp. 365-366 (2d ed. 1902), quoting *Lancaster* v. *Wilson*, 27 Grat. 624, 629 (1876).

In addition to undermining this interest in finality, permitting collateral attacks also leads to the anomaly that courts will, on occasion, be required to sit in review of judgments entered by other courts and of equal — or even greater — authority. Cf. *Asarco Inc.* v. *Kadish*, —— U.S. ——, —— —— (1989); *District of Columbia Court of Appeals* v. *Feldman*, 460 U.S. 462 (1983); *Rooker* v. *Fidelity Trust Co.*, 263 U.S. 413. 415-416 (1923). The rule is also supported by the fact that there is no assur-

spondents have offered no circumstance that might justify reopening the District Court's settled judgment.

The implementation of a consent decree affecting the interests of a multitude of nonparties, and the reliance on that decree as a defense to a charge of discrimination in hiring and promotion decisions, raise a legitimate concern of collusion. No such allegation, however, has been raised. Moreover, there is compelling evidence that the decree was not collusive. In its decision approving the consent decree over the objection of the BFA and individual white firefighters, the District Court observed that there had been "no contention or suggestion" that the decrees were fraudulent or collusive. App. to Pet. for Cert. 238a. The record of the fairness hearing was made part of the record of this litigation and this finding was not contradicted. More significantly, the consent decrees were not negotiated until after the 1976 trial and the court's finding that the City had discriminated against black candidates for jobs as police officers and firefighters, see App. 553, and until after the 1979 trial, at which substantial evidence was presented suggesting that the City also discriminated against black candidates for promotion in the fire department, see n. 12, *supra*. Like the record of the 1981 fairness hearing, the records of both of these prior proceedings were made part of the record in this case. Given this history, the lack of any indication of collusion, and the District Court's finding that "there is more than ample reason for . . . the City of Birmingham to be concerned that [it] would be in time held liable for discrimination against blacks at higher level positions in the police and fire departments," App. to Pet. for Cert. 244a, it is evident that the decree was a product of genuine arm's-length negotiations.

Nor can it be maintained that the consent judgment is subject to reopening and further litigation because the relief it afforded was so out of line with settled legal doctrine that it "was transparently invalid or had only a frivolous pretense to validity." [22] *Walker* v. *Birmingham* 388 U.S. 307, 315

ance that a second round of litigation is more likely than the first to reach a just result or obtain uniformity in the law.

[22] It was argued during the 1981 fairness hearing, in the first complaint filed in this litigation. see App. to Pet. for Cert. 113a, and in at least one of the subsequently filed complaints, see App. 96, that race-conscious relief for persons who are not proven victims of past discrimination is absolutely prohibited by the Equal Protection Clause of the Fourteenth Amendment and by Title VII of the Civil Rights Act of 1964. As I have pointed out. the *Wilks* complaint did not challenge the validity of the decrees. See *id.*, at 135-137.

(1967) (suggesting that a contemnor might be allowed to challenge contempt citation on ground that underlying court order was "transparently invalid"). To the contrary, the type of race-conscious relief ordered in the consent decree is entirely consistent with this Court's approach to affirmative action. Given a sufficient predicate of racial discrimination, neither the Equal Protection Clause of the Fourteenth Amendment [23] nor Title VII of the Civil rights Act of 1964 [24] erects a bar to affirmative action plans that benefit non-victims and have some adverse effect on non-wrongdoers. [25] As JUSTICE O'CONNOR observed

---

[23] See *Wygant* v. *Jackson Bd. of Education*, 476 U.S. 267, 286 [40 FEP Cases 1321, 1329] (1986) (O'Connor, J., concurring in part and concurring in judgment) ("The Court is in agreement that whatever the formulation employed, remedying past discrimination by a state actor is a sufficiently weighty state interest to warrant the remedial use of a carefully constructed affirmative action program"). See also *Sheet Metal Workers*, 478 U.S. at 479–481 [41 FEP Cases, at 130–131] (plurality opinion); *id.*, at 484–489 [41 FEP Cases, at 132–134] (Powell, J., concurring in part and concurring in judgment).

[24] In distinguishing the Court's decision in *Firefighters* v. *Stotts*, 467 U.S. 561 [34 FEP Cases 1702] (1984), the plurality in *Sheet Metal Workers*, 478 U.S., at 474–475 [41 FEP Cases, at 128], asserted: "However, this limitation on *individual* makewhole relief does not affect a court's authority to order race-conscious affirmative action. The purpose of affirmative action is not to make identified victims whole, but rather to dismantle prior patterns of employment discrimination and to prevent discrimination in the future. Such relief is provided to the class as a whole rather than to individual members; no individual is entitled to relief, and beneficiaries need not show that they were themselves victims of discrimination. In this case, neither the membership goal nor the Fund order required petitioners to indenture or train particular individuals, and neither required them to admit to membership individuals who were refused admission for reasons unrelated to discrimination. We decline petitioners' invitation to read *Stotts* to prohibit a court from ordering any kind of race-conscious affirmative relief that might benefit nonvictims. This reading would distort the language of §706(g), and would deprive the courts of an important means of enforcing Title VII's guarantee of equal employment opportunity." See also *id.*, at 483 [41 FEP Cases, at 132] (Powell, J., concurring in part and concurring in judgment) ("plain language of Title VII does not clearly support a view that all remedies must be limited to benefiting victims," and "although the matter is not entirely free from doubt," the legislative history of Title VII indicates that nonvictims may be benefited); *id.*, at 490 [41 FEP Cases, at 134] (O'Connor, J., concurring in part and dissenting in part) ("It is now clear . . . that a majority of the Court believes that the last sentence of §706(g) does not in all circumstances prohibit a court in a Title VII employment discrimination case from ordering relief that may confer some racial preferences with regard to employment in favor of nonvictims of discrimination"); *id.*, at 499 [41 FEP Cases, at 138] (White, J., dissenting) ("I agree that §706(g) does not bar relief for nonvictims in all circumstances").

[25] In my view, an affirmative action plan need not be supported by a predicate of racial discrimination by the employer provided that the plan "serve[s] a valid public purpose, that it was adopted with fair procedures and given a narrow breadth, that it transcends the harm to [the nonminority employees], and that it is a step toward that ultimate goal of eliminating entirely from governmental decisionmaking such irrelevant fac-

---

in *Wygant* v. *Jackson Bd. of Education*, 476 U.S. 267 [40 FEP Cases 1321] (1986), "[t]his remedial purpose need not be accompanied by contemporaneous findings of actual discrimination to be accepted as legitimate as long as the public actor has a firm basis for believing that remedial action is required." *Id.*, at 286 [41 FEP Cases, at 1329] (opinion concurring in part and concurring in judgment). Such a belief was clearly justified in this case. After conducting the 1976 trial and finding against the City and after listening to the five days of testimony in the 1979 trial, the judge was well qualified to conclude that there was sound basis for believing that the City would likely have been found to have violated Title VII if the action had proceeded to a litigated judgment. [26]

Hence, there is no basis for collaterally attacking the judgment as collusive, fraudulent, or transparently invalid. Moreover, respondents do not claim — nor has there been any showing of — mistake, duress, or lack of jurisdiction. Instead, respondents are left to argue that somewhat different relief would have been more appropriate than the relief that was actually granted. Although this sort of issue may provide the basis for a direct appeal, it cannot, and should not, serve to open the door to relitigation of a settled judgment.

III

The facts that respondents are not bound by the decree and that they have no basis for a collateral attack, moreover, do not compel the conclusion that the District Court should have treated the decree as nonexistent for purposes of respondents' discrimination suit. That the decree may not directly interfere with any of respon-

---

tors as a human being's race." *Wygant*, 476 U.S., at 320 [40 FEP Cases, at 1343] (Stevens, J., dissenting). In this case, however, the plan was undoubtedly preceded by an adequate predicate of racial discrimination; thus, I need not consider whether there is some present-day purpose that might justify a race-conscious promotion scheme.

[26] Moreover, the District Court, in its opinion approving the consent decrees, found that the remedies are "reasonably commensurate with the nature and extent of the indicated discrimination," are "limited in duration, expiring as particular positions generally reflect the racial . . . composition of the labor market in the county as a whole," allow for "substantial opportunity for employment advancement of whites and males," and "do not require the selection of blacks . . . who are unqualified or who are demonstrably less qualified than their competitors." App. to Pet. for Cert. 244a–245a. Therefore, it cannot be claimed that the court failed to consider whether the remedies were tailored "to fit the nature of the violation." *Sheet Metal Workers*, 478 U.S., at 476 [41 FEP Cases, at 129]. See also *id.*, at 496 [41 FEP Cases, at 136] (O'Connor, J., concurring in part and dissenting in part).

dents' legal rights does not mean that it may not affect the factual setting in a way that negates respondents' claim. The fact that a criminal suspect is not a party to the issuance of a search warrant does not imply that the presence of a facially valid warrant may not be taken as evidence that the police acted in good faith. *See Malley* v. *Briggs*, 475 U.S. 335, 344–345 (1986); *United States* v. *Leon*, 468 U.S. 897, 921–922, 924 (1984); *United States* v. *Ross*, 456 U.S. 798, 823, n. 32 (1982). Similarly, the fact that an employer is acting under court compulsion may be evidence that the employer is acting in good faith and without discriminatory intent. *Cf. Ashley* v. *City of Jackson*, 464 U.S. 900, 903 [32 FEP Cases 1846, 1848] (1983) (REHNQUIST, J., dissenting from denial of certiorari) (suggesting that compliance with a consent decree "might be relevant to a defense of good-faith immunity"); Restatement (Second) of Judgments §76, Comment *a*, p. 217 (1982) ("If the judgment is held to be not binding on the person against whom it is invoked, it is then ignored in the determination of matters in issue in the subsequent litigation, unless it is relevant for some other purpose such as proving the good faith of a party who relied on it"). Indeed, the threat of a contempt citation provides as good a reason to act as most, if not all, other business justifications.[2]

After reviewing the evidence, the District Court found that the City had in fact acted under compulsion of the consent decree. App. to Pet. for Cert. 107a; App. 280. Based on this finding, the court concluded that the City carried its burden of coming forward with

a legitimate business reason for its promotion policy, and, accordingly, held that the promotion decisions were "not taken with the requisite discriminatory intent" necessary to make out a claim of disparate treatment under Title VII or the Equal Protection Clause. App. to Pet. for Cert. 107a, citing *Texas Dept. of Community Affairs* v. *Burdine*, 450 U.S. 248 [25 FEP Cases 113] (1981). For this reason, and not because it thought that respondents were legally bound by the consent decree, the court entered an order in favor of the City and defendant-intervenors.

Of course, in some contexts a plaintiff might be able to demonstrate that reference to a consent decree is pretextual. See *Burdine, supra*. For example, a plaintiff might be able to show that the consent decree was collusive and that the defendants simply obtained the court's rubber stamp on a private agreement that was in no way related to the eradication of pervasive racial discrimination. The plaintiff, alternatively, might be able to show that the defendants were not bound to obey the consent decree because the court that entered it was without jurisdiction. See *United States* v. *Mine Workers*, 330 U.S. 258, 291–294 [19 LRRM 2346] (1947). Similarly, although more tenuous, a plaintiff might argue that the parties to the consent judgment were not bound because the order was "transparently invalid" and thus unenforceable.[3] If the defendants were as a result not bound to implement the affirmative-action program, then the plaintiff might be able to show that the racial preference was not a product of the court order.

In a case such as this, however, in which there has been no showing that the decree was collusive, fraudulent, transparently invalid, or entered without jurisdiction, it would be "unconscionable" to conclude that obedience to an order remedying a Title VII violation could subject a defendant to additional liability. *Cf. Farmers* v. *WDAY*,

---

[2] Because consent decrees "have attributes both of contracts and judicial decrees," they are treated differently for different purposes. *United States* v. *ITT Continental Baking Co.*, 420 U.S. 223, 236, n.10 (1975). See also *Firefighters* v. *Cleveland*, 478 U.S., at 519 [41 FEP Cases, at 147]. For example, because the content of a consent decree is generally a product of negotiations between the parties, decrees are construed for enforcement purposes as contracts. See *ITT Continental Baking Co., supra*, at 238; *Stotts* v. *Memphis Fire Dept.*, 679 F.2d 541, 557 [28 FEP Cases, 1491, 1502] (CA6 1982), rev'd on other grounds, 467 U.S. 561 [34 FEP Cases 1702] (1984). For purposes of determining whether an employer can be held liable for intentional discrimination merely for complying with the terms of a consent decree, however, it is appropriate to treat the consent decree as a judicial order. Unlike the typical contract, a consent decree, such as the one at issue here, is developed in the context of adversary litigation. Moreover, the court reviews the consent decree to determine whether it is lawful, reasonable, and equitable. In placing the judicial imprimatur on the decree, the court provides the parties with some assurance that the decree is legal and that they may rely on it. Most significantly, violation of a consent decree is punishable as criminal contempt. See 18 U.S.C. §§401, 402; Fed. Rule Crim. Proc. 42.

[3] In *Walker* v. *Birmingham*, 388 U.S. 307 (1967), we held that a party can be held in contempt of court for violating an injunction, even if the injunction was invalid under the Federal Constitution. However, in upholding the contempt citations at issue, we made clear that that was "not a case where the injunction was transparently invalid or had only a frivolous pretense to validity." *Id.*, at 315. Courts and commentators have relied on this reservation in positing that a contempt citation may be collaterally attacked if the underlying order was "transparently invalid". See, *e.g.*, *In re Providence Journal Co.*, 820 F.2d 1342 (CA1 1986), cert. dism'd, *sub nom. Providence Journal* v. *United States*, 485 U.S. —— (1988); 3 C. Wright, Federal Practice and Procedure §702, p. 815, n.17 (2d ed. 1982).

Inc., 360 U.S. 525, 531 (1959). Rather, all of the reasons that support the Court's view that a police officer should not generally be held liable when he carries out the commands in a facially valid warrant apply with added force to city officials, or indeed to private employers, who obey the commands contained in a decree entered by a federal court.[29] In fact, Equal Employment Opportunity Commission regulations concur in this assessment. They assert, "[t]he Commission interprets Title VII to mean that actions taken pursuant to the direction of a Court Order cannot give rise to liability under Title VII." 29 CFR §1608.8 (1989).[30] Assuming that the District Court's findings of fact were not clearly erroneous — which of course is a matter that is not before us — it seems perfectly clear that its judgment should have been affirmed. Any other conclusion would subject large employers who seek to comply with the law by remedying past discrimination to a never-ending stream of litigation and potential liability. It is unfathomable that either Title VII of the Equal Protection Clause demands such a counter-productive result.

IV

The predecessor to this litigation was brought to change a pattern of hiring and promotion practices that had discriminated against black citizens in Birmingham for decades. The white respondents in this case are not responsible for that history of discrimination, but they are nevertheless beneficiaries of the discriminatory practices that the litigation was designed to correct. Any remedy that seeks to create employment conditions that would have obtained if there had been no violations of law will necessarily have an adverse impact on whites, who must now share their job and promotion opportunities with blacks.[31] Just as white employees in the past were innocent beneficiaries of illegal discriminatory practices, so is it inevitable that some of the same white employees will be innocent victims who must share some of the burdens resulting from the redress of the past wrongs.

There is nothing unusual about the fact that litigation between adverse parties may, as a practical matter, seriously impair the interests of third persons who elect to sit on the sidelines. Indeed, in complex litigation this Court has squarely held that a sideline-sitter may be bound as firmly as an actual party if he had adequate notice and a fair opportunity to intervene and if the judicial interest in finality is sufficiently strong. See *Penn-Central Merger and N & W Inclusion Cases*, 389 U.S. 486, 505–506 (1968). Cf. *Bergh* v. *Washington*, 535 F.2d 505, 507 (CA9), cert. denied, 429 U.S. 921 (1976); *Safir* v. *Dole*, 231 U.S. App. D.C. 63, 70–71, 718 F.2d 475, 482–83 (1983), cert. denied, 467 U.S. 1206 (1984); James & Hazard, §11.31, pp. 651–652.

There is no need, however, to go that far in order to agree with the District Court's eminently sensible view that compliance with the terms of a valid decree remedying violations of Title VII cannot itself violate that statute of the Equal Protection Clause.[32] The City of Birmingham, in entering into

---

[29] Both warrants and consent decrees bear the indicium of reliability that a judicial officer has reviewed the proposed act and determined that it is lawful. See *United States* v. *Alexandria*, 614 F.2d 1358, 1361 [22 FEP Cases 872, 874] (CA5 1980) ("trial court must satisfy itself that the consent decree is not unlawful, unreasonable, or inequitable before it can be approved"); App. to Pet. for Cert. 238a. Unlike the police officer in receipt of facially valid warrant, however, an employer with notice of an affirmative injunction has no choice but to act. This added element of compulsion renders imposition of liability for acting pursuant to a valid consent decree all the more equitable.

[30] Section 1608.8 does not differentiate between orders "entered by consent or after contested litigation." 29 CFR §1608.8 (1989). Indeed, the reasoning in the Court's opinion today would seem equally applicable to litigated orders and consent decrees.

The Court's unwillingness to acknowledge that the grounds for a collateral attack on a judgment are significantly narrower than the grounds available on direct review, see *ante*, at 8, n.6 [49 FEP Cases, at 1645], is difficult to reconcile with the host of cases cited in *United States* v. *Frady*, 456 U.S. 152, 165 (1982), the cases cited in n.6, *supra*, and those cited in the scholarly writings cited in n.5, *supra*.

[31] It is inevitable that nonminority employees or applicants will be less well off under an affirmative action plan than without it, no matter what form it takes. For example, even when an employer simply agrees to recruit minority job applicants more actively, white applicants suffer the "nebulous" harm of facing increased competition and the diminished likelihood of eventually being hired. See Schwarzchild, Public Law By Private Bargain: Title VII Consent Decrees and the Fairness of Negotiated Institutional Reform, 1984 Duke L.J. 887, 909–910.

[32] In professing difficulty in understanding why respondents are not "bound" by a decree that provides a defense to employment practices that would otherwise violate Title VII, see *ante*, at 8, n.6 [49 FEP Cases, at 1645], the Court uses the word "bound" in a sense that is different from that used earlier in its opinion. A judgment against an employer requiring it to institute a seniority system may provide the employer with a defense to employment practices that would otherwise violate Title VII. In the sense in which the word "bound" is used in the cases cited by the Court at pages 4 and 5 of its opinion [49 FEP Cases, at 1643], only the parties to the litigation would be "bound" by the judgment. But employees who first worked for the company 180 days after the litigation ended would be "bound" by the judgment in the sense that the Court uses when it responds to my argument. The cases on which the Court relies are entirely consistent with my position. Its facile use of the word "bound" should not be allowed to conceal the obvious flaws in its analysis.

and complying with this decree, has made a substantial step toward the eradication of the long history of pervasive racial discrimination that has plagued its fire department. The District Court, after conducting a trial and carefully considering respondents' arguments, concluded that this effort is lawful and should go forward. Because respondents have thus already had their day in court and have failed to carry their burden, I would vacate the judgment of the Court of Appeals and remand for further proceedings consistent with this opinion.

LORANCE v. AT&T TECHNO-LOGIES

Supreme Court of the United States

LORANCE, et al. v. AT&T TECH-NOLOGIES, INC., et al., No. 87-1428, June 12, 1989

CIVIL RIGHTS ACT OF 1964

1. Timeliness of charge ▶108.563

Limitations period for challenging post-Title VII seniority system begins to run from date of adoption of system, and, therefore, female employees' 1983 charge, filed after they were demoted pursuant to seniority system, challenging alleged discriminatory alteration of system in 1979 is untimely, where they do not allege that seniority system is discriminatory on its face or as presently applied, but merely that system had its genesis in discrimination.

2. Continuing violation ▶108.566

Continuing-violation theory is inapplicable to female employees' claim that they were discriminated against when, in 1983, they were demoted because of discriminatory alteration of seniority system in 1979, since any violation occurred in 1979 with alteration of system and not when effects of alteration were felt in 1983.

3. Seniority ▶108.3301 ▶108.736

Section 703(h) of Civil Rights Act of 1964, which permits employers to act pursuant to bona fide seniority system, does not merely provide affirmative defense to disparate-impact claim, but instead makes intentional discrimination an element of challenge to seniority system.

4. Seniority ▶108.3301 ▶108.561

Facially discriminatory seniority system, which is one that treats similarly situated employees differently, can be challenged at any time, but facially neutral system that is adopted with discriminatory motive can be challenged only within prescribed period after adoption.

———

On writ of certiorari to the U.S. Court of Appeals for the Seventh Circuit (44 FEP Cases 998, 827 F.2d 163). Affirmed.

See also 44 FEP Cases 1817.

Barry Goldstein, Washington, D.C. (Julius L. Chambers, New York, N.Y., Paul Holtzman, Washington, D.C., and Bridget Arimond, Chicago, Ill., with him on briefs), for petitioners.

David W. Carpenter, Washington, D.C. (Rex E. Lee, Patrick S. Casey, and Sidley & Austin, Washington, D.C., Gerald D. Skoning, Charles C. Jackson, and Seyfarth, Shaw, Fairweather & Geraldson, Chicago, Ill., and Joseph Ramirez, Robert W. Benson, and Juanita G. De Roos, of counsel, for employer; Michael H. Gottesman, Robert M. Weinberg, and Bredhoff & Kaiser, Washington, D.C., and Joel A. D'Alba, Stephen J. Feinberg, and Asher, Pavalon, Gittler & Greenfield, Ltd., Chicago, Ill., for union; with him on brief), for respondents.

Charles A. Shanor, General Counsel (Charles Fried, Solicitor General, Donald B. Ayer, Deputy Solicitor General, Richard J. Lazarus, Assistant to the Solicitor General, Gwendolyn Y. Reams, Associate General Counsel, Vincent J. Blackwood, Assistant General Counsel, and Donna J. Brusoski, with him on brief), for United States and EEOC, as amici curiae, urging reversal.

Robert E. Williams, Douglas S. McDowell, and Katrina Grider (McGuiness & Williams), Washington, D.C., filed brief for Equal Employment Advisory Council, as amicus curiae, urging affirmance.

Before REHNQUIST, Chief Justice, and BRENNAN, WHITE, MARSHALL, BLACKMUN, STEVENS, SCALIA, and KENNEDY, Justices.

Full Text of Opinion

JUSTICE SCALIA delivered the opinion of the Court.

Respondent AT&T Technologies, Inc. (AT&T) manufactures electronics products at its Montgomery Works plant. The three petitioners, all of whom are women, have worked as hourly wage employees in that facility since the early 1970's and have been represented by respondent Local 1942, International Brotherhood of Electrical Workers, AFL-CIO. Until 1979 all hourly wage earners accrued competitive seniority exclusively on the basis of years spent in the plant, and a worker promoted to the more highly skilled and better paid "tester" positions retained this plantwide seniority. A collective-bargaining agreement executed by respondents on July 23, 1979, altered the manner of calculating tester seniority.[1] Thenceforth a tester's seniority was to be determined not by length of plantwide service, but by time actually spent as a tester (though it was possible to regain full plantwide seniority after spending 5 years as a tester and completing a prescribed training program). The present action arises from that contractual modification.

Petitioners became testers between 1978 and 1980. During a 1982 economic downturn their low seniority under the 1979 collective-bargaining agreement caused them to be selected for demotion; they would not have been demoted had the former plantwide seniority system remained in place. Claiming that the present seniority system was the product of an intent to discriminate on the basis of sex, petitioners filed complaints with the Equal Employment Opportunity Commission (EEOC) in April 1983. After the EEOC issued right-to-sue letters, petitioners in September 1983 filed the present lawsuit in the District Court for the Northern District of Illinois, and sought certification as class representatives for women employees of AT&T's Montgomery Works plant who had lost plantwide seniority or whom the new system had deterred from seeking promotions to tester positions. Their complaint alleged that among hourly wage earners the tester positions had traditionally been held almost exclusively by men, and nontester positions principally by women, but that in the 1970's an increasing number of women took the steps necessary to qualify for tester positions and exercised their seniority rights to become testers. They claimed that the 1979 alteration of the rules governing tester seniority was the product of a "conspir[acy]" to change the seniority rules, in order to protect incumbent male testers and to discourage women from promoting into the traditionally-

male tester jobs," and that "[t]he purpose and the effect of this manipulation of seniority rules has been to protect male testers from the effects of the female testers' greater plant seniority, and to discourage women from entering the traditionally-male tester jobs." App. 20, 21-22.

On August 27, 1986, before deciding whether to certify the proposed class, the District Court granted respondent's motion for summary judgment on the ground that petitioners had not filed their complaints with the EEOC with the applicable limitations period.[2] 44 FEP Cases 1817, 1821 (ND Ill.). A divided panel of the Court of Appeals for the Seventh Circuit affirmed, concluding that petitioners' claims were time-barred because "the relevant discriminatory act that triggers the period of limitations occurs at the time an employee becomes subject to a facially-neutral but discriminatory seniority system that the employee knows, or reasonably should know, is discriminatory." 827 F.2d 163, 167 [44 FEP Cases 1001] (1987). We granted certiorari, 488 U.S. —— (1988), to resolve a Circuit conflict on when the limitations period begins to run in a lawsuit arising out of a seniority system not alleged to be discriminatory on its face or as presently applied. Compare, e.g., case below, with *Cook* v. *Pan American World Airways*, 771 F.2d 635, 646 [38 FEP Cases 1344, 1353] (CA2 1985), cert. denied, 474 U.S. 1109 [39 FEP Cases 1568] (1986).

Section 706(e) of Title VII of the Civil Rights Act of 1964, 78 Stat. 260, as amended, provides that "[a] charge. . . shall be filed [with the EEOC] within [the applicable period] after the alleged unlawful employment practice occurred." 42 U.S.C. §2000e-5(e). Assessing timeliness therefore "requires us to identify precisely the 'unlawful employment practice' of which [petitioners] complai[n]." *Delaware State College* v. *Ricks*, 449 U.S. 250, 257 [24 FEP Cases 827, 830] (1980). Under §703(a) of Title VII, it is an "unlawful employment practice" for an employer

"(1) . . . to discriminate against any individual with respect to his compensation, terms, conditions, or privileges of employ-

---

[1] The type of seniority at issue here is not "benefit seniority," which is used to "compute *noncompetitive* benefits earned under the contract of employment." *Franks* v. *Bowman Transportation Co.*, 424 U.S. 747, 766 [12 FEP Cases 549, 556] (1976) (emphasis added), but "competitive seniority," which is "used to allocate entitlements to scarce benefits" such as promotion or nondemotion, *id.*, at 766-767 [12 FEP Cases, at 556].

[2] Under 42 U.S.C. §2000e-5(e), a charge must be filed with the EEOC within 180 days of the alleged unfair employment practice unless the complainant has first instituted proceedings with a state or local agency, in which case the period is extended to a maximum of 300 days. Neither the District Court nor the Court of Appeals ruled on the applicable limitations period in the present case, since both courts concluded that petitioners' claims were time-barred even if the applicable period was 300 days. See 827 F.2d 163, 165, and n.2 [44 FEP Cases 998, 1000] (CA7 1987). We may for the same reason avoid ruling on that point here.

ment, because of such individual's race, color, religion, sex, or national origin; or

"(2) to limit, segregate, or classify his employees or applicants for employment in any way which would deprive or tend to deprive any individual of employment opportunities or otherwise adversely affect his status as an employee, because of such individual's race, color, religion sex, or national origin." 42 U.S.C. §2000e-2(a).

Petitioner's allegation of a disparate impact on men and women would ordinarily suffice to state a claim under §703(a)(2), since that provision reaches "practices that are fair in form, but discriminatory in operation," *Griggs* v. *Duke Power Co.*, 401 U.S. 424, 431 [3 FEP Cases 175, 178] (1971); see *Connecticut* v. *Teal*, 457 U.S. 440, 446 [29 FEP Cases 1, 4] (1982). "[S]eniority systems," however, "are afforded special treatment under Title VII," *Trans World Airlines, Inc.* v. *Hardison*, 432 U.S. 63, 81 [14 FEP Cases 1697, 1704] (1977), by reason of §703(h), which states:

"Notwithstanding any other provision of this subchapter, it shall not be an unlawful employment practice for an employer to apply different standards of compensation, or different terms, conditions, or privileges of employment pursuant to a bona fide seniority ... system, ... provided that such differences are not the result of an intention to discriminate because of race, color, religion, sex, or national origin ...." 42 U.S.C. §2000e-2(h).

We have construed this provision to mean that "absent a discriminatory purpose, the operation of a seniority system cannot be an unlawful employment practice even if the system has some discriminatory consequences." *Hardison, supra*, at 82 [14 FEP Cases, at 1705]; see *American Tobacco Co.* v. *Patterson*, 456 U.S. 63, 65, 69 [28 FEP Cases 713, 714, 716] (1982). Thus, for liability to be incurred "there must be a finding of actual intent to discriminate on [statutorily proscribed] grounds on the part of those who negotiated or maintained the [seniority] system." *Pullman-Standard* v. *Swint*, 456 U.S. 273, 289 [28 FEP Cases 1073, 1080] (1982).

[1] Petitioners do not allege that the seniority system treats similarly situated employees differently or that it has been operated in an intentionally discriminatory manner. Rather, they claim that its differential impact on the sexes is unlawful because the system "ha[d] its genesis in [sex] discrimination." *Teamsters* v. *United States*, 431 U.S. 324, 356 [14 FEP Cases 1514, 1527] (1977). Specifically, the complaint alleges that respondents "conspired *to change* the seniority rules, in order to protect incumbent male testers," and that the resulting agreement effected a *"manipulation of* seniority rules" for that "purpose." See App. 20–22 (em-

phasis added). This is in essence a claim of intentionally discriminatory *alteration* of their contractual rights. Seniority is a contractual right, Aaron, Reflections on the Legal Nature and Enforceability of Seniority Rights, 75 Harv. L. Rev. 1532, 1533 (1962), and a competitive seniority *system* establishes a "hierarchy [of such rights] ... according to which ... various employment benefits are distributed," *Franks* v. *Bowman Transportation Co.*, 424 U.S. 747, 768 [12 FEP Cases 549, 557] (1976). Under the collective-bargaining agreements in effect prior to 1979, each petitioner had earned the right to receive a favorable position in the hierarchy of seniority among testers (if and when she became a tester), and respondents eliminated those rights for reasons alleged to be discriminatory. Because this diminution in employment status occurred in 1979 — well outside the period of limitations for a complaint filed with the EEOC in 1983 — the Seventh Circuit was correct to find petitioners' claims time-barred under §706(e).

[2] We recognize, of course, that it is possible to establish a different theoretical construct: to regard the employer as having been guilty of a continuing violation which "occurred," for purposes of §706(e), not only when the contractual right was eliminated but also when each of the concrete effects of that elimination were felt. Or it would be possible to interpret §703 in such fashion that when the proviso of §703(h) is not met ("provided that such differences are not the result of an intention to discriminate because of race, color, religion, sex, or national origin") and that subsection's protection because unavailable, nothing *prevents* suits against the later effects of the system *on disparate impact grounds* under §703(a)(2). The answer to these alternative approaches is that our cases have rejected them.

The continuing violation theory is contradicted most clearly by two decisions, *Delaware State College* v. *Ricks*, 449 U.S. 250 [24 FEP Cases 827] (1980), and *United Air Lines, Inc.* v. *Evans*, 431 U.S. 553 [14 FEP Cases 1510] (1977). In *Ricks*, we treated an allegedly discriminatory denial of tenure — rather than the resulting non-discriminatory termination of employment one year later — as the act triggering the limitations period under §706(e). Because Ricks did not claim "that the manner in which his employment was terminated differed discriminatorily from the manner in which the College terminated other professors who also had been denied tenure," we held that "the only alleged discrimination occurred

— and the filing limitations periods therefore commenced — at the time the tenure decision was made and communicated to Ricks." 449 U.S. at, 258 [24 FEP Cases, at 830]. "That is so," we found, "even though one of the *effects* of the denial of tenure — the eventual loss of a teaching position — did not occur until later." *Ibid.* (emphasis in original) We concluded that " '[t]he proper focus is upon the time of the *discriminatory acts*, not upon the time at which the *consequences* of the acts became most painful." ' ³ *Ibid.* (emphasis in original); accord, *Chardon* v. *Fernandez*. 454 U.S. 6, 8 [27 FEP Cases 57, 57-58] (1981) (*per curiam*).

In *Evans* United Air Lines had discriminatory dismissed the plaintiff after she had worked several years as a flight attendant, and when it rehired her some years later, gave her no seniority credit for her earlier service. Evans conceded that the discriminatory dismissal was time-barred, but claimed that the seniority system impermissibly gave 'present effect to a past act of discrimination." 431 U.S., at 558 [14 FEP Cases, at 1512]. While agreeing with that assessment, we concluded under §703(h) that "a challenge to a neutral system may not be predicated on the mere fact that a past event which has no present legal significance has affected the calculation

---

³ The dissent attempts to distinguish *Delaware State College* v. *Ricks*, 449 U.S. 250 [24 FEP Cases 827] (1980), on the ground that there "[t]he allegedly discriminatory denial of tenure . . . served notice to the plaintiff that his termination a year later would come as a 'delayed, *but inevitable*, consequence.' " *Post*, at 5 [49 FEP Cases, at 1663] (emphasis in original) (citation omitted). This builds on its earlier criticism that "[o]n the day AT&T's seniority system was adopted, there was no reason to believe that a woman who exercised her plantwide seniority to become a tester would *ever* be demoted as a result of the new system," so that at that point the prospect of petitioners' suffering "concret[e] harm" was "speculative." *Post*, at 2 [29 FEP Cases, at 1662] (emphasis in original). Of course the benefits of a seniority system, like those of an insurance policy payable upon the occurrence of a noninevitable event, are by their nature speculative — if only because they depend upon the employee's continuing desire to work for the particular employer. But it makes no more sense to say that no "concrete harm" occurs when an employer provides a patently less desirable seniority guarantee than what the law requires, than it does to say that no concrete harm occurs when an insurance company delivers an accident insurance policy with a face value of $10,000, when what has been paid for is a face value of $25,000. It is true that the injury to the employee becomes substantially *more* concrete when the less desirable seniority system causes his demotion, just as the injury to the policy-holder becomes substantially more concrete when the accident occurs that the payment is $15,000 has than it should be. But that is irrelevant to whether there was *any* concrete injury at the outset. What that dissent means by "concrete harm" is what *Ricks*, *supra*, at 258 [24 FEP Cases, at 830], referred to as the point at which the injury becomes "most painful" — and that case rejected it as the point of reference for liability. Accord, *Chardon* v. *Fernandez*, 454 U.S. 6, 8 [27 FEP Cases 57, 57-58] (1981) *(per curiam)*.

of seniority credit, even if the past event might at one time have justified a valid claim against the employer." 431 U.S., at 560 [14 FEP Cases, at 1513]. Like Evans, petitioners in the present case have asserted a claim that is wholly dependent on discriminatory conduct occurring well outside the period of limitations, and cannot complain of a continuing violation.

[3] The second alternative theory mentioned above would view §703(h) as merely providing an affirmative defense to a cause of action brought under §703(a)(2), rather than as making intentional discrimination an element of any Title VII action challenging a seniority system. The availability of this affirmative defense would not alter the fact that the claim asserted is one of discriminatory impact under §703(a)(2), causing the statute of limitations to run from the time that impact is felt. As an original matter this is a plausible, and perhaps even the most natural, reading of §703(h). (We have construed §703(e), 42 U.S.C. §2000e-2(e) — which deals with bona fide occupational qualifications—in this fashion. See *Dothard* v. *Rawlinson*, 433 U.S. 321, 333 [15 FEP Cases 10, 15] (1977).) But such an interpretation of §703(h) is foreclosed by our cases, which treat the proof of discriminatory intent as a necessary element of Title VII actions challenging seniority systems. At least as concerns seniority plans, we have regarded subsection (h) not as a defense to the illegality described in subsection (a)(2), but as a provision that itself "delineates which employment practices are illegal and thereby prohibited and which are not." *Franks*, 424 U.S., at 758 [12 FEP Cases, at 553]. Thus, in *American Tobacco Co.* we determined §703(h) to mean that "the fact that a seniority system has a discriminatory impact is not alone sufficient to invalidate the system; actual intent to discriminate *must be proved*." 456 U.S., at 65 [28 FEP Cases, at 714] (emphasis added). "To be cognizable," we held, "a claim that a seniority system has discriminatory impact *must* be accompanied by proof of a discriminatory purpose." *Id.*, at 69 [28 FEP Cases, at 716] (emphasis added); accord, *Pullman-Standard*, 456 U.S. at 277, 289; [28 FEP Cases, at 1074, 1080]; *Hardison*, 432 U.S., at 82 [14 FEP Cases, at 1709]. Indeed, in *California Brewers Assn.* v. *Bryant*, 444 U.S. 598 [22 FEP Cases 1] (1980), after deciding that a challenged policy was part of a seniority system, we noted that on remand to the District Court the *plaintiff* would "remain free to show that . . . the seniority system . . . is not 'bona fide' or that the differences in

employment conditions that it has produced are 'the result of an intention to discriminate because of race,' " *id.*, at 610-611 [22 FEP Cases, at 6]. Thus, petitioners' claim depends on proof of intentionally discriminatory adoption of the system, which occurred outside the limitations period.

That being the case, *Machinists* v. *NLRB*, 362 U.S. 411 [45 LRRM 3212] (1960), establishes that the limitations period will run from the date the system was adopted (at least where the adoption occurred after the effective date of Title VII, and a cause of action against it was available). *Machinists* was a decision under the National Labor Relations Act (NLRA), but we have often observed that the NLRA was the model for Title VII's remedial provisions, and have found cases interpreting the former persuasive in construing the latter. See *Ford Motor Co.* v. *EEOC*, 458 U.S. 219, 226, n. 8 [29 FEP Cases 121, 124-125] (1982); *Teamsters*, 431 U.S., at 366 [14 FEP Cases, at 1532]; *Franks, supra*, at 768-770 [12 FEP Cases, at 557-558]; *Albemarle Paper Co.* v. *Moody;* 422 U.S. 405, 419 [10 FEP Cases 1181, 1188] (1975). Such reliance is particularly appropriate in the context presented here, since the highly unusual feature of requiring an administrative complaint before a civil action can be filed against a private party is common to the two statutes. The NLRA's statute of limitations — which provides that "no complaint shall issue based upon any unfair labor practice occurring more than six months prior to the filing of the charge with the Board," 29 U.S.C. §160(b) — is even substantively similar to §706(e) — which states that "[a] charge ... shall be filed [with the EEOC] within one hundred and eighty days after the alleged unlawful employment practice occurred," 42 U.S.C. §2000e-5(e). In *Zipes* v. *Trans World Airlines, Inc.*, 455 U.S. 385 [28 FEP Cases 1] (1982), we specifically relied on cases construing the NLRA's timely filing requirement in determining whether §706(e) — the very provision we construe here — constituted a waivable statute of limitations or rather a jurisdictional prerequisite to a Title VII action. "Because the time requirement for filing an unfair labor practice charge under the National Labor Relations Act operates as a statute of limitations subject to recognized equitable doctrines and not as a restriction of the jurisdiction of the National Labor Relations Board," we said, "the time limitations under Title VII should be treated likewise." 455 U.S., at 395, n.11 [28 FEP Cases, at 5] (citations omitted).

Machinists considered and rejected an approach to the limitations period identical to that advanced here. The suit involved the timeliness of an unfair labor practice complaint directed at a so-called "union security clause," which required all employees to join the union within 45 days of the contract's execution. Under the NLRB's precedents, agreeing to such a clause when the union lacked majority status constituted an unfair labor practice, as did continued enforcement of the clause. 362 U.S., at 413-414. The agreement at issue in *Machinists* had been *adopted* more than 6 months before the complaint issued (outside the limitations period), but had been *enforced* well within the period of limitations. "Conceding that a complaint predicated on the *execution* of the agreement here challenged was barred by limitations," the NLRB contended that "its complaint was nonetheless timely since it was 'based upon' the parties' continued *enforcement*, within the period of limitations, of the union security clause." 362 U.S., at 415 (emphasis in original). We found, however, that "the entire foundation of the unfair labor practice charged was the Union's time-barred lack of majority status when the original collective-bargaining agreement was signed," and that "[i]n the absence of that fact enforcement of this otherwise valid union security clause was wholly benign." *Id.*, at 417. "[W]here a complaint based upon that earlier event is time-barred," we reasoned, "to permit the event itself" "to cloak with illegality that which was otherwise lawful" "in effect results in reviving a legally defunct unfair labor practice." *Ibid.*[a] This analysis is squarely in point here. Because the claimed invalidity of the facially nondiscriminatory and neutrally applied tester seniority system is wholly dependent on the alleged illegality of signing the underlying agreement, it is the date of that signing which governs the limitations period.

---

[a] Like *Ricks* and *United Air Lines, Inc.* v. *Evans*, 431 U.S. 553 [14 FEP Cases 1510] (1977), our decision in *Machinists* v. *NLRB*, 362 U.S. 411 [45 LRRM 3212] (1960), also rejected an attempt to cure untimeliness by asserting a continuing violation:

"The applicability of these principles cannot be avoided here by invoking the doctrine of continuing violation. It may be conceded that the continued enforcement, as well as the execution, of this collective bargaining agreement constitutes an unfair labor practices, and that these are two logically separate violations, independent in the sense that they can be described in discrete terms. Nevertheless, the vice in the enforcement of this agreement is manifestly not independent of the legality of its execution, as would be the case, for example, with an agreement invalid on its face or with one validly executed, but unlawfully administered." *Id.*, at 422-423.

[4] In holding that, when a seniority system is nondiscriminatory in form and application it is the allegedly discriminatory *adoption* which triggers the limitations period, we respect not only §706(e)'s general " 'value judgment concerning the point at which the interests in favor of protecting valid claims are outweighed by the interests in prohibiting the prosecution of stale [claims],' " 449 U.S., at 260 [24 FEP Cases, at 831] (citation omitted), but also the considerations underlying the "special treatment" accorded to seniority systems under §703(h), see *Hardison*, 432 U.S., at 81 [14 FEP Cases, at 1704]. This "special treatment" strikes a balance between the interests of those protected against discrimination by Title VII and those who work — perhaps for many years — in reliance upon the validity of a facially lawful seniority system. There is no doubt, of course, that a facially discriminatory seniority system (one that treats similarly situated employees differently) can be challenged at any time,' and that even a facially neutral system, if it is adopted with unlawful discriminatory motive, can be challenged within the prescribed period after adoption. But allowing a facially neutral system to be challenged, and entitlements under it to be altered many years after its adoption would disrupt those valid reliance interests that §703(h) was meant to protect. In the context of the present case, a female tester could defeat the settled (and worker-for) expectations of her co-workers whenever she is demoted or not promoted under the new systems, be that in 1983, 1993, 2003, or beyond. Indeed, a given plaintiff could in theory sue successively for not being promoted, for being demoted, for being laid off, and for not being awarded a sufficiently favorable pension, so long as these acts — even if nondiscriminatory in themselves — could be attributed to the 1979 change in seniority.

' The dissent is mistaken to equate the application of facially neutral but discriminatorily adopted system with the application of a system that is facially discriminatory. See *Post*, at 4 [49 FEP Cases, at 1663]. With a facially neutral system the discriminatory act occurs *only* at the time of adoption, for each application is nondiscriminatory (seniority accrues for men and women on an identical basis). But a facially discriminatory system (e.g., one that assigns men twice the seniority that women receive for the same amount of time served) by definition discriminates each time it is applied. This is a material difference for purposes of the analysis we employed in *Evans* and *Ricks* — which focuses on the timing of the *discriminatory* acts for purposes of the statute of limitations. It is also why the dissent's citation, *Post*, at 3 [49 FEP Cases, at 1662], of *Bazemore* v. *Friday*, 478 U.S. 385 [41 FEP Cases 92] (1986) — in which "[e]ach week's paycheck . . . deliver[ed] less to a black than to a similarly situated white," *id.*, at 395 [41 FEP Cases, at 97] — is misplaced.

Our past cases, to which we adhere today, have declined to follow an approach that has such disruptive implications.

* * *

For the foregoing reasons, the judgment of the Court of Appeals is

Affirmed.

JUSTICE O'CONNOR took no part in the consideration or decision of this case.

Concurring Opinion

JUSTICE STEVENS, concurring.

Although I remain convinced that the Court misconstrued Title VII in *American Tobacco Co.* v. *Patterson*, 456 U.S. 63 [28 FEP Cases 713] (1982), *see id.*, at 86–90 [28 FEP Cases, at 724–725] (dissenting opinion) and in *Delaware State College* v. *Ricks*, 449 U.S. 250 [24 FEP Cases 827] (1980), see *id.*, at 265–267 [24 FEP Cases, at 833–834] (dissenting opinion), the Court has correctly applied those decisions to the case at hand. And it is the Court's construction of the statute — rather than the views of an individual Justice — that becomes a part of the law. See *Johnson* v. *Transportation Agency*, 480 U.S. 616, 644 [43 FEP Cases 411, 423–424] (1987) (STEVENS, J., concurring); *Dougherty County Board of Education* v. *White*, 439 U.S. 32, 47 (1978) (STEVENS, J., concurring). Accordingly, I join the Court's opinion.

Dissenting Opinion

JUSTICE MARSHALL, with whom JUSTICE BRENNAN and JUSTICE BLACKMUN join, dissenting.

The majority holds today that, when it is alleged that an employer and a union have negotiated and adopted a new seniority system with the intention of discriminating against women in violation of Title VII, 42 U.S.C. §2000e *et seq.*, the limitations period set forth in §706(e), §2000e-5(e), begins to run immediately upon the adoption of that system. *Ante*, at 9–10 [49 FEP Cases, at 1660]. This is so even if the employee who subsequently challenges that system could not reasonably have expected to be demoted or otherwise concretely harmed by the new system at the time of its adoption, and, indeed, even if the employee was not working in the affected division of the company at the time of the system's adoption.

This severe interpretation of §706(e) will come as a surprise to Congress, whose goals in enacting Title VII surely never included conferring absolute immunity on discriminatorily adopted seniority systems that survive their first 300 days.[1] Because the harsh reality of today's decision, requiring employees to sue anticipatorily or forever hold their peace, is so glaringly at odds with the purposes of Title VII, and because it is compelled neither by the text of the statute nor our precedents interpreting it, I respectfully dissent.

The facts of this case illustrate the austere practical consequences of the majority's holding. On the day AT&T's seniority system was adopted, there was no reason to believe that a woman who exercised her plantwide seniority to become a tester would *ever* be demoted as a result of the new system. Indeed, under the new system, after five years a woman tester would regain her plantwide seniority; only in the intervening five years was she potentially endangered. Patricia Lorance, who was already a tester when the new system was adopted, almost made it; only after four years as a tester was she demoted under the terms of the new system. That the new system would concretely harm petitioners Janice King and Carol Bueschen was even more speculative. They became testers several months *after* the seniority system was modified, and like Lorance, they were not adversely affected by the restructured seniority system until 1982. (Indeed, absent the nationwide recession in the early 1980's, the petitioners might never have been affected.) Today, however, the majority concludes that these women are barred from bringing this suit because they failed to anticipate, within 300 days of the new system's adoption, that these contingencies would one day place them among the new system's casualties.

Nothing in the text of Title VII compels this result. On the contrary, even the majority concedes that a plausible reading of Title VII would regard the employer as having violated §703(a)(1), 42 U.S.C. §2000e-2(a)(1), the disparate treatment wing of the statute, not only at the time of the system's adoption, but also when each concrete effect of that system is felt. *Ante*, at 5-6 [49 FEP Cases, at 1658]; see also 827 F.2d 163, 166 [44 FEP Cases 998, 1000] (CA7 1987)

(describing this interpretation as "logically appealing"). Under this continuing violation theory, each time a discriminatory seniority system is applied, like each time a discriminatory salary structure is applied, an independent "unlawful employment practice" under §703(a)(1) takes place, triggering the limitations period anew. See *Bazemore* v. *Friday*, 478 U.S. 385, 395-396 [41 FEP Cases 92, 97] (1986) ("Each week's paycheck that delivers less to a black than to a similarly situated white is a wrong actionable under Title VII"); cf. *Havens Realty Corp.* v. *Coleman*, 455 U.S. 363, 380 (1982) ("Where the challenged violation is a continuing one, the staleness concern disappears"). Viewing each application of a discriminatory system as a new violation serves the equal opportunity goals of Title VII by ensuring that victims of discrimination are not prevented from having their day in court.

Today's decision is the latest example of how this Court, flouting the intent of Congress, has gradually diminished the application of Title VII to seniority systems. First, the Court held that §703(h), 42 U.S.C. §2000e-2(h), requires special treatment for bona fide seniority systems under Title VII so that "absent a discriminatory purpose, the operation of a seniority system cannot be an unlawful employment practice even if the system has some discriminatory consequences." *Trans World Airlines, Inc.* v. *Hardison*, 432 U.S. 63, 82 [14 FEP Cases 1697, 1705] (1977); see also *Pullman-Standard* v. *Swint*, 456 U.S. 273, 289 [28 FEP Cases 1073, 1080] (1982).[2] Then, the Court held by a narrow margin that §703(h) protects even those seniority systems put into place *after* the passage of Title VII. *American Tobacco Co.* v. *Patterson*, 456 U.S. 63, 71 [28 FEP Cases 713, 716] (1982).

---

[1] Or, in the case of a complaint not previously filed with a state or local agency, their first 180 days. 42 U.S.C. §2000e-(5)(e); *ante*, at 3, n. 2. [49 FEP Cases, at 1657].

[2] It remains astonishing to me that seniority systems are sheltered from disparate-impact claims, see *Teamsters* v. *United States*, 431 U.S. 324, 377-394 [14 FEP Cases 1514, 1536-1543] (1977) (opinion of Marshall, J.). Even the majority concedes that "[a]s an original matter ... a plausible, and perhaps even the most natural, reading of §703(h)" regards that subsection as merely providing an affirmative defense to a disparate impact action brought under §703(a)(2). *Ante*, at 8 [49 FEP Cases, at 1659].

But even accepting our precedents, I do not believe, as the majority does, that they prohibit the Court from finding that petitioners have made a timely and colorable claim of disparate impact under §703(a)(2), 42 U.S.C. §2000e-2(a)(2). In *Trans World Airlines* v. *Hardison*, 432 U.S. 63 [14 FEP Cases 1697] (1977) we held only that bona fide seniority systems were exempted by §703(h) from disparate-impact claims. Accepting as true petitioners' allegation that AT&T and its union restructured the seniority system for discriminatory reasons, this system should not qualify as a bona fide one entitled to immunity from disparate-impact claims.

The majority contends that the result it reaches today is dictated by these and other ill-advised precedents involving seniority systems, but in my view, today's decision compounds the Court's prior decisional errors by giving them unnecessarily broad scope. This extension is particularly inappropriate because it forces the Court to reach such a bizarre and impractical result. Never have we held or even intimated that, in the context of a statute of limitations inquiry, one must evaluate challenges to a seniority system born of discriminatory intent as of the moment of its adoption. Indeed, had we so held, the majority's concession that a worker may *at any time* challenge a facially discriminatory seniority plan under §703(a)(1) would be flatly contradicted by precedent. *Ante*, at 11 [49 FEP Cases, at 1661]. The discriminatory intent that goes into the creation of even a facially flawed seniority plan is, after all, no different than the discriminatory intent that informs the creation of a facially neutral one. To impute ongoing intent in the former situation but not in the latter is untenable. The distinction the majority erects today serves only to reward those employers ingenious enough to cloak their acts of discrimination in a facially neutral guise, identical though the effects of this system may be to those of a facially discriminatory one.

Neither *United Air Lines Inc.* v. *Evans*, 431 U.S. 553 [14 FEP Cases 1510] (1977), nor *Delaware State College* v. *Ricks*, 449 U.S. 250 [24 FEP Cases 827] (1980), on which the majority premises its rejection of the continuing violation theory, compel today's result. In *Evans*, unlike the instant case, the plaintiff never alleges that the seniority system itself was set up in order to discriminate. Indeed, we observed that Evans "does not attack the bona fides of United's seniority system" and "makes no charge that the system is intentionally designed to discriminate." 431 U.S., at 560 [14 FEP Cases, at 1513]; see also *id.*, at 557 [14 FEP Cases, at 1512]. The sole discrimination alleged in *Evans* was in the plaintiff's prior discharge, the impact of which, she alleged, had been enhanced upon her return to work by the failure of the seniority system to accord her credit for time she would have served had she not been discharged. In denying her challenge to that system, we held that "a challenge to a neutral system may not be predicated on the mere fact that a past event [Evan's prior discharge] which has no present legal significance has affected the calculation of seniority credit." *Id.*, at 560

[14 FEP Cases, at 1513]. That holding is plainly inapposite here, where the very essence of petitioners' claim is that AT&T's discriminatorily adopted seniority system is *not* neutral. Thus, the majority's conclusion that the "past event" cited in this case — the discriminatory adoption of the very seniority system under legal challenge — has "'no present legal significance,'" *ibid.*, quoted *ante*, at 7 [49 FEP Cases, at 1659], is *ipse dixit*.

Ricks is likewise inapposite. The allegedly discriminatory denial of tenure in that case served notice to the plaintiff that his termination a year later would come as a "delayed, *but inevitable* consequence," 449 U.S., at 257-258 [24 FEP Cases, at 830] (emphasis added). It was thus appropriate, as in so many areas involving statutes of limitations doctrine, to set the limitations clock running upon the plaintiff's discovery of harm to herself. Petitioners Lorance, King, and Bueschen, however, were given no such advance warning. For them, the majority holds, the limitations clock began running, and ran out, long before it was apparent that they would be demoted by AT&T's discriminatory system. Like *Evans*, *Ricks* stands for the proposition that neutral employment practices that passively perpetuate the consequences of prior time-barred discrimination but are not themselves bred of discriminatory intent do not constitute actionable wrongs under Title VII. Neither case suggests that the operation of a seniority system set up *in order* to discriminate should be treated the same way as a legitimate seniority (or tenure) system, born of nondiscriminatory motives, which in a particular case may have the effect of passively reinforcing prior time-barred acts of discrimination.

Nor, finally, is it correct to say that *Machinists* v. *NLRB*, 362 U.S. 411 [45 LRRM 3212] (1960), "establishes that the limitations period will run from the date the system was adopted," *ante*, at 9 [49 FEP Cases, at 1660], and therefore controls this case. Initially, it bears mention that *Machinists* arose under a different statute, the Labor Management Relations Act (NLRA), 29 U.S.C. §151-169, and that *Machinists* did not involve a seniority system, but instead a union security clause which, it was alleged, had been defectively adopted. Significant though the role of the NLRA was as a model for Title VII's remedial provisions, these are hardly the indicia of a controlling precedent. Moreover, sound reasons support the finding of a time-bar in *Machinists*, but no time-bar here. In *Machinists*, as in *Ricks* the enforcement of the challenged security clause was the inevitable consequence of its execution. The clause affected all non-union employees alike, and from its very inception there was no mystery about which employees would be affected and about the impact it would have on them. By contrast, in this case, the very essence of petitioners' claim is that AT&T's new seniority system was designed to have a long-range discriminatory impact, hurting women employees as a group but, as of the time of its inception, only theoretically hurting particular women employees. Unlike *Machinists* there is no indication that anyone employed at AT&T was, during the limitations period chosen by the majority, so tangibly affected by the new plan as to create any incentive to sue.[5]

---

[5] Tellingly, none of the Courts of Appeals presented with a claim of a continuing violation has reached the result the majority today reaches. Indeed, two of the Courts of Appeals have interpreted our precedents to *permit* claims of continuing violation. *Cook* v. *Pan American World Airways, Inc.*, 771 F.2d 635, 646 [38 FEP Cases 1344, 1353] (CA2 1985); cf. *Johnson* v. *General Electric*, 840 F.2d 132, 135 [46 FEP Cases 81, 83–84] (CA1 1988). Even the Seventh Circuit, finding petitioners' claim time-barred in the judgment under review, adopted a

The majority today continues the process of immunizing seniority systems from the requirement of Title VII. In addition to the other hurdles previously put in place by the Court, employees must now anticipate, and initiate suit to prevent, future adverse applications of a seniority system, no matter how speculative or unlikely these applications may be. This Court's observation that "limitations periods should not commence to run so soon that it becomes difficult for a layman to involve the protection of the civil rights statutes," *Ricks*, 449 U.S., at 262, n.16 [24 FEP Cases, at 832], has an increasingly hollow ring. Because I do not believe that Congress, in framing Title VII, even remotely contemplated putting employees into the predicament which the majority today makes inevitable, I dissent.

---

far narrower interpretation than the majority, under which the limitations period begins to run on the date when the employee first becomes subject to the seniority system. 827 F.2d 163, 167 [44 FEP Cases 998, 1001] (1987).

WARDS COVE PACKING CO. v. ATONIO

Supreme Court of the United States

WARDS COVE PACKING COMPANY, INC., et al. v. ATONIO, et al., No. 87-1387, June 5, 1989

CIVIL RIGHTS ACT OF 1964

1. Disparate impact ►108.0407 ►108.8128

Comparison between pool of mostly unskilled, mostly non-white cannery workers and pool of mostly skilled, mostly white non-cannery workers working for same employer does not establish prima facie case of disparate impact without reference to pools of qualified job applicants or qualified population in labor force available to fill skilled and non-skilled jobs at issue.

2. Disparate impact ►108.0407 ►108.8128

Racial imbalance in one segment of work force does not, without more, establish prima facie case of disparate impact with respect to selection of workers elsewhere, even where workers for the different positions may have somewhat fungible skills; employer's selection mechanism probably does not operate with disparate impact on minority-group persons if percentage of selected applicants who are non-white is not significantly less than percentage of qualified applicants who are non-white, as long as there are no barriers or practices deterring qualified non-whites from applying.

3. Disparate impact ►108.0407

Disparate impact is not made out simply by showing racial imbalance in work force; it must be shown that it is application of specific or particular employment practice that created impact in question, and such showing is integral part of prima facie case.

4. Disparate impact ►108.0407 ►108.736

Challenged practice need not be "essential" or "indispensable' to employer's business for it to pass muster; this degree of scrutiny would be almost impossible for most employers to meet.

5. Disparate impact ►108.0407 ►108.736 ►108.7331

Once prima facie case of disparate impact is made out, burden of producing evidence of business justification shifts to employer, but burden of persuasion remains with litigant, since this rule conforms with usual method for allocating persuasion and production burdens in federal courts and with rule in disparate-treatment cases.

6. Disparate impact ►108.0407 ►108.7331

Burden of persuasion in disparate-impact case remains with individual who brought it, since he is required by Title VII to prove that he was denied desired employment opportunity "because of" his race or color.

7. Disparate impact ►108.0407

Individuals who cannot persuade trier of fact in Title VII disparate-impact action not to accept employer's business-necessity defense may still be able to prevail by coming forward with alternatives to employer's hiring practices that reduce racially disparate impact of practices currently being used, but such alternatives must be equally effective as employer's chosen hiring procedures in achieving employer's legitimate hiring goals, and costs or other burdens of proposed alternative selection devices are relevant in determining whether they would be equally effective.

8. Disparate impact ►108.0407

Fact that courts are generally less competent than employers to restructure business practices requires that they should proceed with care, in evaluating proposed alternative selection or hiring devices, before requiring employer to adopt alternative practice in response to showing of disparate impact.

———

On writ of certiorari to the U.S. Court of Appeals for the Ninth Circuit (47 FEP Cases 163, 827 F.2d 439). Reversed and remanded.

See also 31 FEP Cases 728, 703 F.2d 329; 38 FEP Cases 1170, 768 F.2d 1120; and 43 FEP Cases 130, 810 F.2d 1477.

Douglas M. Fryer (Douglas M. Duncan, Richard L. Phillips, and Mikkelborg, Broz, Wells & Fryer, with him on briefs), Seattle, Wash., for petitioners.

Abraham A. Arditi, Seattle, Wash. (Bobbe J. Bridge and Garvey, Schubert & Barer, Seattle, Wash., with him on brief), for respondents.

Charles Fried, Solicitor General, W. Bradford Reynolds, Assistant Attorney General, Roger Clegg, Deputy Assistant Attorney General, Richard G. Taranto, Assistant to the Solicitor

General, and David K. Flynn and Lisa J. Stark, U.S. Department of Justice, filed brief for United States, as amicus curiae, urging that the judgment of the court of appeals be vacated.

Robert E. Williams, Douglas S. McDowell, and Edward E. Potter (McGuiness & Williams), Washington, D.C., filed brief for Equal Employment Advisory Council, as amicus curiae, urging reversal.

Lawrence Z. Lorber and J. Robert Kirk (Breed, Abbott & Morgan, of counsel), Washington, D.C., filed brief for American Society for Personnel Administration, as amicus curiae, urging reversal.

Glen D. Nager, Andrew M. Kramer, David A. Copus, and Patricia A. Dunn (Jones, Day, Reavis & Pogue), Washington, D.C. (Stephen A. Bokat and Mona C. Zeiberg, Washington, D.C., of counsel), filed brief for Chamber of Commerce of the United States, as amicus curiae, urging reversal.

Clint Bolick, Jerald L. Hill, and Mark J. Bredemeier, Washington, D.C., and Arthur H. Abel (Faegre & Benson), Minneapolis, Minn., filed brief for Center for Civil Rights, as amicus curiae, urging the vacation of the judgment below.

Joan E. Bertin, Kary L. Moss, Isabelle K. Pinzler, and John A. Powell, New York, N.Y., filed brief for American Civil Liberties Union, National Women's Law Center, NOW Legal Defense and Education Fund, and Women's Legal Defense Fund, as amici curiae, urging affirmance.

Grover G. Hankins and Samuel M. Walters, Baltimore, Md., and Alfred W. Blumrosen, Newark, N.J., filed brief for National Assn. for the Advancement of Colored People, as amicus curiae, urging affirmance of the court of appeals' holding and remanding with instructions.

Julius L. Chambers, Charles S. Ralston, and Ronald L. Ellis, New York, N.Y., Bill L. Lee, Patrick O. Patterson, Jr., and Theodore M. Shaw, Los Angeles, Calif., Antonio Hernandez, E. Richard Larson, and Jose R. Juarez, Jr., Los Angeles, Calif., and Ruben Franco and Kenneth Kimmerling, New York, N.Y., filed brief for NAACP Legal Defense and Educational Fund, Inc., The Mexican American Legal Defense and Educational Fund, and The Puerto Rican Legal Defense and Educational Fund, as amici curiae, urging affirmance.

Conrad Harper, Stuart J. Land, Norman Redlich, Richard T. Seymour, and James C. Gray, Jr., Washington, D.C., and Nicholas deB. Katzenbach, Alan E. Kraus, and David Arciszewski (Riker, Danzig, Scherer, Hyland & Perretti), Morristown, N.J., filed brief for Lawyers' Committee for Civil Rights Under Law, as amicus curiae, urging affirmance.

Before REHNQUIST, Chief Justice, and BRENNAN, WHITE, MARSHALL, BLACKMUN, STEVENS, O'CONNOR, SCALIA, and KENNEDY, Justices.

Full Text of Opinion

JUSTICE WHITE delivered the opinion of the Court.

Title VII of the Civil Rights Act of 1964, 42 U.S.C. §2000e-2(a) makes it an unfair employment practice for an employer to discriminate against any individual with respect to hiring or the terms and condition of employment because of such individual's race, color, religion, sex, or national origin; or to limit, segregate or classify his employees in ways that would adversely affect any employee because of the employee's race, color, religion, sex, or national origin.[1] Griggs v. Duke Power Co., 401 U.S. 424, 431 [3 FEP Cases 175, 178] (1971), construed Title VII to proscribe "not only overt discrimination but also practices that are fair in form but discriminatory in practice." Under this basis for liability, which is known as the "disparate impact" theory and which is involved in this case, a facially neutral employment practice may be deemed violative of Title VII without evidence of the employer's subjective intent to discriminate that is required in a "disparate treatment" case.

I

The claims before us are disparate-impact claims, involving the employ-

---

[1] Title VII of the Civil Rights Act of 1964, 42 U.S.C. §2000e-2(a), provides:

"(a) It shall be an unlawful employment practice for an employer —

"(1) to fail or refuse to hire or to discharge any individual, or otherwise to discriminate against any individual with respect to his compensation, terms, conditions, or privileges of employment, because of such individual's race, color, religion, sex, or national origin; or

"(2) to limit, segregate, or classify his employees or applicants for employment in any way which would deprive or tend to deprive any individual of employment opportunities or otherwise adversely affect his status as an employee, because of such individual's race, color, religion, sex, or national origin."

ment practices of petitioners, two companies that operate salmon canneries in remote and widely separated areas of Alaska. The canneries operate only during the salmon runs in the summer months. They are inoperative and vacant for the rest of the year. In May or June of each year, a few weeks before the salmon runs begin, workers arrive and prepare the equipment and facilities for the canning operation. Most of these workers posses a variety of skills. When salmon runs are about to begin, the workers who will operate the cannery lines arrive, remain as long as there are fish to can, and then depart. The canneries are then closed down, winterized, and left vacant until the next spring. During the off season, the companies employ only a small number of individuals at their headquarters in Seattle and Astoria, Oregon, plus some employees at the winter shipyard in Seattle.

The length size of salmon runs vary from year to year and hence the number of employees needed at each cannery also varies. Estimates are made as early in the winter as possible; the necessary employees are hired, and when the time comes, they are transported to the canneries. Salmon must be processed soon after they are caught, and the work during the canning season is therefore intense.[2] For this reason, and because the canneries are located in remote regions, all workers are housed at the canneries and take their meals in company-owned mess halls.

Jobs at the canneries are of two general types: "cannery jobs" on the cannery line, which are unskilled positions; and "noncannery jobs," which fall into a variety of classifications. Most noncannery jobs are classified as skilled positions.[3] Cannery jobs are

---

[2] "Independent fishermen catch the salmon and turn them over to company-owned boats called 'tenders,' which transport the fish from the fishing grounds to the canneries. Once at the cannery, the fish are eviscerated, the eggs pulled, and they are cleaned. Then, operating at a rate of approximately four cans per second, the salmon are filled into cans. Next, the canned salmon are cooked under precise time-temperature requirement established by the FDA, and the cans are inspected to ensure that proper seals are maintained on the top, bottom and sides." 768 F.2d 1120, 1123 [38 FEP Cases 1170, 1172-1173], vacated, 787 F.2d 462 (CA9 1985).

[3] The noncannery jobs were described as follows by the Court of Appeals: "Machinists and engineers are hired to maintain the smooth and continuous operation of the canning equipment. Quality control personnel conduct the FDA-required inspections and recordkeeping. Tenders are staffed with a crew necessary to operate the vessel. A variety of support personnel are employed to operate the entire cannery community, including, for example, cooks, carpenters, store-keepers, bookkeepers, beach gangs for dock yard labor and construction, etc." 768 F.2d, at 1123 [38 FEP Cases, at 1173].

filled predominantly by nonwhites, Filipinos and Alaska Natives. The Filipinos are hired through and dispatched by Local 37 of the International Longshoremen Workers Union pursuant to a hiring hall agreement with the Local. The Alaska natives primarily reside in villages near the remote cannery locations. Noncannery jobs are filled with predominantly white workers, who are hired during the winter months from the companies' offices in Washington and Oregon. Virtually all of the noncannery jobs pay more than cannery positions. The predominantly white noncannery workers and the predominantly nonwhite cannery employees live in separate dormitories and eat in separate mess halls.

In 1974, respondents, a class of nonwhite cannery workers who were (or had been) employed at the canneries, brought this Title VII action against petitioners. Respondents alleged that a variety of petitioners' hiring/promotion practices — e.g., nepotism, a rehire preference, a lack of objective hiring criteria, separate hiring channels, a practice of not promoting from within — were responsible for the racial stratification of the work force, and had denied them and other nonwhites employment as noncannery workers on the basis of race. Respondents also complained of petitioners' racially segregated housing and dining facilities. All of respondents' claims were advanced under both the disparate-treatment and disparate-impact theories of Title VII liability.

The District Court held a bench trial, after which it entered 172 findings of fact. App. to Pet. for Cert. I-1-I-94. It then rejected all of respondents' disparate-treatment claims. It also rejected the disparate-impact challenges involving the subjective employment criteria used by petitioners to fill these noncannery positions, on the ground that those criteria were not subject to attack under a disparate-impact theory. Id., at I-102. Petitioner's "objective" employment practices (e.g., an English language requirement, alleged nepotism in hiring, failure to post noncannery openings, the rehire preference, etc.) were found to be subject to challenge under the disparate-impact theory, but these claims were rejected for failure of proof. Judgment was entered for petitioners.

On appeal, a panel of the Ninth Circuit affirmed, 768 F.2d 1120 [38 FEP Cases 1170] (1985), but that decision was vacated when the Court of Appeals agreed to hear the case en banc.

787 F.2d 462 (1985). The en banc hearing was ordered to settle an intra-circuit conflict over the question whether subjective hiring practices could be analyzed under a disparate-impact model; the Court of Appeals held — as this Court subsequently ruled in *Watson* v. *Fort Worth Bank & Trust*, 487 U.S. —— [47 FEP Cases 102] (1988) — that disparate-impact analysis could be applied to subjective hiring practices. 810 F.2d 1477, 1482 [43 FEP Cases 130, 134] (1987). The Ninth Circuit also concluded that in such a case, "[o]nce the plaintiff class has shown disparate-impact caused by specific, identifiable employment practices or criteria, the burden shifts to the employer," *id.*, at 1485 [43 FEP Cases, at 137], to "prov[e the] business necessity" of the challenged practice. *Id.*, at 1486 [43 FEP Cases, at 137]. Because the en banc holding on subjective employment practices reversed the District Court's contrary ruling, the en banc Court of Appeals remanded the case to a panel for further proceedings.

On remand, the panel applied the en banc ruling to the facts of this case. 827 F.2d 439 [47 FEP Cases 163] (1987). It held that respondents had made out a prima facie case of disparate-impact in hiring for both skilled and unskilled noncannery positions. The panel remanded the case for further proceedings, instructing the District Court that it was the employer's burden to prove that any disparate impact caused by its hiring and employment practices was justified by business necessity. Neither the en banc court nor the panel disturbed the District Court's rejection of the disparate-treatment claims.[4]

---

[4] The fact that neither the District Court, nor the Ninth Circuit *en banc*, nor the subsequent Court of Appeals, panel ruled for respondents on their disparate treatment claims — *i.e.*, their allegations of intentional racial discrimination — warrants particular attention in light of the dissents' comment that the canneries "bear an unsettling resemblance to aspects of a plantation economy." *Post*, at 2 n.4 [49 FEP Cases, at 1528] (Stevens, J., dissenting); *post*, at 1 [49 FEP Cases, at 1528] (Blackmun, J., dissenting).

Whatever the "resemblance," the unanimous view of the lower courts in this litigation has been that respondents did not prove that the canneries practice intentional racial discrimination. Consequently, Justice Blackmun's hyperbolic allegation that our decision in this case indicates that this Court no longer "believes that race discrimination ... against nonwhites ... is a problem in our society," *post*, at 2, [49 FEP Cases, at 1529], is inapt. Of course, it is unfortunately true that race discrimination exists in our country. That does not mean, however, that it exists at the canneries — or more precisely, that it has been proven to exist at the canneries.

Indeed, Justice Stevens concedes that respondents did not press before us the legal theories under which the aspects of cannery life that he finds to most resemble a "plantation economy"

Petitioners sought review of the Court of Appeals' decision in this court, challenging it on several grounds. Because some of the issues raised by the decision below were matters on which this Court was evenly divided in *Watson* v. *Fort Worth Bank & Trust Co.*, *supra*, we granted certiorari, 487 U.S. —— (1988), for the purpose of addressing these disputed questions of the proper application of Title VII's disparate-impact theory of liability.

II

In holding that respondents had made out a prima facie case of disparate impact, the court of appeals relied solely on respondents' statistics showing a high percentage of nonwhite workers in the cannery jobs and a low percentage of such workers in the noncannery positions.[5] Although statistical proof can alone make out a prima facie case, see *Teamsters* v. *United States*, 431 U.S. 324, 339 [14 FEP Cases 1514, 1520] (1977); *Hazelwood School Dist.* v. *United States*, 433 U.S. 299, 307–308 [15 FEP Cases 1, 4–5] (1977), the Court of Appeals' ruling here misapprehends our precedents and the purposes of Title VII, and we therefore reverse.

"There can be no doubt," as there was when a similar mistaken analysis had been undertaken by the courts below in *Hazelwood, supra*, at 308 [15 FEP Cases, at 4–5] "that the ... comparison ... fundamentally misconceived the role of statistics in employment discrimination cases." The "proper comparison [is] between the racial composition of [the at-issue jobs] and the racial composition of the qualified ... population in the relevant labor market." *Ibid.* It is such a comparison — between the racial composition of the qualified persons in the

---

might be unlawful. *Post*, at 3 n.4 [49 FEP Cases, at 1528]. Thus, the question here is not whether we "approve" of petitioner's employment practices or the society that exists at the canneries, but rather, whether respondents have properly established that these practices violate Title VII.

[5] The parties dispute the extent to which there is a discrepancy between the percentage of nonwhite employed as cannery workers, and those employed in noncannery positions. Compare, *e.g.*, Brief for Petitioners 4–9 with Brief for Respondents 4–6. The District Court made no precise numerical findings in this regard, but simply noted that there were "significant disparities between the at-issue jobs [i.e., noncannery jobs] and the total workforce at the canneries" which were explained by the fact that "nearly all employed in the 'cannery worker' department are non-white." See App. to Pet. for Cert. I-111, I-42.

For reasons explained below, the degree of disparity between these groups is not relevant to our decision here.

labor market and the persons holding at-issue jobs — that generally forms the proper basis for the initial inquiry in a disparate impact case. Alternatively, in cases where such labor market statistics will be difficult if not impossible to ascertain, we have recognized that certain other statistics — such as measures indicating the racial composition of "otherwise-qualified applicants" for at-issue jobs — are equally probative for this purpose. See, e.g., New York City Transit Authority v. Beazer, 440 U.S. 568, 585 [19 FEP Cases 149, 155-156] (1979).⁶

[1] It is clear to us that the Court of Appeals' acceptance of the comparison between the racial composition of the cannery work force and that of the noncannery work force, as probative of a prima facie case of disparate impact in the selection of the latter group of workers, was flawed for several reasons. Most obviously, with respect to the skilled noncannery jobs at issue here, the cannery work force in no way reflected "the pool of qualified job applicants" or the "qualified population in the labor force." Measuring alleged discrimination in the selection of accountants, managers, boat captains, electricians, doctors, and engineers — and the long list of other "skilled" noncannery positions found to exist by the District Court, see App. to Pet. for Cert. I-56-I-58 — by comparing the number of nonwhites occupying these jobs to the number of nonwhites filling cannery worker positions is nonsensical. If the absence of minorities holding such skilled positions is due to a dearth of qualified nonwhite applicants (for reasons that are not petitioners' fault),⁷ petitioners' selection methods or employment practices cannot be said to have had a "disparate impact" on nonwhites.

One example illustrates why this must be so. Respondents' own statistics concerning the noncannery work force at one of the canneries at issue here indicate that approximately 17% of the new hires for medical jobs, and 15% of the new hires for officer worker

---

⁶ In fact, where "figures for the general population might . . . accurately reflect the pool of qualified job applicants," cf. Teamsters v. United States, 431 U.S. 324, 340, n. 20 [14 FEP Cases 1514, 1521] (1977), we have even permitted plaintiffs to rest their prima facie cases on such statistics as well. See, e.g., Dothard v. Rawlinson, 433 U.S. 321, 329-330 [15 FEP Cases 10, 14] (1977).

⁷ Obviously, the analysis would be different if it were found that the dearth of qualified nonwhite applicants was due to practices on petitioner's part which — expressly or implicitly — deterred minority group members from applying for noncannery positions. See, e.g., Teamsters v. United States, supra, at 365 [14 FEP Cases, at 1531].

positions, were nonwhite. See App. to Brief for Respondents B-1. If it were the case that less than 15-17% of the applicants for these jobs were nonwhite and that nonwhites made up a lower percentage of the relevant qualified labor market, it is hard to see how respondents without more, cf. Connecticut v. Teal, 457 U.S. 440 [29 FEP Cases 1] (1982), would have made out a prima facie case of disparate impact. Yet, under the Court of Appeals' theory, simply because nonwhites comprise 52% of the cannery workers at the cannery in question, see App. to Brief for Respondents B-1, respondents would be successful in establishing a prima facie case of racial discrimination under Title VII.

Such a result cannot be squared with our cases or with the goals behind the statute. The Court of Appeals' theory, at the very least, would mean that any employer who had a segment of his work force that was — for some reason — racially imbalanced, could be haled into court and forced to engage in the expensive and time-consuming task of defending the "business necessity" of the methods used to select the other members of his work force. The only practicable option for many employers will be to adopt racial quotas, insuring that no portion of his work force deviates in racial composition from the other portions thereof; this is a result that Congress expressly rejected in drafting Title VII. See 42 U.S.C. §2000e-2(j); see also Watson v. Fort Worth Bank & Trust Co., 487 U.S. at — - - —, and n. 2 [47 FEP Cases, at 108-109] (opinion of O'CONNOR, J.). The Court of Appeals' theory would "leave the employer little choice . . . but to engage in a subjective quota system of employment selection. This, of course, is far from the intent of Title VII." Albemarle Paper Co. v. Moody, 422 U.S. 405, 449 [10 FEP Cases 1181, 1197] (1975) (BLACKMUN, J., concurring in judgment).

[2] The Court of Appeals also erred with respect to the unskilled noncannery positions. Racial imbalance in one segment of an employer's work force does not, without more, establish a prima facie case of disparate impact with respect to the selection of workers for the employer's other positions, even where workers for the different positions may have somewhat fungible skills (as is arguably the case for cannery and unskilled noncannery workers). As long as there are no barriers or practices deterring qualified nonwhites from applying for noncannery positions, see supra n. 6, if the percentage of selected applicants who are non-

white is not significantly less than the percentage of qualified applicants who are nonwhite, the employer's selection mechanism probably does not operate with a disparate impact on minorities.[8] Where this is the case, the percentage of nonwhite workers found in other positions in the employer's labor force is irrelevant to the question of a prima facie statistical case of disparate impact. As noted above, a contrary ruling on this point would almost inexorably lead to the use of numerical quotas in the workplace, a result that Congress and this Court have rejected repeatedly in the past.

Moreover, isolating the cannery workers as the potential "labor force" for unskilled noncannery positions is at once both too broad and too narrow in its focus. Too broad because the vast majority of these cannery workers did not seek jobs in unskilled noncannery positions; there is no showing that many of them would have done so even if none of the arguably "deterring" practices existed. Thus, the pool of cannery workers cannot be used as a surrogate for the class of qualified job applicants because it contains many persons who have not (and would not) be noncannery job applicants. Conversely, if respondents propose to use the cannery workers for comparison purposes because they represent the "qualified labor population" generally, the group is too narrow because there are obviously many qualified persons in the labor market for noncannery jobs who are not cannery workers.

The peculiar facts of this case further illustrate why a comparison between the percentage of nonwhite cannery workers and nonwhite noncannery workers is an improper basis for making out a claim of disparate impact. Here, the District Court found that nonwhites were "overrepresent-[ed]" among cannery workers because petitioners had contracted with a predominantly nonwhite union (Local 37) to fill these positions. See App. to Pet. for Cert. I-42. As a result, if petitioners

(for some permissible reason) ceased using Local 37 as its hiring channel for cannery positions, it appears (according to the District Court's findings) that the racial stratification between the cannery and noncannery workers might diminish to statistical insignificance. Under the Court of Appeals' approach, therefore, it is possible that *with no change whatsoever* in their hiring practices for noncannery workers — the jobs at-issue in this lawsuit — petitioners could make respondents' prima facie case of disparate impact "disappear." But *if* there would be no prima facie case of disparate impact in the selection of noncannery workers absent petitioners' use of Local 37 to hire cannery workers, surely the petitioners' reliance on the union to fill the cannery jobs not at-issue here (and its resulting "overrepresentation" of nonwhite in those positions) does not — standing alone — make out a prima facie case of disparate impact. Yet it is precisely such an ironic result that the Court of Appeals reached below.

Consequently, we reverse the Court of Appeals' ruling that a comparison between the percentage of cannery workers who are nonwhite and the percentage of noncannery workers who are nonwhite makes out a prima facie case of disparate impact. Of course, this leaves unresolved whether the record made in the District Court will support a conclusion that a prima facie case of disparate impact has been established on some basis other than the racial disparity between cannery and noncannery workers. This is an issue that the Court of Appeals or the District Court should address in the first instance.

III

Since the statistical disparity relied on by the Court of Appeals did not suffice to make out a prima facie case, any inquiry by us into whether the specific challenged employment practices of petitioners caused that disparity is pretermitted, as is any inquiry into whether the disparate impact that any employment practice may have had was justified by business considerations.[9] Because we remand

---

[8] We qualify this conclusion — observing that it is only "probable" that there has been no disparate impact on minorities in such circumstances — because bottom-line racial balance is not a defense under Title VII. See *Connecticut* v. *Teal*, 457 U.S. 440 [29 FEP Cases 1] (1982). Thus, even if petitioners could show that the percentage of selected applicants who are nonwhite is not significantly less than the percentage of qualified applicants who are nonwhite, respondents would still have a case under Title VII, if they could prove that some particular hiring practice has a disparate impact on minorities, notwithstanding the bottom-line racial balance in petitioners' workforce. See *Teal, supra,* at 450 [29 FEP Cases, at 6] see also n.8, *infra.*

[9] As we understand the opinions below, the specific employment practices were challenged only insofar as they were claimed to have been responsible for the overall disparity between the number of minority cannery and noncannery workers. The Court of Appeals did not purport to hold that any specified employment practice produced its own disparate impact that was action-

for further proceedings, however, on whether a prima facie case of disparate impact has been made in defensible fashion in this case, we address two other challenges petitioners have made to the decision of the Court of Appeals.

A

First is the question of causation in a disparate-impact case. The law in this respect was correctly stated by JUSTICE O'CONNOR'S opinion last Term in *Watson* v. *Fort Worth Bank & Trust*, 487 U.S. at, —— [47 FEP Cases, at 109]:

"[W]e note that the plaintiff's burden in establishing a prima facie case goes beyond the need to show that there are statistical disparities in the employer's work force. The plaintiff must begin by identifying the specific employment practice that is challenged. . . . Especially in cases where an employer combines subjective criteria with the use of more rigid standardized rules or tests, the plaintiff is in our view responsible for isolating and identifying the specific employment practices that are allegedly responsible for any observed statistical disparities."

Cf. also *Id.*, at —— [47 FEP Cases, at 111] (BLACKMUN, J., concurring in part and concurring in judgment).

Indeed, even the Court of Appeals — whose decision petitioners assault on this score — noted that "it is . . . essential that the practices identified by the cannery workers be linked causally with the demonstrated adverse impact." 827 F.2d, at 445 [47 FEP Cases, at 167]. Notwithstanding the Court of Appeals' apparent adherence to the proper inquiry, petitioners contend that the court erred by permitting respondents to make out their case by offering "only [one] set of cumulative comparative statistics as evidence of the disparate impact of each and all of [petitioners' hiring] practices." Brief for Petitioners 31.

[3] Our disparate-impact cases have always focused on the impact of *particular* hiring practices on employment opportunities for minorities. Just as an employer cannot escape liability under Title VII by demonstrat-

able under Title VII. This is not to say that a specific practice, such as nepotism, if it were proved to exist, could not itself be subject to challenge if it had a disparate impact on minorities. Nor is it to say that segregated dormitories and eating facilities in the workplace may not be challenged under 42 U.S.C. §2000e-2(a)(2) without showing a disparate impact on hiring or promotion.

ing that, "at the bottom line," his work force is racially balanced (where particular hiring practices may operate to deprive minorities of employment opportunities), see *Connecticut* v. *Teal*, 457 U.S., at 450 [29 FEP Cases, at 6], a Title VII plaintiff does not make out a case of disparate impact simply by showing that, "at the bottom line," there is racial *imbalance* in the work force. As a general matter, a plaintiff must demonstrate that it is the application of a specific or particular employment practice that has created the disparate impact under attack. Such a showing is an integral part of the plaintiff's prima facie case in a disparate-impact suit under Title VII.

Here, respondents have alleged that several "objective" employment practices (*e. g.*, nepotism, separate hiring channels, rehire preferences), as well as the use of "subjective decision making" to select noncannery workers, have had a disparate impact on nonwhites. Respondents base this claim on statistics that allegedly show a disproportionately low percentage of nonwhites in the at-issue positions. However, even if on remand respondents can show that nonwhites are underrepresented in the at-issue jobs in a manner that is acceptable under the standards set forth in Part II, *supra*, this alone will *not* suffice to make out a prima facie case of disparate impact. Respondents will also have to demonstrate that the disparity they complain of is the result of one or more of the employment practices that they are attacking here, specifically showing that each challenged practice has a significantly disparate impact on employment opportunities for whites and nonwhites. To hold otherwise would result in employers being potentially liable for "the myriad of innocent causes that may lead to statistical imbalances in the composition of their work forces." *Watson* v. *Fort Worth Bank & Trust*, *supra*, at —— [47 FEP Cases, at 108].

Some will complain that this specific causation requirement is unduly burdensome on Title VII plaintiffs. But liberal civil discovery rules give plaintiffs broad access to employers' records in an effort to document their claims. Also, employers falling within the scope of the Uniform Guidelines on Employee Selection Procedures, 29 CFR §1607.1 *et seq.* (1988), are required to "maintain . . . records or other information which will disclose the impact which its tests and other selection procedures have upon employment opportunities of persons by identifiable race, sex, or ethnic group[s.]" See §1607.4(A). This includes records concerning "the individual components of the selection process" where there is a significant disparity in the selection rates of whites and non-whites. See §1607.4(C). Plaintiffs as a general matter will have the benefit of these tools to meet their burden of showing a causal link between challenged employment practices and racial imbalances in the work force; respondents presumably took full advantage of these opportunities to build their case before the trial in the District Court was held.[10]

Consequently, on remand, the courts below are instructed to require, as part of respondents' prima facie case, a demonstration that specific elements of the petitioners' hiring process have a significantly disparate impact on nonwhites.

B

If, on remand, respondents meet the proof burdens outlined above, and establish a prima facie case of disparate impact with respect to any of petitioners' employment practices, the case will shift to any business justification petitioners offer for their use of these practices. This phase of the disparate-impact case contains two components: first, a consideration of the justifications an employer offers for his use of these practices; and second, the availability of alternate practices to achieve the same business ends, with less racial impact. See, e. g., Albemarle Paper Co. v. Moody, 422 U.S., at 425 [10 FEP Cases, at 1190]. We consider these two components in turn.

(1)

[4] Though we have phrased the query differently in different cases, it is generally well-established that at the justification stage of such a disparate impact case, the dispositive issue is whether a challenged practice serves, in a significant way, the legitimate employment goals of the employer. See, e. g., Watson v. Fort Worth Bank & Trust Co., 487 U.S., at —— [47 FEP Cases, at 110]; New York Transit Authority v. Beazer, 440 U.S., at 587, n.31 [19 FEP Cases, at 156]; Griggs v. Duke Power Co., 401 U.S., at 432 [3 FEP Cases, at 178]. The touchstone of this

---

[10] Of course, petitioners' obligation to collect or retain any of these data may be limited by the Guidelines themselves. See 29 CFR §1602.14(b) (1988) (exempting "seasonal" jobs from certain record-keeping requirements).

inquiry is a reasoned review of the employer's justification for his use of the challenged practice. A mere insubstantial justification in this regard will not suffice, because such a low standard of review would permit discrimination to be practiced through the use of spurious, seemingly neutral employment practices. At the same time, though, there is no requirement that the challenged practice be "essential" or "indispensable" to the employer's business for it to pass muster: this degree of scrutiny would be almost impossible for most employers to meet, and would result in a host of evils we have identified above. See supra, at 8 [49 FEP Cases, at 1524].

[5, 6] In this phase, the employer carries the burden of producing evidence of a business justification for his employment practice. The burden of persuasion, however, remains with the disparate-impact plaintiff. To the extent that the Ninth Circuit held otherwise in its en banc decision in this case, see 810 F.2d, at 1485–1486 [43 FEP Cases, at 137], or in the panel's decision on remand, see 827 F.2d, at 445, 447 [47 FEP Cases, at 168, 169] — suggesting that the persuasion burden should shift to the petitioners once the respondents established a prima facie case of disparate impact — its decisions were erroneous. "[T]he ultimate burden of proving that discrimination against a protected group has been caused by a specific employment practice remains with the plaintiff at all times." Watson, supra, at —— [47 FEP Cases, at 110] (O'CONNOR, J.) (emphasis added). This rule conforms with the usual method for allocating persuasion and production burdens in the federal courts, see Fed. Rule Evid. 301, and more specifically, it conforms to the rule in disparate-treatment cases that the plaintiff bears the burden of disproving an employer's assertion that the adverse employment action or practice was based solely on a legitimate neutral consideration. See Texas Dept. of Community Affairs v. Burdine, 450 U.S. 248, 256–258 [25 FEP Cases 113, 115–116] (1981). We acknowledge that some of our earlier decisions can be read as suggesting otherwise. See Watson, supra, at —— [47 FEP Cases, at 111–113] (BLACKMUN, J., concurring). But to the extent that those cases speak of an employer's "burden of proof" with respect to a legitimate business justification defense, see e. g., Dothard v. Rawlinson, 433 U.S. 321, 329 [15 FEP Cases 10, 14] (1977), they should have been understood to mean an employer's production — but not persuasion — burden. Cf., e. g., NLRB

v. *Transportation Management Corp.,*
462 U.S. 393, 404, n.7 [113 LRRM 2857]
(1983). The persuasion burden here
must remain with the plaintiff, for it
is he who must prove that it was "because of such individual's race, color,"
etc., that he was denied a desired employment opportunity. See 42 U.S.C.
§2000e-2(a).

(2)

[7] Finally, if on remand the case
reaches this point, and respondents
cannot persuade the trier of fact on
the question of petitioner's business
necessity defense, respondent may still
be able to prevail. To do so, respondents will have to have to persuade the
factfinder that "other tests or selection devices, without a similarly unde-
sirable racial effect, would also serve
the employer's legitimate [hiring] interest[s];" by so demonstrating, respondents would prove that "[petitioners
were] using [their] tests merely as a
'pretext' for discrimination." *Albemarle Paper Co., supra,* at 425 [10 FEP
Cases, at 1190]; see also *Watson,* 487
U.S., at —— [47 FEP Cases, at 110]
(O'CONNOR, J.); *Id.,* at —— [47 FEP
Cases, at 113-114] (BLACKMUN, J.). If
respondents, have established a prima
facie case, come forward with alternatives to petitioners' hiring practices
that reduce the racially-disparate impact of practices currently being used,
and petitioners refuse to adopt these
alternatives, such a refusal would belie
a claim by petitioners that their incumbent practices are being employed
for nondiscriminatory reasons.

[8] Of course, any alternative practices which respondents offer up in
this respect must be equally effective
as petitioners' chosen hiring procedures in achieving petitioners' legitimate employment goals. Moreover,
"[f]actors such as the cost or other
burdens of proposed alternative selection devices are relevant in determining whether they would be equally as
effective as the challenged practice in
serving the employer's legitimate business goals." *Watson, supra,* at —— [47
FEP Cases, at 110] (O'CONNOR, J.).
"Courts are generally less competent
than employers to restructure business practices," *Furnco Construction
Corp.* v. *Waters,* 438 U.S. 567, 578 [17
FEP Cases 1062, 1066] (1978); consequently, the judiciary should proceed
with care before mandating that an
employer must adopt a plaintiff's alternate selection or hiring practice in
response to a Title VII suit.

IV

For the reasons given above, the
judgment of the Court of Appeals is

reversed, and the case is remanded for
further proceedings consistent with
this opinion.

It is so ordered.

————

Dissenting Opinions

JUSTICE STEVENS, with whom
JUSTICE BRENNAN, JUSTICE MAR-
SHALL, and Justice BLACKMUN
join, dissenting.

Fully 18 years ago, this Court unani-
mously held that Title VII of the Civil
Rights Act of 1964 [1] prohibits employment practices that have discriminatory effects as well as those that are
intended to discriminate. *Griggs* v.
Duke Power Co., 401 U.S. 424 [3 FEP
Cases 175] (1971). Federal courts and
agencies consistently have enforced
that interpretation, thus promoting
our national goal of eliminating barriers that define economic opportunity
not by aptitude and ability but by
race, color, national origin, and other
traits that are easily identified but ut-
terly irrelevant to one's qualification
for a particular job.[2] Regrettably, the
Court retreats from these efforts in its
review of an interlocutory judgment
respecting the "peculiar facts" of this
lawsuit.[3] Turning a blind eye to the
meaning and purpose of Title VII, the
majority's opinion perfunctorily rejects a longstanding rule of law and

————

[1] 78 Stat. 253, as amended, 42 U.S.C. §2000e *et
seq.*
[2] Title VII also bars discrimination because of
religion or sex. 42 U.S.C. §2000e-2(a). Discrimination based on other characteristics has been challenged under other statutes. See, *e.g., School Board
of Nassau County* v. *Arline,* 480 U.S. 273 [43 FEP
Cases 81] (1987) (determining scope of protection
for handicapped schoolteacher under §504 of the
Rehabilitation Act of 1973, 87 Stat. 394, 29 U.S.C.
§794); *Newport News Shipbuilding & Dry Dock Co.*
v. *EEOC,* 462 U.S. 669 [32 FEP Cases 1] (1983) (Preg-
nancy Discrimination Act of 1978, Pub. L. 95-555,
§1, 92 Stat. 2076, 42 U.S.C. §2000e-(k)); *Lorillard* v.
Pons, 434 U.S. 575 [16 FEP Cases 885] (1978) (Age
Discrimination in Employment Act of 1967, 81
Stat. 602, as amended, 29 U.S.C. §621 *et seq.*); *Cor-
ning Glass Works* v. *Brennan,* 417 U.S. 188 [9 FEP
Cases 919] (1974) (Equal Pay Act of 1963, 77 Stat.
56, §3, enacted as §6(d) of the Fair Labor Standards
Act of 1938, 29 U.S.C. §206(d)).
[3] See *ante,* at 10 [49 FEP Cases, at 1525]. The
majority purports to reverse the Court of Appeals
but in fact directs the District Court to make
additional findings, some of which had already
been ordered by the Court of Appeals. Compare 827
F.2d 439, 445 [47 FEP Cases 163, 167] (CA9 1987),
with *ante,* at 13-14 [49 FEP Cases, at 1526]. Furthermore, nearly half the majority's opinion is
devoted to two questions not fairly raised at this
point: "the question of causation in a disparate
impact case," *ante,* at 12 [49 FEP Cases, at 1525],
and the nature of the employer's defense, *id.,* at 14
[49 FEP Cases, at 1526], at an interlocutory stage of
such a factually complicated case, I believe the
Court should have denied certiorari and allowed
the District Court to make the additional findings
directed by the Court of Appeals.

underestimates the probative value of evidence of a racially stratified work force.[4] I cannot join this latest sojourn into judicial activism.

I

I would have though it superfluous to recount at this late date the development of our Title VII jurisprudence, but the majority's facile treatment of settled law necessitates such a primer. This Court initially considered the meaning of Title VII in *Griggs* v. *Duke Power Co.*, 401 U.S. 424 [3 FEP Cases 175] (1971), in which a class of utility company employees challenged the conditioning of entry into higher paying jobs upon a high school education or passage of two written tests. Despite evidence that "these two requirements operated to render ineligible a markedly disproportionate number of Negroes,"[5] the Court of Appeals had held that because there was no showing of an intent to discriminate on account of race, there was no Title VII violation. *Id.* at 429, [3 FEP Cases, at 177]. Chief Justice Burger's landmark

opinion established that an employer may violate the statute even when acting in complete good faith without any invidious intent.[6] Focusing on §703(a)(2),[7] he explained:

"The objective of Congress in the enactment of Title VII is plain from the language of the statute. It was to achieve equality of employment opportunities and remove barriers that have operated in the past to favor a identifiable group of white employees over other employees. Under the Act, practices, procedures, or tests neutral on their face, and even neutral in terms of intent, cannot be maintained if they operate to 'freeze' the status quo of prior discriminatory employment practices." *Griggs*, 401 U.S., at 429–430 [3 FEP Cases, at 177].

The opinion in *Griggs* made it clear that a neutral practice that operates to exclude minorities is nevertheless lawful if it serves a valid business purpose. "The touchstone is business necessity," the Court stressed. *Id.*, at 431 [3 FEP Cases, at 178]. Because "Congress directed the thrust of the Act to the *consequences* of employment practices, not simply the motivation[,]. . . Congress has placed on the employer the burden of showing that any given requirement must have a manifest relationship to the employment in question." [8] *Id.*, at 432 [3 FEP Cases, at 178] (emphasis in original). Congress has declined to act — as the Court now sees fit — to limit the reach of this "disparate impact" theory, see *Teamsters* v. *United States*, 431 U.S. 324, 335,

---

[4] Respondents comprise a class of present and former employees of petitioners, two Alaskan salmon canning companies. The class members, described by the parties as "nonwhite," include persons of Samoan, Chinese, Filipino, Japanese, and Alaska Native descent, all but one of whom are United States citizens. 34 EPD ¶34,437, pp. 33,822, 33,836–33.838 (WD Wash. 1983). Fifteen years ago they commenced this suit, alleging that petitioners engage in hiring, job assignment, housing, and messing practices that segregate nonwhites from whites, in violation of Title VII. Evidence included this response in 1971 by a foreman to a college student's inquiry about cannery employment:
" 'We are not in a position to take many young fellows to our Bristol Bay canneries as they do not have the background for our type of employees. Our cannery labor is either Eskimo or Filipino and we do not have the facilities to mix other with these groups.' " *Id.*, at 33,836.
Some characteristics of the Alaska salmon industry described in this litigation — in particular, the segregation of housing and dining facilities and the stratification of jobs along racial and ethnic lines — bear an unsettling resemblance to aspects of a plantation economy. See generally Plantation, Town, and County, Essays on the Local History of American Slave Society 163–334 (E. Miller & E. Genovese eds. 1974). Indeed the maintenance of inferior, segregated facilities for housing and feeding nonwhite employees, see 34 EPD ¶34,437, pp. 33.836, 33,843–33,844, strikes me as a form of discrimination that, although it does not necessarily fit neatly into a disparate impact or disparate treatment mold, nonetheless violates Title VII. See generally Brief for National Association for the Advancement of Colored People as *Amicus Curiae*, Respondents, however, do not press this theory before us.
[5] This Court noted that census statistics showed that in the employer's State, North Carolina, "while 34% of white males had completed high school, only 12% of Negro males had done so. . . . Similarly, with respect to standardized tests, the EEOC in one case found that use of a battery of tests, including the Wonderlic and Bennett tests used by the Company in the instant case, resulted in 58% of whites passing the tests, as compared with only 6% of the blacks." *Griggs*, 401 U.S., at 430, n. 6 [3 FEP Cases, at 177].

[6] "The Court of Appeals held that the Company had adopted the diploma and test requirements without any 'intention to discriminate against Negro employees.' We do not suggest that either the District Court or the Court of Appeals erred in examining the employer's intent; but *good intent or absence of discriminatory intent does not redeem employment procedures or testing mechanisms that operate as 'built-in headwinds' for minority groups and are unrelated to measuring job capability.*" *Id.*, at 432 [3 FEP Cases, at 178] (emphasis added) (citation omitted).
[7] See *id.*, at 426, n. 1 [3 FEP Cases, at 176]. This subsection provides that "[i]t shall be an unlawful employment practice for an employer —
"(a) to limit, segregate, or classify his employees or applicants for employment in any way which would deprive or tend to deprive any individual of employment opportunities or otherwise adversely affect his status as an employee, because of such individual's race, color, religion, sex, or national origin." 42 U.S.C. §2000e-2(a)(2).
[8] The opinion concluded:
"Nothing in the Act precludes the use of testing or measuring procedures; obviously they are useful. What Congress has forbidden is giving these devices and mechanisms controlling force unless they are demonstrably a reasonable measure of job performance. Congress has not commanded that the less qualified be preferred over the better qualified simply because of minority origins. Far from disparaging job qualifications as such, Congress has made such qualifications the controlling factor, so that race, religion, nationality, and sex become irrelevant. *What Congress has commanded is that any test used must measure the person for the job and not the person in the abstract.*" 401 U.S., at 436 [3 FEP Cases, at 180] (emphasis added).

n. 15 [14 FEP Cases 1514, 1519] (1977); indeed it has extended its application.[9] This approval lends added force to the *Griggs* holding.

The *Griggs* framework, with its focus on ostensibly neutral qualification standards, proved inapposite for analyzing an individual employee's claim, brought under §703(a)(1),[10] that an employer intentionally discriminated on account of race.[11] The means for determining intent absent direct evidence was outlined in *McDonnell Douglas Corp.* v. *Green*, 411 U.S. 792 [5 FEP Cases 965] (1973), and *Texas Dept. of Community Affairs* v. *Burdine*, 450 U.S. 248 [25 FEP Cases 113] (1981), two opinions written by Justice Powell for unanimous Courts. In such a "disparate treatment" case, see *Teamsters*, 431 U.S., at 335, n. 15, [14 FEP Cases, at 1519] the plaintiff's initial burden, which is "not onerous," 450 U.S., at 253 [25 FEP Cases, at 115], is to establish "a prima facie case of racial dis-

---

[9] Voting Rights Act Amendments of 1982, Pub. L. 97-205, 96 Stat. 131, 134, as amended, codified at 42 U.S.C. §§1973, 1973b (1982 ed. and Supp. V). Legislative reports leading to 1972 amendments to Title VII also evince support for disparate impact analysis. H.R. Rep. No. 92-238, pp. 8, 20-22 (1971); S. Rep. No. 92-415, p. 5, and n. 1 (1971); accord *Connecticut* v. *Teal*, 457 U.S. 440, 447, n. 8 [29 FEP Cases 1, 4] (1982). Moreover, the theory is employed to enforce both housing and age discrimination statutes. See Note, Business Necessity in Title VII: Importing an Employment Discrimination Doctrine into the Fair Housing Act, 54 Ford. L. Rev. 563 (1986); Note, Disparate Impact Analysis and the Age Discrimination in Employment Act, 68 Minn. L. Rev. 1038 (1984).

[10] This subsection makes it unlawful for an employer:
"to fail or refuse to hire or to discharge any individual, or otherwise to discriminate against any individual with respect to his compensation, terms, conditions, or privileges of employment, because of such individual's race, color, religion, sex, or national origin. . . ." 42 U.S.C. §2000e-2(a)(1).

[11] In *McDonnell Douglas Corp.* v. *Green*, 411 U.S. 792 [5 FEP Cases 965] (1973), Justice Powell explained:
"*Griggs* differs from the instant case in important respects. It dealt with standardized testing devices which, however neutral on their face, operated to exclude many blacks who were capable of performing effectively in the desired positions. *Griggs* was rightly concerned that childhood deficiencies in the education and background of minority citizens, resulting from forces beyond their control, not be allowed to work a cumulative and invidious burden on such citizens for the remainder of their lives. Respondent, however, appears in different clothing. He had engaged in a seriously disruptive act against the very one from whom he now seeks employment. And petitioner does not seek his exclusion on the basis of a testing device which overstates what is necessary for competent performance, or through some sweeping disqualification of all those with any past record of unlawful behavior, however remote, insubstantial, or unrelated to applicant's personal qualifications as an employee. Petitioner assertedly rejected respondent for unlawful conduct against it and, in the absence of proof of pretext or discriminatory application of such a reason, this cannot be thought the kind of 'artificial' arbitrary, and unnecessary barriers to employment' which the Court found to be the intention of Congress to remove" *Id.*, at 806 [5 FEP Cases, at 970] (citations omitted).

crimination," 411 U.S., at 802 [5 FEP Cases, at 969]; that is, to create a presumption of unlawful discrimination by "eliminat[ing] the most common nondiscriminatory reasons for the plaintiff's rejection." [12] 450 U.S., at 254 [25 FEP Cases, at 116]. "The burden then must shift to the employer to articulate some legitimate, nondiscriminatory reason for the employee's rejection." 411 U.S., at 802 [5 FEP Cases, at 969]; see 450 U.S., at 254 [25 FEP Cases, at 116]. Finally, because "Title VII does not . . . permit [the employer] to use [the employees'] conduct as a pretext for the sort of discrimination prohibited by §703(a)(1)," the employee "must be given a full and fair opportunity to demonstrate by competent evidence that the presumptively valid reasons for his rejection were in fact a cover up for a racially discriminatory decision." 411 U.S., at 804-805 [5 FEP Cases, at 970]; see 450 U.S., at 256 [25 FEP Cases, at 116]. While the burdens of producing evidence thus shift, the "ultimate burden of persuading the trier of fact that the defendant intentionally discriminated against the plaintiff remains at all times with the plaintiff." [13] 450 U.S., at 253 [25 FEP Cases, at 115].

Decisions of this Court and other federal courts repeatedly have recognized that while the employer's burden in a disparate treatment case is simply one of coming forward with evidence of legitimate business purpose, its burden in a disparate impact case is proof of an affirmative defense of business necessity.[14] Although the

---

[12] "This may be done by showing (i) that he belongs to a racial minority; (ii) that he applied and was qualified for a job for which the employer was seeking applicants; (iii) that, despite his qualifications, he was rejected; and (iv) that, after his rejection, the position remained open and the employer continued to seek applicants from persons of complainant's qualifications." *Id.*, at 802 [5 FEP Cases, at 969].

[13] Although disparate impact and disparate treatment are the most prevalent modes of proving discrimination violative of Title VII, they are by no means exclusive. See generally B. Schlei & P. Grossman, Employment Discrimination Law 13-289 (2d ed. 1983) (four chapters discussing "disparate treatment," "present effects of past discrimination," "adverse impact," and "reasonable accommodation" as "categories" of discrimination). Cf. n. 4, *supra*. Moreover, either or both of the primary theories may be applied to a particular set off facts. See *Teamsters* v. *United States*, 431 U.S. 324, 336, n. 15 [14 FEP Cases 1514, 1519] (1977).

[14] See *McDonnell Douglas*, 411 U.S., at 802, n. 14 [5 FEP Cases, at 969]. See also, *e.g.*, *Teal*, 457 U.S., at 446 [29 FEP Cases, at 4] ("employer must . . . demonstrate that 'any given requirement [has] a manifest relationship to the employment in question' "); *New York City Transit Authority* v. *Beazer*, 440 U.S. 568, 587 [19 FEP Cases 149, 156] (1979) (employer "rebutted" prima facie case by "demonstration that its narcotics rule . . . 'is job related' "); *Dothard* v. *Rawlinson*, 433 U.S. 321, 329 [15 FEP Cases 10, 14] (1977) (employer has to "prov[e] that the challenged requirements are job related"); *Albemarle*

majority's opinion blurs that distinction, thoughtful reflection on common-law pleading principles clarifies the fundamental differences between the two types of "burdens of proof." [15] In the ordinary civil trial, the plaintiff bears the burden of persuading the trier of fact that the defendant has harmed her. See, e.g., 2 Restatement (Second) of Torts §§328 A, 433 B (1965) (hereinafter Restatement). The defendant may undercut plaintiff's efforts both by confronting plaintiff's evidence during her case in chief and by submitting countervailing evidence during its own case. [16] But if the plaintiff proves the existence of the harmful act, the defendant can escape liability only by persuading the factfinder that the act was justified or excusable. See, e.g., Restatement §§454-461, 463-467. The plaintiff in turn may try to refute this affirmative defense. Although the burdens of producing evidence regarding the existence of harm or excuse thus shift between the plaintiff and the defendant, the burden of proving either proposition remains throughout on the party asserting it.

In a disparate treatment case there is no "discrimination" within the meaning of Title VII unless the employer intentionally treated the employee unfairly because of race. Therefore, the employee retains the burden of proving the existence of intent at all times. If there is direct evidence of intent, the employee may have little difficulty persuading the factfinder that discrimination has occurred. But in the likelier event that intent has to be established by inference, the employee may resort to the McDonnell/Burdine inquiry. In either instance, the employer may undermine the employee's evidence but has no independent burden of persuasion.

In contrast, intent plays no role in the disparate impact inquiry. The question, rather, is whether an employment practice has a significant, adverse effect on an identifiable class of workers — regardless of the cause or motive for the practice. The employer may attempt to contradict the factual basis for this effect; that is, to prevent the employee from establishing a prima facie case. But when an employer is faced with sufficient proof of disparate impact, its only recourse is to justify the practice by explaining why it is necessary to the operation of business. Such a justification is a classic example of an affirmative defense. [17]

Failing to explore the interplay between these distinct orders of proof, the Court announces that our frequent statements that the employer shoulders the burden of proof respecting business necessity "should have been understood to mean an employer's production — but not persuasion — burden." [18] Ante, at 16 [49 FEP

Paper Co. v. Moody, 422 U.S. 405, 425 [10 FEP Cases 1181, 1190] (1975) (employer has "burden of proving that its tests are 'job related' "); Griggs, 401 U.S., at 432 [3 FEP Cases, at 178] (employer has "burden of showing that any given requirement must have a manifest relationship to the employment"). Court of Appeals opinions properly treating the employer's burden include Bunch v. Bullard, 795 F.2d 384, 393-394 [41 FEP Cases 515, 523] ((CA5 1986); Lewis v. Bloomsburg Mills, Inc., 773 F.2d 561, 572 [38 FEP Cases 1692, 1701] (CA4 1985); Nash v. Consolidated City of Jacksonville, Duvval City., Fla., 763 F.2d 1393, 1397 [38 FEP Cases, 151, 153-154] (CA11 1985); Segar v. Smith, 238 U.S. App. D.C. 103, 121, 738 F.2d 1249, 1267 [35 FEP Cases 31. 42] (1984), cert. denied sub nom. Meese v. Segar, 471 U.S. 1115 [37 FEP Cases 1312] (1985); Moore v. Hughes Helicopters, Inc., a Div. of Summa Corp., 708 F.2d 475, 481 [32 FEP Cases 97, 101] (CA9 1983); Hawkins v. Anheuser-Busch, Inc., 697 F.2d 810, 815 [30 FEP Cases 1170, 1175] (CA8 1983); Johnson v. Uncle Ben's, Inc., 657 F.2d 750 [26 FEP Cases 1417] (CA5 1981), cert. denied, 459 U.S. 967 [30 FEP Cases 56] (1982); contra Croker v. Boeing Co., 662 F.2d 975, 991 [26 FEP Cases 1569, 1579] (CA3 1981) (en banc). Cf. Equal Employment Opportunity Comm'n Uniform Guidelines on Employee Selection Procedures, 29 CFR §1607.1 et seq. (1988).

[15] See, e.g., 9 J. Wigmore, Evidence §§2485-2498 (J. Chadbourn rev. 1981); D. Louisell & C. Mueller, Federal Evidence §§65-70 (1977) (hereinafter Louisell); 21 C. Wright & K. Graham, Federal Practice and Procedure §5122 (1977) (hereinafter Wright); J. Thayer, A Preliminary Treatise on Evidence 353-389 (1898) (hereinafter Thayer); C. Langdell, Equity Pleading 108-115 (2d ed. 1883).

[16] Cf. Thayer 357 (quoting Caldwell v. New Jersey S.B. Co., 47 N.Y. 282, 290 (1872) (" 'The burden of maintaining the affirmative of the issue, and, properly speaking, the burden of proof, remained upon the plaintiff throughout the trial; but the burden or necessity was cast upon the defendant, to relieve itself from the presumption of negligence raised by the plaintiff's evidence' ").

[17] Accord Fed. Rule Civ. Proc. 8(c) ("In pleading to a preceding pleading, a party shall set forth affirmatively . . . any . . . matter constituting an avoidance or affirmative defense"). Cf. Thayer 368-369:

"An admission may, of course, end the controversy, but such an admission may be, and yet not end it; and if that be so, it is because the party making the admission sets up something that avoids the apparent effect of it. . . . When this happens, the party defending becomes, in so far, the actor or plaintiff. In general, he who seeks to move a court in his favor, whether as an original plaintiff whose facts are merely denied, or as a defendant, who, in admitting his adversary's contention and setting up an affirmative defense, takes the role of actor (reus excipiendo fit actor), — must satisfy the court of the truth and adequacy of the grounds of his claim, both in point of fact and law."

Similarly, in suits alleging price discrimination in violation of §2 of the Clayton Act, as amended by the Robinson Patman Act, 15 U.S.C. §13, it is well settled that the defendant has the burden of affirmatively establishing as a defense either a cost justification, under the proviso to subsection (a), United States v. Borden Co., 370 U.S. 460, 467 (1962), or a good-faith attempt to meet a competitor's equally low price, pursuant to subsection (b). Standard Oil Co. v. FTC, 340 U.S. 231, 250 (1951).

[18] The majority's only basis for this proposition is the plurality opinion in Watson v. Fort Worth Band & Trust, 487 U.S. ——, —— [47 FEP Cases 102, 110] (1988), which in turn cites no authority. As Justice Blackmun explains in Watson, 487 U.S., at —— - —— [47 FEP Cases, at 111-114] (concurring in part and concurring in judgment), and as I

Cases, at 1527]. Our opinions always have emphasized that in a disparate impact case the employer's burden is weighty. "The touchstone," the Court said in *Griggs*, "is business necessity." 401 U.S., at 431 [3 FEP Cases, at 178]. Later, we held that prison administrators had failed to "rebut[t] the prima facie case of discrimination by showing that the height and weight requirements are . . . essential to effective job performance," *Dothard* v. *Rawlinson*, 433 U.S. 321, 331 [15 FEP Cases 10, 15] (1977). Cf. n. 14, *supra*. I am thus astonished to read that the "touchstone of this inquiry is a reasoned review of the employer's justification for his use of the challenged practice. . . . [T]here is no requirement that the challenged practice be . . . 'essential,' " *ante*, at 15 [49 FEP Cases, at 1527]. This casual — almost summary — rejection of the statutory construction that developed in the wake of *Griggs* is most disturbing. I have always believed that the *Griggs* opinion correctly reflected the intent of the Congress that enacted Title VII. Even if I were not so persuaded, I could not join a rejection of a consistent interpretation of a federal statute. Congress frequently revisits this statutory scheme and can readily correct our mistakes if we misread its meaning. *Johnson* v. *Transportation Agency, Santa Clara, Cty., Cal.*, 480 U.S. 616, 644 [43 FEP Cases 411, 423-424] (1987) (STEVENS, J., concurring); *Runyon* v. *McCrary*, 427 U.S. 160, 190-192 (1976) (STEVENS, J., concurring). See *McNally* v. *United States*, 483 U.S. 350, 376 (1987) (STEVENS, J., dissenting); *Commissioner* v. *Fink*, 483 U.S. 89, 102-105 (1987) (STEVENS, J., dissenting); see also *Rodriguez de Quijas* v. *Shearson/American Express, Inc.*, 490 U.S. ——, —— - —— (11989) (STEVENS, J., dissenting).

Also troubling is the Court's apparent redefinition of the employees' burden of proof in a disparate impact case. No prima facie case will be made, it declares, unless the employees " 'isolat[e] and identif[y] the specific employment practices that are allegedly responsible for any observed statistical disparities.' " *Ante*, at 12 [49 FEP Cases, at 1525] (quoting *Watson* v. *Fort Worth Bank & Trust*, 487 U.S. ——,

have shown here, the assertion profoundly misapprehends the difference between disparate impact and disparate treatment claims.
  The Court also makes passing reference to Federal Rule of Evidence 301. *Ante*, at 15 [49 FEP Cases, at 1527]. That Rule pertains only to shifting of evidentiary burdens upon establishment of a presumption and has no bearing on the substantive burdens of proof. See Louisell §§65-70; Wright §5122.

—— [47 FEP Cases 102, 109]. (1988) (plurality opinion)). This additional proof requirement is unwarranted.[19] It is elementary that a plaintiff cannot recover upon proof of injury alone; rather, the plaintiff must connect the injury to an act of the defendant in order to establish prima facie that the defendant is liable. *E.g.*, Restatement §430. Although the causal link must have substance, the act need not constitute the sole or primary cause of the harm. §§431-433; cf. *Price Waterhouse* v. *Hopkins*, 490 U.S. —— [49 FEP Cases 954] (1989). Thus in a disparate impact case, proof of numerous questionable employment practices caused racial disparities.[20] Ordinary principles of fairness require that Title VII actions be tried like "any lawsuit." Cf. *USPS Board of Governors* v. *Aikens*, 460 U.S. 711, 714, n. 3 [31 FEP Cases 609, 610] (1983). The changes the majority makes today, tipping the scales in favor of employers, are not faithful to those principles.

II

Petitioners seek reversal of the Court of Appeals and dismissal of this suit on the ground that respondents' statistical evidence failed to prove a prima facie case of discrimination. Brief for Petitioners 48. The District Court concluded "there were 'significant disparities' " between the racial composition of the cannery workers and the noncannery workers, but it "made no precise numerical findings" on this and other critical points. See *ante*, at 6 n. 5 [49 FEP Cases, at 1523]. Given this dearth of findings and the Court's newly articulated preference for individualized proof of causation, it would be manifestly unfair to consider respondents' evidence in the aggregate and deem it insufficient. Thus the Court properly rejects petitioners' request for a final judgment and remands for further determination of the strength of respondents' prima facie case. See *ante*, at 11 [49 FEP Cases,

[19] The Solicitor General's brief *amicus curiae* on behalf of the employers agrees:
  "[A] decision rule for selection may be complex: it may, for example, involve consideration of multiple factors. And certainly if the factors combine to produce a single ultimate selection decision and it is not possible to challenge each one, that decision may be challenged (and defended) as a whole." Brief for United States as *Amicus Curiae* 22 (footnote omitted).
[20] The Court discounts the difficulty its causality requirement presents for employees, reasoning that they may employ "liberal civil discovery rules" to obtain the employer's statistical personnel records. *Ante*, at 13. Even assuming that this generally is true, it has no bearing in this litigation, since it is undisputed that petitioners did not preserve such records. Brief for Respondents 42-43; Reply Brief for Petitioners 18-19.

at 1525]. Even at this juncture, however, I believe that respondents' evidence deserves greater credit than the majority allows.

Statistical evidence of discrimination should compare the racial composition of employees in disputed jobs to that " 'of the qualified . . . population in the relevant labor market.' " *Ante*, at 6-7 [49 FEP Cases, at 1523] (quoting *Hazelwood School District* v. *United States*, 433 U.S. 299, 308 [15 FEP Cases 1, 4-5] (1977)). That statement leaves open the definition of the qualified population and the relevant labor market. Our previous opinions, *e.g.*, *New York City Transit Authority* v. *Beazer*, 440 U.S. 568, 584-586 [19 FEP Cases 149, 155-156] (1970); *Dothard* v. *Rawlinson*, 433 U.S. 321, 329-330 [15 FEP Cases 10, ——] (1977); *Albemarle Paper Co.* v. *Moody*, 422 U.S. 405, 425 [10 FEP Cases 1181, 1190] (1975); *Griggs*, 401 U.S. at 426, 430, n. 6 [3 FEP Cases, at 177] demonstrate that in reviewing statistical evidence, a court should not strive for numerical exactitude at the expense of the needs of the particular case.

The District Court's findings of fact depict a unique industry. Canneries often are located in remote, sparsely populated areas of Alaska. 34 EPD ¶34,437, p. 33,825 (WD Wash. 1983). Most jobs are seasonal, with the season's length and the canneries' personnel needs varying not just year-to-year but day-to-day. *Ibid.* To fill their employment requirements, petitioners must recruit and transport many cannery workers and noncannery workers from States in the Pacific Northwest. *Id.*, at 33,828. Most cannery workers come from a union local based outside Alaska or from Native villages near the canneries. *Ibid.* Employees in the noncannery positions — the positions that are "at issue" — learn of openings by word of mouth; the jobs seldom are posted or advertised, and there is no promotion to non-cannery jobs from within the cannery workers' ranks. *Id.*, at 33,827-33,828.

In general, the District Court found the at-issue jobs to require "skills," ranging from English literacy, typing, and "ability to use seam micrometers, gauges, and mechanic's hand tools" to "good health" and a driver's license.[21]

---

[21] The District Court found that of more than 100 at-issue job titles, all were skilled except these 15: kitchen help, waiter/waitress, janitor, oildock crew, night watchman, tallyman, laundry, gasman, roustabout, store help, stockroom help, assistant caretaker (winter watchman and watchman's assistant), machinist helper/trainee, deckhand, and apprentice carpenter/carpenter's helper. 34 EPD ¶34,437, p. 33-835.

Id., at 33,833-33,834. All cannery workers' jobs, like a handful of at-issue positions, are unskilled, and the court found that the intensity of the work during canning season precludes on-the-job training for skilled noncannery positions. *Id.*, at 33,825. It made no findings regarding the extent to which the cannery workers already are qualified for at-issue jobs: individual plaintiffs testified persuasively that they were fully qualified for such jobs,[22] but the court neither credited nor discredited this testimony. Although there are no findings concerning wage differentials, the parties seem to agree that wages for cannery workers are lower than those for noncannery workers, skilled or unskilled. The District Court found that "nearly all" cannery workers are nonwhite, while the percentage of nonwhites employed in the entire Alaska salmon canning industry "has stabilized at about 47% to 50%." *Id.*, at 33,829. The precise stratification of the work force is not described in the findings, but the parties seem to agree that the noncannery jobs are predominantly held by whites.

Petitioners contend that the relevant labor market in this case is the general population of the " 'external' labor market for the jobs at issue." Brief for Petitioners 17. While they would rely on the District Court's finding in this regard, those findings are ambiguous. At one point the District Court specifies "Alaska, the Pacific Northwest, and California" as "the geographical region from which [petitioners] draw their employees," but its next finding refers to "this relevant geographical area for cannery worker, laborer, and the other non-skilled jobs," 34 EPD ¶34,437, p. 33,828. There is no express finding of the relevant labor market for noncannery jobs.

Even assuming that the District Court properly defined the relevant geographical area, its apparent assumption that the population in that area constituted the "available labor supply," *ibid.*, is not adequately founded. An undisputed requirement for employment either as a cannery or noncannery worker is availability for seasonal employment in the far reaches of Alaska. Many noncannery

---

[22] Some cannery workers later became architects, an Air Force officer, and a graduate student in public administration. Some had college training at the time they were employed in the canneries. See *id.*, at 33,837-33,838; App. 38, 52-53; Tr. 76, 951-952, 1036, 1050, 2214.

workers, furthermore, must be available for preseason work. *Id.*, at 33,829, 33,833–33,834. Yet the record does not identify the portion of the general population in Alaska, California, and the Pacific Northwest that would accept this type of employment.[23] This deficiency respecting a crucial job qualification diminishes the usefulness of petitioners' statistical evidence. In contrast, respondents' evidence, comparing racial compositions within the work force, identifies a pool of workers willing to work during the relevant times and familiar with the workings of the industry. Surely this is more probative than the untailored general population statistics on which petitioners focus. Cf. *Hazelwood*, 433 U.S., at 308, n. 13 [15 FEP Cases, at 5]; *Teamsters*, 431 U.S., at 339–340, n. 20 [14 FEP Cases, at 1521].

Evidence that virtually all the employees in the major categories of at-issue jobs were white,[24] whereas about two-thirds of the cannery workers were nonwhite,[25] may not by itself suffice to establish a prima facie case of discrimination.[26] But such evidence of

racial stratification puts the specific employment practices challenged by respondents into perspective. Petitioners recruit employees for at-issue jobs from outside the work force rather than from lower-paying, overwhelmingly nonwhite, cannery worker positions. 34 EPD ¶34,437, p. 33,828–33,829. Information about availability of at-issue positions is conducted by word of mouth;[27] therefore, the maintenance of housing and mess halls that separate the largely white noncannery work force from the cannery workers, *id.*, at 33,836, 33,843–33,844, coupled with the tendency toward nepotistic hiring,[28] are obvious barriers to employment opportunities for nonwhites. Putting to one side the issue of business justifications, it would be quite wrong to conclude that these practices have no discriminatory consequence.[29] Thus I agree with the Court of Appeals, 827 F.2d 439, 444–445 [47 FEP Cases 163, 167] (CA9 1987), that when the District Court makes the additional findings prescribed today, it should treat the evidence of racial stratification in the work force as a significant element of respondents' prima facie case.

---

[23] The District Court's justification for use of general population statistics occurs in these findings of fact:

"119. Most of the jobs at the canneries entail migrant, seasonal labor. While as a general proposition, most people prefer full-year, fixed location employment near their homes, seasonal employment in the unique salmon industry is not comparable to most other types of migrant work, such as fruit and vegetable harvesting which, for example, may or may not involve a guaranteed wage.

"120. Thus, while census data is [sic] dominated by people who prefer full-year, fixed-location employment, such data is [sic] nevertheless appropriate in defining labor supplies for migrant, seasonal work." 34 EPD ¶34,437, p. 33,829.
The court's rather confusing distinction between work in the cannery industry and other "migrant, seasonal work" does not support its conclusion that the general population composes the relevant labor market.

[24] For example, from 1971 to 1980, there were 443 persons hired in the job departments labeled "machinists," "company fishing boat," and "tender" at petitioner Castle & Cooke, Inc.'s Bumble Bee cannery; only three of them were nonwhites. Joint Excerpt of Record 35 (Exh. 588). In the same categories at the Red Salmon cannery of petitioner Wards Cove Packing Co., Inc., 488 whites and 42 nonwhites were hired. *Id.*, at 36 (Exh. 589).

[25] The Court points out that nonwhites are "overrepresented" among the cannery workers. *Ante*, at 10–11 [49 FEP Cases, at 1525]. Such an imbalance will be true in any racially stratified work force; its significance becomes apparent only upon examination of the pattern of segregation within the work force. In the cannery industry nonwhites are concentrated in positions offering low wages and little opportunity for promotion. Absent any showing that the "underrepresentation" of whites in this stratum is the result of a barrier to access, the "overrepresentation" of nonwhites does not offend Title VII.

[26] The majority suggests that at-issue work demands the skills possessed by "accountants, managers, boat captains, electricians, doctors, and engineers." See *ante*, at 7 [49 FEP Cases, at 1523]. It is at least theoretically possible that a disproportion-

ate number of white applicants possessed the specialized skills required by some at-issue jobs. In fact, of course, many at-issue jobs involved skills not at all comparable to these selective examples. See 34 EPD ¶34,437, p. 33,833–33,834. Even the District Court recognized that in a year-round employment setting, "some of the positions which this court finds to be skilled, *e. g.*, truckdriving on the beach, [would] fit into the category of jobs which require skills that are readily acquirable by persons in the general public." *Id.*, at 33,841.

[27] As the Court of Appeals explained in its remand opinion:
"Specifically, the companies sought cannery workers in Native villages and through dispatches from ILWU Local 37, thus securing a work force for the lowest paying jobs which was predominantly Alaska Native and Filipino. For other departments the companies relied on informal word-of-mouth recruitment by predominantly white superintendents and foremen, who recruited primarily white employees. That such practices can cause a discriminatory impact is obvious." 827 F.2d, at 446 [47 FEP Cases, at 169].

[28] The District Court found but downplayed the fact that relatives of employees are given preferential consideration. See 34 EPD ¶34,437, p. 33,840. But "of 349 nepotistic hires in four upper-level departments during 1970–75, 332 were of whites, 17 of nonwhites," the Court of Appeals noted. "If nepotism exists, it is by definition a practice of giving preference to relatives, and where those doing the hiring are predominantly white, the practice necessarily has an adverse impact on nonwhites." 827 F.2d, at 445 [47 FEP Cases, at 168].

[29] The Court suggests that the discrepancy in economic opportunities for white and nonwhite workers does not amount to disparate impact within the meaning of Title VII unless respondents show that it is "petitioners' fault." *Ante*, at 7 [49 FEP Cases, at 1524]; see also *ante*, at 9–10 [49 FEP Cases, at 1524–1525]. This statement distorts the disparate impact theory, in which the critical inquiry is whether an employer's practices *operate* to discriminate. *E. g.*, *Griggs*, 401 U.S., at 431 [3 FEP Cases, at 178]. Whether the employer intended such discrimination is irrelevant.

III

The majority's opinion begins with recognition of the settled rule that that "a facially neutral employment practice may be deemed violative of Title VII without evidence of the employer's subjective intent to discriminate that is required in a 'disparate treatment' case." *Ante*, at 2 [49 FEP Cases, at 1521]. It then departs from the body of law engendered by this disparate impact theory, reformulating the order of proof and the weight of the parties' burdens. Why the Court undertakes these unwise changes in elementary and eminently fair rules is a mystery to me.

I respectfully dissent.

JUSTICE BLACKMUN, with whom JUSTICE BRENNAN and JUSTICE MARSHALL join, dissenting.

I fully concur in JUSTICE STEVENS' analysis of this case. Today a bare majority of the Court takes three major strides backwards in the battle against race discrimination. It reaches out to make last Term's plurality opinion in *Watson* v. *Fort Worth Bank & Trust*, 487 U.S. —— [47 FEP Cases 102] (1988), the law, thereby upsetting the longstanding distribution of burdens of proof in Title VII disparate-impact cases. It bars the use of internal workforce comparisons in the making of a prima facie case of discrimination, even where the structure of this industry in question renders any other statistical comparison meaningless. And it requires practice-by-practice statistical proof of causation, even where, as here, such proof would be impossible.

The harshness of these results is well demonstrated by the facts of this case. The salmon industry as described by this record takes us back to a kind of overt and institutionalized discrimination we have not dealt with in years: a total residential and work environment organized on principles of racial stratification and segregation, which, as JUSTICE STEVENS points out, resembles a plantation economy. *Post* at 2, n. 4, [49 FEP Cases, at 1528]. This industry long has been characterized by a taste for discrimination of the old-fashioned sort: a preference for hiring nonwhites to fill its lowest-level positions, on the condition that they stay there. The majority's legal rulings essentially immunize these practices from attack under a Title VII disparate-impact analysis.

Sadly, this comes as no surprise. One wonders whether the majority still believes that race discrimination — or, more accurately, race discrimination against nonwhites — is a problem in our society, or even remembers that it ever was. Ct. *City of Richmond* v. *J. A. Croson Co.*, —— U.S. —— (1989).

APPENDIX C

SAMPLE CORPORATE PROMOTION PLANS

Gannett Company Inc. (C-3)

Xerox Corporation (C-23)

Aetna Life & Casualty (C-51)

Reprinted with permission.

GANNETT COMPANY INC.

BUILDING YOUR MINORITY PROGRAM

The action items that follow will help you cover the bases necessary to make progress in the area of minority hiring. When you can check most of these areas, your model program will be on its way.

RECRUITMENT

_____ 1. Attend minority job opportunity conferences (job fairs) offered by individual newspapers and minority media organizations and newspaper associations.

_____ 2. Write an in-paper ad that emphasizes your newspaper's commitment to minority hiring.

_____ 3. Enlist the help of minorities working at your newspaper to spread information about positions available by word of mouth.

_____ 4. Send your job announcements and internship/fellowship information to local minority community service organizations and minority-oriented businesses.

_____ 5. Support the activities of local minority media organizations such as the Asian American Journalists Association, National Association of Black Journalists, National Association of Hispanic Journalists and the Native American Press Association. Do you contribute to the publications of these groups, and let them know about employment opportunities at your newspaper?

_____ 6. Contact business schools, art departments and student newspaper advisors of schools with sizable minority populations when there are positions available at your newspaper.

_____ 7. Develop job descriptions or definitions identifying goals of jobs, traits needed and skills that can be taught? For example, how much typing does a classified advisor really need--compared with knowledge of prices and the potential audience for the ad?

_____ 8. Use the job application form to seek information about non-newspaper experience that could translate into credentials conducive to success in newspaper jobs.

_____ 9. Make certain sources refer a mix of candidates to you whether for jobs or routes of permanent employment. You may need to establish other sources or have straight talk with the current ones.

_____ 10. Use search firms that specialize in minority hiring, especially for mid-level and upper level positions.

_____ 11. Advertise positions in minority newspapers.

(Rev. 10/7/88)

_____ 12. Keep track of the progress of promising minority candidates you meet. Invite candidates with potential to attend job fairs in your area to keep informal track of their progress.

_____ 13. Use the services of JOB/NET or the California Chicano News Media Association JOBank or Asian American Journalists Association job bank, or the SPJ/SDX hotline to find minorities.

_____ 14. Use your own newspaper as a recruiting tool. If you already have good minority people on your staff, run house ads promoting your people and the newspaper. Be certain to run house ads on all your good people.

_____ 15. Make sure that recruiters belong to sales organizations. Food, liquor, and automotive sales clubs hold regular meetings at which you can meet qualified recruits.

Other ideas (your own suggestions):

_____ 1. _____

_____

_____ 2. _____

_____

_____ 3. _____

_____

EDUCATION

_____ 1. Consider operating a summer minority high school workshop.

_____ 2. "Adopt" a minority school in your area as a way of interesting young minorities in the newspaper business.

_____ 3. Develop an internship program for all departments of the newspaper How many minorities are selected? What percentage result in permanent hires?

_____ 4. Take part in ASNE's Project Focus, which places freshman and sophomore college students at newspapers near their hometown for the summer.

_____ 5. Participate in the INROADS program. In this program you would contribute to the salary and education of a minority youth while he/she works at your newspaper. INROADS provides counseling and career development programs.

_____ 6. Set up training programs for inexperienced new employees with checks along the way to make sure they're progressing.

_____ 7. Give college scholarships to minorities, and consider combining these with summer and holiday job opportunities.

Other ideas (your own suggestions):

_____ 1. _____

_____ 2. _____

_____ 3. _____

STAFF DEVELOPMENT/PROMOTING

_____ 1. Consider existing minority staff to move into front-line decision making positions as they arise.

_____ 2. Send minority staff people to newspaper related training sessions (ANPA, API, Institute for Journalism Education, or the University of Missouri Multicultural Management Program).

_____ 3. Nominate minority employees for ANPA Foundation fellowships.

_____ 4. Assign mentors to new minority staff members—to all new staff members.

_____ 5. Consider an employee's outside activities in looking for signs of interests and abilities.

_____ 6. Pay dues for memberships in minority professional organizations in proportion to non-minority organizations.

_____ 7. List what are considered dead-end jobs. Must they remain that way? Can abilities used transfer to other jobs and indicate possibility of success?

_____ 8. Don't forget that vacation fill-ins offer chances for employees to show facility at other jobs, possibly even in other departments. Posting vacation lists in advance lets employees "bid" for fill-in opportunities.

Other ideas (your own suggestions):

_____ 1. _____

_____ 2. _____

_____ 3. _____

RETENTION

_____ 1. Publish an in-house staff newsletter. This is a good way to make sure minorities know what's happening when they may not be "on the grapevine."

_____ 2. Assign minorities to ad hoc committees, such as planning company picnics, to make sure their interests are represented and that they feel more a part of the company. Do committees offer opportunities to find and develop leadership and management ability, and chances to work with people from other departments?

_____ 3. Assure that minority salaries are commensurate with effort and ability.

_____ 4. Provide social opportunities for staff to interact outside of normal business.

_____ 5. Make certain personnel evaluations identify strength, weakness and ways to deal with both, including commitment from supervisors and management to follow through.

_____ 6. Know the turnover in job categories—to help local contacts know what opportunities exist. What percentage of jobs are filled from the local market? Identify opportunities that may improve the mix.

_____ 7. Encourage community-wide agencies to diversify their boards, i.e., the Chamber of Commerce, United Way and other "big" organizations. You can make a statement to the community by helping them to improve the mix.

_____ 8. Remove any unconscious bias from top offices. Who has access to be publisher? How do they gain it? Ask yourself if the same people would have access if the next publisher was a minority.

_____ 9. Your presence on advisory boards, community meetings, coffees—to account for your newspaper's commitment, ascertain community perception of it—will help broaden perspectives.

_____ 10. Ensure that non-minorities who work for you understand that creating regular channels for evaluation, contact, etc., offers benefits for them.

_____ 11. Consider an outside personnel consultant if you feel there are unconscious barriers to minority hiring among supervisors and managers—grooming or promoting one type of employee, steering overtime in favor of one group, taking complaints of one group more seriously than complaints of another, overlooking equivalent credentials of minority applicants or the merits of diversifying the mix.

_____ 12. Organize regular sessions with minority leaders in your community. Ask what perceptions they and their associates have with regard to the newspaper. Prepare to hear the truth. Take the feedback seriously.

_____ 13. In purchasing services, seek minority-owned. Consider the variety of janitorial services, repair shops, florists, etc. Often, a little money spent at one of these businesses has great public relations impact rather than the same amount spent at the usual place.

_____ 14. Examine every aspect of your newspaper to determine whether minorities are being excluded. Do you buy from minority vendors? Does your advertising sales staff approach minority businesses? Does your circulation cover minority neighborhoods?

_____ 15. Hire minority candidates who would make good additions to the staff even if there isn't a position open. When a slot becomes available, make a transfer.

_____ 16. Assign someone to coordinate the minority program at your newspaper. Consider the personnel director, the EEO officer, or someone else. Your support of this person will set the tone for increased attention in this area.

_____ 17. Make a schedule for yourself to examine these issues on a continuing basis--at least quarterly. Assess with the staff what has worked, what is not, and what needs more attention.

_____ 18. What tickets were purchased by the newspaper last year? Can mix be improved? Remember pancake suppers in the suburbs, but support inner city fellowships as well.

INTERNAL ASSIGNMENTS

In order for your program to be successful, everyone has to get the order. Assign a coordinator and make sure he/she gives each department a role, and that all individuals know their responsibilities.

Obtain approval and commitment from top management in starting to expand your minority hiring program.

Write a memo, if necessary, on reasons for establishing a minority program, and goals and objectives of such a program.

Publisher/Top Management

_____ 1. Show your commitment by assigning minorities to the board of directors.

_____ 2. Make a clear statement to your staff in written and oral communications, that your aim is to include minorities in all levels of operations. consider adding minority hiring and advancement to your organization's MBO's.

_____ 3. Establish staff incentives for bringing in minority candidates and becoming involved with community work.

_____ 4. Are community service dollars given to traditional
          establishment charities and organizations, or reaching a
          fair share of non-traditional, newly identified community
          needs? People who are not used to corporate dollar support
          can make the money you give go much farther than those who
          get the support routinely (and perhaps are no longer asked
          to account for it or re-justify the need).

_____ 5. Is some of each manager's time invested in organizations
          providing contact with segments of the community of their
          every day routine?

NEWSROOM

_____ 1. Develop lists of minority community contacts for news
          staff use (churches, business and labor, schools, other
          professionals, civic clubs, and volunteers).

_____ 2. Review staff make up in the newsroom. Assess the gaps
          left in likelihood of picking up tips, providing contacts
          that lead to news stories or information. Make sure your
          activities fill those gaps at least until hiring can
          correct them.

_____ 3. Inventory pictures in the newspaper. Do they reflect
          the population mix? Analyze why or why not to help
          determine action needed.

_____ 4. Contact minority church pastors and funeral directors--they
          can help with weddings and engagements, funerals, job
          candidates, and general community information, especially
          regarding minority community, professional and fraternity
          or sorority groups.

_____ 5. Hold after-work discussion sessions for news staff. Include
          minorities in the mix of people invited.

_____ 6. Conduct "How to Get Coverage" workshops and include minority
          organizations.

_____ 7. Review wire budgets regularly. Do selections used reflect
          information news of the whole community?

_____ 8. Check regular handling of news in other newspapers or news
          media when you suspect that traditional values may have
          interfered with broader understanding of events or issues.

ADVERTISING DEPARTMENT

_____ 1. Does the sales staff approach minority businesses?

_____ 2. Are non-traditional skills that could translate to success in advertising being considered when minorities apply for positions?

_____ 3. Does the personnel mix preclude the possibilities of broadening your outreach to minority businesses? Do your activities compensate for the situation until hiring can correct it?

PROMOTIONS DEPARTMENT

_____ 1. Speeches to the community should reflect a cross-section. See opportunities for minority managers to speak to mainstream groups.

_____ 2. Do your promotional materials reflect diversity? (Brochures, orientation packets, slide shows, etc.)

_____ 3. Do you run house ads to promote good people, including minorities.

CIRCULATION

_____ Assess the racial mixture of the carrier force. Determine the turnover in minority neighborhoods. Consider reducing the number of carriers assigned to a distribution manager or the size of the routes in neighborhoods where parental involvement is low.

PERSONNEL

_____ 1. Determine where part-time staffers are obtained. Does network prevent minorities from getting jobs?

_____ 2. Enlist the assistance of English instructors, coaches, music instructors, publications advisors, and other educators to help in recruiting minority high school students to clerk in the newsroom and other departments.

_____ 3. Post pictures of all new employees on a bulletin board.

_____ 4. Establish business-side internships for college students.

GENERAL

_____ 1. Share newspaper and magazine articles on minority issues
with your staff.

_____ 2. Select minority employees to help organize staff functions.

_____ 3. Organize activities out of the office to enable employees
to interact with each other.

_____ 4. Make industry information available to all including
Editor & Publisher, Presstime, NAB, NPRA, INAME, and ICMA
publications.

_____ 5. Check the library subscription lists, special
interest publications and newspapers.

_____ 6. Ask your minority staff members and community contacts to
help with any or all of this.

COMMUNITY PROMOTIONAL TECHNIQUES

In-Paper Ads

_____   Write an ad for your newspaper emphasizing the newspaper commitment to minority hiring.

_____   Create a brochure that emphasizes all the programs you are conducting to widen opportunities for minorities.

_____   Use minorities in the newspaper's advertising and promotional material.

In writing your ads, find out which ad size would be used most in your newspaper.

Run your ads throughout the year. If possible, an ad a week—if not, one every two weeks. Send these to the local minority media groups each quarter for publication in their newsletter.

There are some basic rules to remember in writing these ads:

Direct all ads to the minority community.

Always list telephone number readers can call for additional information.

If you use a coupon, make it large enough for them to write in legibly.

Headline is important—make sure it will catch the reader's eye.

Direct Mail

Write letters directed to:

_____   Minority Community Service Organizations

_____   Minority Media Organizations

_____   Minority Businesses

_____   Educators

Letters can be sent to promote your availability for meetings. This letter should go to community service organizations.

Letters on the program and services available should go to minority media organizations.

Letters that promote the availability of newspaper personnel for speaking engagements can be sent to schools with a sizable minority population and to community organizations.

Letters on topics appearing in the newspapers which might be of interest to minorities should be sent to minority organizations and minority businesses.

Letters can also have a coupon attached for readers to send in for more information.

ALWAYS include your telephone number and address in all correspondence.

Other ideas:

> Develop a brochure to explain all the programs and services available to minorities.

> Your brochure can be sent to organizations and schools for posting.

> Develop a poster to be placed in schools, community centers, etc.

PARTNERS IN PROGRESS
Year-end Report
September 30, 1988

Unit: _____   Unit No.: _____

Prepared by _____   Phone No.: _____

Reviewed by _____   Date Submitted: _____
                    (Unit Head)

SECTION I (EMPLOYEE PROFILE)

Number of Employees — 9/30/88
(Full and part-time positions)

Top Four Job Categories	TOTAL	MALE					FEMALE					TOTAL FEMALE	TOTAL MINORITY
		W	B	H	A	AI	W	B	H	A	AI		
Officials & Managers													
Professionals													
Technicians													
Sales													
TOTAL TOP FOUR													
% of Top Four	100%											%	%
Top Four SMSA* **												%	%
TOTAL ALL EMPLOYEES													
% of Total	100%											%	%
TOTAL SMSA*												%	%

	Total	Female	Minority
Top Four Employment at 9/30/88			
Top Four Employment at 9/30/87			
Variance (1988 minus 1987)			

	Total	Female	Minority
Total Employment at 9/30/88			
Total Employment at 9/30/87			
Variance (1988 minus 1987)			

*Standard Metropolitan Statistical Area (SMSA) labor statistics can be obtained from the Department of Labor. Or, you may use the percentages derived from availability analysis (8-factor analysis) provided that information has been submitted for approval.

**If Top Four statistics are not available, use Total SMSA %.

PIP Year-end Report — Page 2   UNIT:_____ No.:_____

SECTION II (JOB OPPORTUNITIES — TOP FOUR JOB CATEGORIES)
(Review of openings and how they were filled)

Top Four Job Opportunities (10/1/87 — 9/30/88)
(Full and part-time opportunities)

Job Categories	TOTAL	MALE					FEMALE					TOTAL FEMALE	TOTAL MINORITY
		W	B	H	A	AI	W	B	H	A	AI		
NEW HIRES													
Officials & Managers													
Professionals													
Technicians													
Sales													
TOTAL NEW HIRES													
LOCAL INTERNAL APPOINTMENTS													
Officials & Managers													
Professionals													
Technicians													
Sales													
TOTAL INTERNAL APPOINTMENTS													
COMPANY TRANSFERS IN													
Officials & Managers													
Professionals													
Technicians													
Sales													
TOTAL TRANSFERS IN													
TOTAL JOB OPPORTUNITIES (Total new hires, internal appointments and transfers.)													
Officials & Managers													
Professionals													
Technicians													
Sales													
TOTAL TOP FOUR OPPORTUNITIES													
% of Job Opportunities	100%											%	%
Top Four SMSA*												%	%

Position Type	New	Replacement	Total Jobs Filled
Officials and managers			
Professionals			
Technicians			
Sales			
TOTAL TOP FOUR POSITIONS			

* Use total SMSA if top four statistics not available.

PIP Year-end Report—Page 3   UNIT:_____ No.:_____

SECTION III (EMPLOYEE SEPARATIONS)

Voluntary Employee Separations (10/1/87 — 9/30/88)
(Full and part-time)

Job Categories	TOTAL	MALE					FEMALE					TOTAL FEMALE	TOTAL MINORITY
		W	B	H	A	AI	W	B	H	A	AI		
Officials & Managers													
Professionals													
Technicians													
Sales													
TOTAL VOLUNTARY TOP FOUR SEPARATIONS													
TOTAL VOLUNTARY ALL SEPARATIONS													

Involuntary Employee Separations (10/1/87 — 9/30/88)
(Full and part-time)

Job Categories	TOTAL	MALE					FEMALE					TOTAL FEMALE	TOTAL MINORITY
		W	B	H	A	AI	W	B	H	A	AI		
Officials & Managers													
Professionals													
Technicians													
Sales													
TOTAL INVOLUNTARY TOP FOUR SEPARATIONS													
TOTAL INVOLUNTARY ALL SEPARATIONS													
*TOTAL TOP FOUR SEPARATIONS													
*TOTAL ALL SEPARATIONS													

*Add voluntary and involuntary separations.

SECTION IV — INTERNS (College level)

Interns (10/1/87 — 9/30/88)

Job Categories	NUMBER OF INTERNS									MALE					FEMALE				
	TOTAL			MINORITY			FEMALE												
	N	S	G	N	S	G	N	S	G	W	B	H	A	AI	W	B	H	A	AI
Professionals																			
Technicians																			
Sales																			
Other																			
TOTAL																			

N = non-paid or working for college credit
S = interns whose salary is completely paid by the unit.
G = interns whose salary is partially or fully paid by Corporate.

UNIT:_____ No.:_____

SECTION V (MINORITY/FEMALE VENDOR ANALYSIS)

	Vendor Analysis (10/1/87 — 9/30/88)				
	White Female Vendors	Minority Female Vendors	White Male Vendors	Minority Male Vendors	Total All Vendors
Number of Vendors used					
Total Dollars spent	$	$	$	$	$

Total Dollars Spent with Female Vendors $_____

Percent of Total Vendor Dollars Spent with Female Vendors _____%

Total Dollars Spent with Minority Vendors $_____

Percent of Total Vendor Dollars Spent with Minority Vendors _____%

Total Dollars Spent with Female and Minority Vendors $_____

Percent of Total Vendor Dollars Spent with Female and Minority Vendors _____%

SECTION VI (Community Relations/Special Achievements)

Describe any special outreach efforts aimed at enhancing a strong presence in your community.

These activities may be reported by type:

Educational, Minority/Female Organizations, Civil, Organizational Support, and Volunteerism

You might also include such special activities as: Volunteer work organized by your unit, representation at special community functions, recruitment at job fairs, contributions/grants to local organizations that impact minority and female issues.

COMMUNITY RELATIONS

ACTIVITIES	OBJECTIVE	RESULTS

(Please use additional sheets if more space is needed.)

SPECIAL ACHIEVEMENTS

List minority/female appointments at the department head level and above and other special achievements relating to affirmative action progress at your unit.

_____

_____

_____

_____

_____

(Please use additional sheets if more space is needed.)

PIP Year-end Report—Page 5 UNIT:_____ No.:_____

SECTION VII: FORMAL EEO COMPLAINTS FILED

List all formal EEO complaints filed between October 1, 1987 and September 30, 1988. Indicate type (Race, handicap, sex, age, etc.) and current status (Pending, Closed, Withdrawn, Settled) of complaint.

COMPLAINTS	DATE	TYPE	STATUS

Number of Formal Complaints filed this year: _____

Number of Formal Complaints filed this year, by Type:

Race _____   Handicap _____   National Origin _____

Sex _____   Age _____   Religion _____   Other _____

Number of Formal Complaints filed this year, by Status:

Pending	(Under investigation)	_____
Closed	(Agency determined no cause)	_____
Withdrawn	(Complainant withdrew complaint)	_____
Settled	(Decided for or against unit)	_____

List all unresolved formal complaints filed before October 1, 1987.

COMPLAINTS	DATE	TYPE	STATUS

UNIT:_____ No.:_____

Part-Time Employee Analysis

SECTION VIII (PART-TIME EMPLOYEE PROFILE)

Number of Part-Time Employees — 9/30/88

Top Four Job Categories	TOTAL	MALE					FEMALE					TOTAL FEMALE	TOTAL MINORITY
		W	B	H	A	AI	W	B	H	A	AI		
Officials & Managers													
Professionals													
Technicians													
Sales/Advertising													
Sales/Circulation													
Sales/Other													
TOTAL TOP FOUR—P/T													
TOTAL ALL EMPLOYEES—P/T													

SECTION IX (PART-TIME JOB OPPORTUNITIES — TOP FOUR JOB CATEGORIES)
(Review of part-time openings and how they were filled)

Top Four Job Opportunities (10/1/87 — 9/30/88) — Part-Time

	TOTAL	MALE					FEMALE					TOTAL FEMALE	TOTAL MINORITY
		W	B	H	A	AI	W	B	H	A	AI		
TOTAL PART-TIME JOB OPPORTUNITIES (Total P/T hires, internal appointments and transfers.)													
Officials & Managers													
Professionals													
Technicians													
Sales/Advertising													
Sales/Circulation													
Sales/Other													
TOTAL TOP FOUR OPPORTUNITIES—P/T													

Part-Time Position Type	New	Replacement	Total Part-Time Jobs Filled
Officials and managers			
Professionals			
Technicians			
Sales/Advertising			
Sales/Circulation			
Sales/Other			
TOTAL TOP FOUR POSITIONS—P/T			

UNIT:_____ No.:_____

Part-Time Employee Analysis (Cont'd.)

SECTION X (PART-TIME EMPLOYEE SEPARATIONS)

Part-Time Voluntary Employee Separations — 10/1/87—9/30/88)

Job Categories	TOTAL	MALE					FEMALE					TOTAL FEMALE	TOTAL MINORITY
		W	B	H	A	AI	W	B	H	A	AI		
Officials & Managers													
Professionals													
Technicians													
Sales/Advertising													
Sales/Circulation													
Sales/Other													
TOTAL VOLUNTARY P/T TOP FOUR SEPARATIONS													
TOTAL VOLUNTARY P/T ALL SEPARATIONS													

Part-Time Involuntary Employee Separations (10/1/87 — 9/30/88)

Job Categories	TOTAL	MALE					FEMALE					TOTAL FEMALE	TOTAL MINORITY
		W	B	H	A	AI	W	B	H	A	AI		
Officials & Managers													
Professionals													
Technicians													
Sales/Advertising													
Sales/Circulation													
Sales/Other													
TOTAL INVOLUNTARY TOP FOUR SEPARATIONS													
TOTAL INVOLUNTARY ALL SEPARATIONS													

Part-Time Voluntary and Involuntary Separations (10/1/87 — 9/30/88)

	TOTAL	MALE					FEMALE					TOTAL FEMALE	TOTAL MINORITY
		W	B	H	A	AI	W	B	H	A	AI		
*TOTAL PART-TIME TOP FOUR SEPARATIONS													
*TOTAL ALL PART-TIME SEPARATIONS													

*Add Voluntary and Involuntary Separations

UNIT EVALUATION SELF-RATING SHEET (1000 POINT SCALE)

UNIT NAME _____   UNIT # _____

	1988			1987		
	Minority	Female	Total	Minority	Female	Total
Number of Top Four Employees	___	___	___	___	___	___
PERCENT MINORITY/FEMALE	___%	___%		___%	___%	
TOP FOUR SMSA	___%	___%		___%	___%	
PERCENT OF TOP FOUR SMSA ACHIEVED	___%	___%		___%	___%	
Total Number of Employees	___	___	___	___	___	___
PERCENT MINORITY/FEMALE	___%	___%		___%	___%	
TOTAL SMSA	___%	___%		___%	___%	
PERCENT OF TOTAL SMSA ACHIEVED	___%	___%		___%	___%	

SECTION I — CREDIT FOR ACHIEVEMENT OF TOP FOUR AND TOTAL SMSA GOALS

If your unit has achieved 100% or more of the minority and female Top Four and Total Employment SMSA, score 900 points, transfer to overall score on reverse, and complete comments. If not, complete Sections II–V.

TOTAL SCORE
☐

SECTION II — CREDIT FOR ACHIEVEMENT OF TOP FOUR SMSA GOALS (Maximum 400 points)

Circle points earned for minorities and females, and add them for point score.

% of Top Four SMSA achieved	Minority	Female
0% – 49%	0	0
50% – 74%	50	50
75% – 89%	100	100
90% – 99%	150	150
100% or more	200	200

Points
☐
Section II

SECTION III — CREDIT FOR ACHIEVEMENT OF TOTAL SMSA GOALS (Maximum 200 points)

Circle points earned for minorities and females, and add them for point score.

% of Total SMSA achieved	Minority	Female
0% – 49%	0	0
50% – 74%	25	25
75% – 89%	50	50
90% – 99%	75	75
100% or more	100	100

Points
☐
Section III

SECTION IV — CREDIT FOR TOP FOUR MINORITY/FEMALE EMPLOYMENT PROGRESS

Number of Top Four Job Opportunities _____			
% Filled by Minorities	_____	% Filled by Females	_____
Minority Top Four SMSA	_____	Female Top Four SMSA	_____
Minority SMSA X 150%	_____	Female SMSA X 150%	_____

A. If your unit had two or fewer top four opportunities and 100% went to minorities and/or females. OR if your unit had no top four opportunities, score 150 points.

B. If your unit had more than two top four job opportunities circle points earned for minorities and females, and add them for your point score.

	Points	
Top Four Placements	Minority	Female
If no placements were made	0	0
If placement rate < SMSA %	25	25
If placement rate = or > SMSA, BUT < 150% of SMSA	50	50
If placement rate > 150% of SMSA	75	75

Points
☐
Section IV

SUBTOTAL (Sum points from Sections II, III, and IV)   ☐
Sections II, III, & IV

(Continued on reverse)

SECTION V — CREDIT FOR SPECIAL ACHIEVEMENTS (Maximum 250 points)

	Minority	Female
INTERN PERCENTAGES	_____ %	_____ %
PERCENT OF TOTAL VENDOR DOLLARS	_____ %	_____ %

If your <u>intern</u> percentages were equal to or greater than your SMSA% for minorities or females, and/or at least 5% of your <u>total vendor dollars</u> went to females or minorities, circle the points earned below and add them for your point scores (A & B). Please attach a brief explanation for points awarded for community relations activities (C), significant placements (D), and other special achievements (E).

		Minority	Female		Points
A.	If Intern percentage < SMSA %	0	0		
	If Intern percentage = or > SMAS %	25	25	A	
B.	If Percent of Vendor Dollars < 5%	0	0		
	If Percent of Vendor Dollars = or > 5%	50	50	B	
C.	Special Achievements in Community Relations (Maximum 25 pts)			C	
D.	Placements to Operating Committee/50 pts; to other Management positions/25 points (Maximum 50 points)			D	
E.	Other Special Achievements (Maximum 25 pts)			E	

SUBTOTAL (Sum points A, B, C, D, E from Section V) [Section V]

SUBTOTAL (Sections II, III, IV from Page 1) [Sections II, III, IV]

OVERALL TOTAL (Sum Sections II-V) [   ]

1988 RATING

☐ Exceptional (900-1000) ☐ Superior (700-899) ☐ Commendable (500-699)
☐ Below Expectations (300-499) ☐ Change Needed (0-299)

UNIT EXECUTIVE'S COMMENTS — NAME: _____ DATE: _____

REGIONAL/DIVISIONAL
EXECUTIVE'S COMMENTS — NAME: _____ DATE: _____

CORPORATE EMPLOYEE
RELATIONS COMMENTS — NAME: _____ DATE: _____

Balancing the Xerox Workforce

We are on a course to balance the Xerox workforce by the 1990s. By balanced workforce we mean achieving and maintaining equitable representation of all employee groups—majority females, majority males, minority females and minority males—at all grade bands, in all functions and organizations.

We want all Xerox managers to understand why it is important to balance our workforce, what we have achieved in the three years since we implemented this strategy, and what they can do to help achieve their operating units' goals.

Balancing our workforce is sound business practice. In the short-term it will help us achieve our revenue and profit plans. Many of our major accounts, like the City of New York and the Department of the Navy, require that we demonstrate equal employment opportunity and offer upward mobility for all employees, including minorities and women.

The long-term impact may be even more significant. The U.S. workforce is shrinking, and it will continue to shrink over the next several decades. As the "baby boomers"—those born between 1946 and 1964—grow older and eventually retire, there will be fewer and fewer workers to replace them. More and more employers will be vying for fewer and fewer employees. Staying competitive demands being able to take advantage of all our human resources, regardless of race, age or sex, for all positions, from entry-level through senior management.

Achieving a balanced workforce is also one of our key human resource objectives. These half-dozen objectives, which include workforce preparedness, competitive pay and benefits, and employee communications, are focused on strategic issues of vital importance to the company and its future.

But we would balance our workforce even if we didn't have compelling business reasons. It is absolutely the right thing to do. We value our employees—minority and majority, male and female. Our role as a responsible corporate citizen demands that we be aggressive in demonstrating that Xerox is, and will continue to be, an equal opportunity employer. We will not discriminate in any aspect of employment or in any business dealings. We will take affirmative and corrective steps whenever necessary.

Responsibility for achieving a balanced workforce lies with our operating units and the corporate staff. In that respect it is treated like any other business objective. And every member of the management team, from the senior staff through first-line managers, shares in that responsibility. Managers must treat their employees fairly and equitably, in the ways they manage, recognize, appraise, reward and promote them.

Balanced Workforce: A Short Definition

A balanced workforce means that all four employee groups—majority females, majority males, minority females and minority males—are represented in all functions and at all levels in the organization. The Xerox workforce will be balanced when each group's representation equals its end-point goal.

Achieving balance starts with defining these end-point goals. Xerox uses U.S. census data and internal headcount data to calculate goals for job categories and grade bands (e.g., non-exempt clerical; exempt grades 7-9). These goals are defined in terms of percent representation, so the total for all four groups in a given category always equals 100 percent. And the goals remain constant, whether the population increases or decreases.

To measure progress in achieving their balanced workforce goals, operating units set annual targets. These targets are designed to create gradual changes in percent representation so that the end-point goals can be achieved over a number of years.

Affirmative Action: The First 20 Years

Like most employers in the 1960s, Xerox did little in the area of affirmative action until required to do so by law. But in the next 20 years the company was consistently at the forefront, taking aggressive action, while some companies adopted a wait-and-see attitude. We are, and will continue to be, one of the most progressive American companies in affirmative action.

The Beginning.
The first major piece of legislation was Title VII of the Civil Rights Act of 1964, which outlawed discrimination—in education, housing and employment—on any basis. The following year President Johnson issued Executive Order 11246. This order established affirmative action as a means to improve education and employment opportunities for minorities and, later, women. It required employers to initiate affirmative action plans and established the Office of Federal Contract and Compliance Programs to monitor them. Like other government suppliers, Xerox was required to comply with the order or risk losing government contracts.

The First Decade: Plans and Programs.
The company responded by initiating programs to hire minorities in both Rochester and field locations. These early programs, which were focused primarily on black males, received public praise.

In 1968 Chairman Joseph Wilson and President Peter Mc-Colough wrote to all Xerox managers. They acknowledged that the company—despite a number of significant steps—"simply has not gone far enough." They committed to intensive recruiting of minorities, and they charged Xerox managers with the responsibility of hiring and training them. "We must do more," they said, "because Xerox will not condone the waste of a great national resource. It will not compromise the conviction on which the success of this enterprise and the nation depends."

Later that year the company funded and provided management consulting to a minority-owned and -operated plant that supplied Xerox parts. In the following year Xerox initiated training to make managers aware of the legal requirements of affirmative action and the changes taking place in the workforce.

The company also became involved from a social action perspective. When Rochester, then site of corporate headquarters, suffered race riots in the mid-sixties, senior managers worked actively with civic and religious leaders to seek solutions to the city's problems. In the late sixties and early seventies Xerox sponsored television programs, like *Of Black America*, designed to raise public awareness of racial problems. Both *The Autobiography of Miss Jane Pittman*, the most popular show the company sponsored, and *I Will Fight No More Forever*, the story of Chief Joseph of the Nez Perce Indians, received critical acclaim.

In 1971 Chairman C. Peter McColough established a "million dollar fund" to set up affirmative action programs throughout Xerox. The following year he wrote to all Xerox managers and supervisors, identifying affirmative action as a business priority. Each of them, he said, would be held accountable for progress in affirmative action. McColough's action was without precedent among major employers at that time. He placed Xerox in a leadership position with respect to affirmative action.

The company set up procedures and systems to support the manager's affirmative action responsibility. First, Xerox began to develop numerical targets for representation of minorities at various levels. The process for developing these targets was based on eight "availability" factors defined by the federal government (see page 7). A key element of this process was identifying pivotal jobs and targeting minorities and women to fill them. A pivotal job is one that typically leads to upper-level positions and, ultimately, to the executive level. Sales manager and district manager are examples of pivotal jobs.

Second, by the mid-seventies every manager's performance appraisal included a section on affirmative action. Up to 15 percent of a manager's appraisal in human resources depended on the actions taken to hire and promote minorities and women.

The Availability Approach.

The federal government had developed a method for establishing representation targets for minorities and women. The availability estimates help answers questions like:

- What percent of new-hire engineers in El Segundo should be Hispanic?

- What percent of new hire engineers in Rochester should be women?

Availability estimates are based on weighted averages of the eight factors listed in the box on page 7. Initial targets focused on the hiring of minorities. Their scope was later expanded to include women as well as minorities, and promotions as well as hiring.

The Second Decade: Progress.

During the late 1970s affirmative action efforts began to emphasize opportunities for women. The expansion of Xerox businesses into Texas and California led to increased hiring of Hispanics and Asian Americans.

By the early eighties affirmative action had formally become part of the human resources strategic plan. This plan's objective is to incorporate human resource issues into the business planning process, so that resources will match the needs of the business.

Five affirmative action objectives were established to support the human resources plan. These objectives focused on defining and achieving a balanced workforce; aggressively pursuing upward mobility for minorities and women; integrating affirmative action into the everyday process of doing business, both within the company and with our external customers and suppliers; and communicating the role of affirmative action to Xerox people.

Availability Factors

National, state, city and county data is reported by the U.S. Census; Xerox data is collected internally.

The employable population	People age 16 and over residing in the state
Unemployment	The number of unemployed people in the state
Total labor force	People who are either employed or seeking employment in the local area (usually defined as a county or metropolitan area)
Requisite skills available locally	People in the local labor market who have the required skills to perform a given job (e.g., drafting)
Requisite skills recruitable	People in the recruitable labor market who have the required skills to perform a given job
Available internally	Xerox people in the specific internal "feeder" job group
College enrollment	People enrolled in college or professional school programs that will equip them with the required skills
Available internally with training	Xerox people enrolled in Xerox training programs related to a given job (not currently included in calculating availability estimates used by Xerox)

Xerox senior management endorsed these objectives in 1983 and specifically committed to an action plan to move women into executive-level positions throughout Xerox.

1984 Assessment.

In 1984 the company took stock of what had been achieved during the two decades since Congress outlawed discrimination in employment. This assessment identified both accomplishments and problems.

On the positive side:

• Goals had been achieved for both minorities and women in non-exempt jobs and entry-level exempt positions

• For minority males, a number of goals in middle- and upper-level grade bands had been achieved

• Affirmative action had been firmly established as the manager's responsibility.

On the negative side:

• Goals had not been achieved for upper-level and executive positions. Women, both majority and minority, were significantly under-represented

• Although minorities and women were still significantly under-represented in some organizations and functions, a number of employees perceived affirmative action as having "gone overboard," thereby limiting the opportunities available to white males.

How to improve both upper-level representation and employees' perceptions while maintaining the progress to date was the problem confronting the company. The solution, which has made Xerox the benchmark company in affirmative action, is explained in the next article.

A Balanced Workforce: The Goal for the 1990s

Xerox has consistently been in the forefront of affirmative action, a leader among progressive companies working to solve a major national problem.

In the sixties that meant aggressively recruiting and developing blacks. In the seventies it meant hiring women sales representatives and sponsoring technical training programs to prepare women for service jobs. It meant hiring Hispanics and Asians, as well as blacks, as we expanded our operations in California and Texas.

We intend to continue our preeminent position in the eighties and nineties. In this decade it means breaking the "glass ceiling" that has prevented large numbers of minorities and women from moving into executive positions. It means balancing our entire workforce, so that all kinds of people are represented in all functions at all levels in the organization.

The key word is balance. Over-representation of a minority group—minority males, for example—is just as much of an imbalance as over-representation of majority males. We have a strategy that addresses all employee groups, not just minorities and women.

We want to achieve balance by the mid-1990s. We'll know we've reached it when Xerox family groups—including those at the highest level—reflect the diversity of the American workforce. When a region senior staff and a district sales team both have the same mix of employee groups. When a chief engineer can be a black woman or an Hispanic man. When the president of an operating unit can be a woman. When an operating unit's head financial officer can be black. When a region general manager can be a native American. And we'll know we have achieved balance when the novelty of minorities and women in these positions has long since passed.

The Balanced Workforce Strategy.

How are we going to get there? We have long-range goals and annual targets to bring us to those goals by the mid-nineties. We hold our managers accountable for meeting their targets. Managers are responsible for developing their people's skills and giving them the opportunity for upward mobility. When we have openings in middle management and executive-level jobs, we want to have a diversity of employees —black and white, Hispanic and Asian, male and female— ready to fill them.

Balanced Workforce Goals.

The first step of the strategy is to define precisely what we mean by a balanced workforce. Each operating unit has determined the percent representation of employee groups —majority female, majority male, minority female, minority male—that will "balance" the organization.

The goals must be quantitative and realistic, and they must comply with federal requirements. Xerox operating units have used a combination of existing approaches and innovative techniques to calculate their goals.

Non-exempt and entry-level exempt jobs.

Non-exempt job categories include skilled craft workers, labor and service workers, office and clerical workers, and operatives. Entry-level exempt jobs are those in grades 1-6 and grades 7-9.

Employees in these jobs are usually hired from outside the company. So Xerox uses the availability estimates (see page 7) as the balanced workforce goals for these categories. These estimates give an accurate picture of the proportions of the four employee groups available for hire in the operating unit's local area. There are separate goals for each job family (e.g., sales, engineering, finance) and work location (e.g., Monroe County, El Segundo) to reflect local demographics.

Upper-level exempt jobs.
These include jobs in exempt grade bands 10-12, 13-14, and 15-18. Depending on the function and level, Xerox fills from 50 to 95 percent of these positions by promoting current employees, rather than by hiring from the outside labor market. But the availability estimates provide accurate goals only if the majority of employees are hired externally. So the goals for these grade bands are calculated by giving the internal availability factor and current headcount proportionately more weight than the factors relating to external hiring. Not only are these goals more accurate, but they also reflect the dynamics of the Xerox workforce.

Most operating units have achieved relatively good balance in these grade bands by bringing minorities and women into the workforce in entry-level exempt positions. With the right development, these employees can move into upper-level jobs (grades 10 and above) just like their majority male counterparts.

Senior-level and executive jobs. These are jobs in grades 19 and above. Senior corporate management, rather than individual operating units, is responsible for both setting and achieving the goals in this grade band.

If you would like more information about the procedures for calculating balanced workforce goals, ask your affirmative action or personnel manager. He or she can provide you with a streamlined explanation of the complex procedures used.

Xerox operating units calculated their balanced workforce goals in 1985. At that time each unit projected a date for reaching its goals. For most units this time frame was about ten years (1985-1995).

Balanced Workforce Targets.

A long-term goal is easier to reach if it's broken into smaller steps. Balanced workforce targets are annual milestones to chart progress toward the goals. For each goal, there is a corresponding annual target. Targets were designed to increase the representation of groups currently below the balanced workforce goal in a series of incremental steps leading to that goal. An operating unit that achieves its targets each year will reach its goals on schedule.

The balanced workforce performance report on the next page shows the goals and this year's targets for a sample operating unit. Although based on a hypothetical operating unit, this example is similar to the actual reports used in your unit.

The report shows headcount, current representation, the balanced workforce goal and the current year's balanced workforce target. In many cases the balanced workforce goals have already been achieved, so there is no target. In this organization, majority females are under-represented in all grade bands except 1-6. Majority males are under-rep-

resented in grade bands 7-9 and 1-6. Minority females are under-represented in grade bands 15-18, 13-14 and 10-12. Minority males are under-represented in the 13-14 grade band. Under-represented groups have been targeted for opportunities (see page 14).

Measuring Progress.

At least three times a year operating units review their progress toward balanced workforce goals. The senior management team looks at several factors to assess progress.

First, they look at current representation with respect to this year's target and the long-term goal. Is representation moving in the right direction? Will this year's target be achieved? If not, what recovery plans will be necessary to ensure progress next year? (Next year's target, based on the assumption that this year's target will be met, represents even more of a challenge.)

Balanced Workforce Performance Report

Grade Band	Employee Group	Head- count	Current Rep (%)	End-Point BWF Goal (%)	Annual BWF Target (%)
15-18	MajFem	10	5	23	8
	MajMal	168	77	57	N/M
	MinFem	4	2	7	2
	MinMal	36	16	13	N/M
Total		218	100	100	
13-14	MajFem	38	8	20	10
	MajMal	377	76	58	N/M
	MinFem	9	2	7	3
	MinMal	71	14	15	15
Total		495	100	100	
10-12	MajFem	126	9	18	11
	MajMal	954	69	60	N/M
	MinFem	38	3	6	3
	MinMal	265	19	16	N/M
Total		1383	100	100	
07-09	MajFem	326	19	23	21
	MajMal	821	49	57	57
	MinFem	150	9	7	N/M
	MinMal	391	23	13	N/M
Total		1688	100	100	
01-06	MajFem	164	29	16	N/M
	MajMal	169	30	67	35
	MinFem	96	17	4	N/M
	MinMal	138	24	13	N/M
Total		567	100	100	

N/M: no measurement; balanced workforce goal has already been achieved.

Second, they look at the distribution of opportunities among the four employee groups. An opportunity is a personnel "transaction" that moves an individual into a job or grade level, including:

- A promotion

- A transfer-in from another operating unit (e.g., into marketing from corporate headquarters)

- Hiring a new employee from outside the company.

Opportunities represent the means to achieve balanced workforce targets and goals. If opportunities are not used to adjust representation in the right direction, the goal will never be achieved. In the sample organization (see page 13), majority women should participate in the current-year opportunities to achieve the annual target in the 15-18 grade band. In the 7-9 grade band, however, majority males are the underrepresented groups. To the extent that they share in the opportunities in this grade band, their representation will increase.

Finally, senior management looks at details below the summary level shown in the chart. Balanced workforce implies balance among all minorities and across all functions. That means an operating unit should not achieve a minority female goal exclusively with blacks; Hispanics, Asians and other minority groups must be represented as well. Likewise, a grade-band goal should not be achieved with representation in a limited number of functions like Sales or Personnel. Women and minorities have to be represented in all functions, including finance, data processing, engineering and service.

A Progress Report.

Three years after its implementation, the balanced workforce strategy has achieved significant results. With their attention focused on under-represented employee groups, managers are preparing longer-term plans for developing and moving their employees. And that has led to upward mobility for all employee groups. Annual measurements indicate that women now represent 29 percent of managers, a three-fold increase since 1977. During the same time the representation of minorities has doubled in the categories of managers (from 9 to 18 percent) and professionals (from 10 to 20 percent).

Xerox has also been recognized as the benchmark company for its approach to affirmative action. Other Fortune 500 companies have sought us out and requested information on how the company achieved the results to date, and how the balanced workforce strategy, with its long-term goals and annual targets, works.

Most operating units have achieved some of their balanced workforce goals, but no operating unit has reached all its goals. There is much to be accomplished over the next decade.

Balancing the Workforce: The Manager's Role

As an individual manager, you may not have been directly involved in setting your operating unit's balanced workforce goals and targets. But you are involved in reaching them. Actions that you take can either help or hinder achieving balanced workforce targets and, ultimately, goals.

Develop your people. Give your people growth assignments that will challenge them and help them acquire new skills. High-visibility assignments—task forces, problem solving and quality improvement teams—can give your employees exposure to your manager and others in the organization. Check that minorities and women get their share of these assignments.

Find out what Xerox training and development courses will help employees develop their potential, and make sure they have the opportunity to attend. Talk realistically with all your employees about their career paths.

Find out what your operating unit's balanced workforce goals and targets are. Ask your manager to review the goals and targets for your organization, so that you can better understand where the "under representation" is. If you have an opening, find out if a specific group is targeted for an "opportunity" before you fill it. If your unit is having difficulty reaching its targets, work with other managers and use the quality tools and processes to address the issue.

Use the Management Resources Planning (MRP) process.
Xerox has a planning tool to help managers prepare employees for middle- and senior-management positions. Look for long-range opportunities for employees in under-represented groups. Talk with your manager about the minorities and women in your group with potential for these jobs and your plans for developing them.

Ensure that your human resource practices are fair and equitable. When you appraise people, evaluate them on their performance against their objectives. Don't make assumptions—positive or negative—about any particular employee group. Make sure all employees get the benefit of your coaching and counseling.

Find out what motivates each of your employees. Employees with different cultural backgrounds may not respond to the same kind of motivation that you do. Some people enjoy public recognition, for example, while it makes others uncomfortable. If you know your employees as individuals, you'll be able to tailor your management style to bring out their best performance.

Make sure that your people understand the goals of affirmative action. Talk with your employees about what Xerox affirmative action is trying to achieve and why balancing our workforce is the right thing to do.

With 7,000 Xerox managers working on achieving balanced workforce goals, success is virtually assured.

Summary of Terms

affirmative action
process of correcting imbalances in the representation of minorities and women in the workforce. First enacted into law by Executive Order 11246 (1965), requiring that all government contractors establish affirmative action plans with stated goals and timetables for achieving targeted levels of minorities and women. Affirmative action addresses specific classes of employees; equal employment opportunity, on the other hand, focuses on the individual.

availability
percentage of minority females, majority females, minority males and majority males accessible to hiring in a specific city, county or state, usually within a 35-mile radius of the place of employment

balanced workforce
key objective of the long-term direction of affirmative action, as defined by the end-point goals (see balanced workforce goals)

balanced workforce goals
end-point goals, by operating unit and grade band, for representation of majority females, majority males, minority females and minority males to be achieved within a designated time frame, and then maintained

balanced workforce targets
incremental steps for achieving balanced workforce goals; planned for achievement on an annual basis

eight-factor availability analysis
calculated percentage of four employee groups (majority female, majority male, minority female, minority male) and minorities (Asian, black, Hispanic and native American) accessible for hiring as a result of weighting the statistical estimates of population, unemployment, total labor force, skills in the local labor market, skills in the recruitable labor market, internal Xerox representation and college enrollment data

equal employment opportunity
the right of an individual to be
considered as a candidate for
hire or promotion solely on the
basis of his or her qualifications and ability to meet the
job requirements. Enacted into
law as the Civil Rights Act of
1964, which prohibited discrimination in personnel practices on the basis of race,
color, sex or national origin.
These categories have been expanded (e.g., by the Equal
Employment Opportunity Act
of 1972) and now include handicapped individuals, persons
between the ages of 40 and 70,
and disabled and Vietnam
veterans.

feeder base
workforce population used to
generate balanced workforce
goals in the 10-12, 13-14 and
15-18 grade bands. For most
calculations, the feeder base
consists of employees in the 1-
6 and 7-9 grade bands (calculations for marketing organizations include grade bands for
sales and service as well as 1-6
and 7-9).

grade band
grouping of employees in
Xerox exempt job grades 1
through 6; 7 through 9; 10
through 12; 13 and 14 ; 15
through 18; and 19 and above

job family
grouping of Xerox job codes
into functional areas, such as
data processing, engineering,
finance, legal, manufacturing,
management, marketing, personnel, scientific and service

majority
grouping of all employees
with the race classification of
white (origins in any of the
original peoples of Europe,
North Africa or the Middle
East)

minority
grouping of all employees
with race classifications of
black (origins in any of the
black racial groups of Africa);
Asian or Pacific islander (origins in any of the original
peoples of the Far East, South-
east Asia, the Indian subcon-
tinent, or the Pacific islands);
American Indian or Alaskan
native (origins in any of the
original peoples of North
America); and Hispanic (Mexican, Puerto Rican, Cuban, Central or South American, or
other Spanish culture or origin, regardless of race).

operating unit
major group (e.g., U. S. Marketing Group, Business Products and Systems Group) or
division (e.g., Real Estate /
General Services Division)
within Xerox Corporation

opportunity
a personnel "transaction"—
like hiring, promotion or transfer—that moves an individual
into a new job or grade level

pivotal job
a job—like sales manager or
district manager—that typically leads to upper-level and executive positions

representation
percentage of a given
employee group (majority females, majority males, minority females and minority
males) currently employed in a
specific operating unit, grade
band

upward mobility
process by which employees
are identified, developed and
moved into middle- and senior-
management positions

AFFIRMATIVE ACTION AT XEROX

JOURNEY TO WORKFORCE 2000

XEROX HAS BEEN RECOGNIZED AS A (SOME SAY *THE*) BENCHMARK COMPANY IN AFFIRMATIVE ACTION. THIS HAS BEEN CONFIRMED IN THE MOST CONCRETE MANNER - *WE HAVE BEEN CALLED ON BY OTHER FORTUNE 5OO COMPANIES TO SHARE THE SECRETS OF OUR SUCCESS* AND *XEROX WAS RECOGNIZED BY THE DEPARTMENT OF LABOR WITH ITS EXEMPLARY VOLUNTARY EFFORT (EVE) AWARD.*

SINCE PRESIDENT JOHNSON SIGNED THE EXECUTIVE ORDER ESTABLISHING AFFIRMATIVE ACTION AS A MANDATORY REQUIREMENT FOR COMPANIES DOING BUSINESS WITH THE FEDERAL GOVERNMENT, THIS SUBJECT HAS BEEN DEBATED, LITIGATED, CASTIGATED AND SOME HAVE EVEN TRIED TO TERMINATE IT.

WE AT XEROX HAVE DEBATED THE ISSUE FROM TIME TO TIME; AND UNFORTUNATELY, WE HAVE ALSO BEEN LITIGANTS, ALWAYS FROM THE DEFENDANT POSITION. HOWEVER IN NO CASE HAVE WE EVER BEEN AMONG THE PEOPLE WHO CASTIGATED OR TRIED TO TERMINATE AFFIRMATIVE ACTION. IN FACT, WE EMBRACED AFFIRMATIVE ACTION FULLY (IN SOME RESPECTS, IT COULD BE SAID AFFIRMATIVE ACTION EMBRACED US.)

WE ARE EXTREMELY PROUD OF OUR RECORD AND ACCOMPLISHMENTS IN *AFFIRMATIVE ACTION AT XEROX.*

WE ARE ALSO VERY MUCH AWARE OF HOW MUCH MORE WORK WE HAVE TO DO IN *AFFIRMATIVE ACTION AT XEROX* TO ACHIEVE THE GOALS WE HAVE SET FOR OURSELVES.

AFFIRMATIVE ACTION AT XEROX HAS BEEN A 20 + YEAR JOURNEY; THERE HAVE BEEN TIMES WHEN THIS JOURNEY HAS BEEN CALLED AN ODYSSEY. AND IN SOME RESPECTS THAT WOULD BE AN APT DESCRIPTION, ODYSSEY BEING DEFINED AS "AN EXTENDED ADVENTUROUS WANDERING."

AFFIRMATIVE ACTION AT XEROX HAS BEEN ANYTHING BUT <u>WANDERING</u>. SINCE WE UNDERTOOK THIS JOURNEY, WE HAVE BEEN FOCUSED WITH CLEAR OBJECTIVES. WE HAVE MODIFIED OUR OBJECTIVES AS WE DETERMINED APPROPRIATE.

FROM ITS INCEPTION, *AFFIRMATIVE ACTION AT XEROX* WAS DECLARED BY TOP MANAGEMENT TO BE A COMPANY VALUE, A BUSINESS OBJECTIVE AND A MANAGEMENT PRIORITY. WITH THIS COMMITMENT BEING MADE EARLY IN THE GAME, *AFFIRMATIVE ACTION AT XEROX*, WHILE DIFFICULT AND CHALLENGING, IS ACHIEVABLE.

WE HAVE BEEN WORKING THIS ISSUE FOR A LONG TIME AT XEROX; AND WE STILL HAVE A GREAT DEAL MORE WORK AHEAD OF US.

MANAGING A DIVERSE WORK FORCE

AS WE MOVE AHEAD WITH OUR EFFORTS TO ACHIEVE A BALANCED WORKFORCE, WE ARE AWARE THAT THE CHALLENGES WILL INCREASE AND NEW ISSUES WILL ARISE. WE ARE NOW BEGINNING TO DEAL WITH SOME OF THESE ISSUES:

- THE NEED FOR BETTER UNDERSTANDING BETWEEN THE DIFFERENT GROUPS - MALES AND FEMALES; BLACKS, WHITES HISPANICS, ASIANS AND AMERICAN INDIDANS;

- THE NEED FOR MINORITY AND FEMALE GROUP MEMBERS TO LEARN TO WORK WITH AND *FOR* EACH OTHER.

SUMMARY

FOUR KEY MANAGEMENT PRACTICES HAVE RESULTED IN XEROX BEING *"THE EMPLOYER OF CHOICE"*:

- VISIBLE TOP MANAGEMENT COMMITMENT AND CONTINUING INVOLVEMENT

  (STEADFAST COMMITMENT OF CEO)

- EXPLICIT OBJECTIVES, STRATEGIES AND DIRECTION

  (GOAL AND TARGE SETTING AND CONSTANT INSPECTION)

- HEALTHY AND PRODUCTIVE INTERCHANGES WITH OUR EMPLOYEES - FEMALE & MALE, MINORITY & MAJORITY

- STAYING THE COURSE IN GOOD TIMES AND BAD TIMES

AT XEROX, MANAGEMENT NOT ONLY TALKS AFFIRMATIVE ACTION, WE LIVE IT.

AS WE SAY AT XEROX, *WE WALK LIKE WE TALK*!

KEY TRENDS - WORKFORCE 2000

■   U. S. ECONOMY EXPECTED TO GROW AT A RELATIVELY HEALTHY PACE

■   MANUFACTURING SECTOR WILL BE A MUCH SMALLER SHARE OF THE U. S. ECONOMY

■   U. S. WORKFORCE WILL GROW SLOWLY - BECOME OLDER, MORE FEMALE, MORE MINORITY

■   NEW JOBS WILL PRIMARILY BE IN THE SERVICE INDUSTRIES AND WILL DEMAND MUCH
    HIGHER SKILL LEVELS

DEMOGRAHPIC FACTS OF WORKFORCE 2000

■   THE U. S. POPULATION AND WORKFORCE WILL GROW MORE SLOWLY THAN AT ANYTIME
    SINCE THE 1930's.

■   THE AVERAGE AGE OF THE POPULATION AND THE WORKFORCE WILL RISE WHILE THE POOL
    OF YOUNG WORKERS ENTERING THE LABOR MARKET WILL SHRINK.

■   MORE WOMEN WILL ENTER THE WORKFORCE, ALTHOUGH THE RATE ON INCREASE WILL
    TAPER OFF.

■   MINORITIES WILL BE A LARGER SHARE OF NEW ENTRANTS INTO THE LABOR FORCE.

■   IMMINGRANTS WILL REPRESENT THE LARGEST SHARE OF THE INCREASE IN THE
    POUPULATION AND THE WORKFORCE SINE THE FIRST WORLD WAR.

CHALLENGES TO SUCCESS - 2000 & BEYOND

- **STIMULATE AND ACHIEVE BALANCED WORLD GROWTH**

- **IMPROVE PRODUCTIVITY IN SERVICE INDUSTRIES**

- **MAINTAIN THE DYANMISM OF AN AGING WORKFORCE**

- **RECONCILE THE CONFLICTING NEEDS OF WOMEN, WORK AND FAMILIES**

- **INTEGRATE BLACK AND HISPANIC WORKERS FULLY INTO THE WORKFORCE**

- **IMPROVE THE EDUCATIONAL PREPARATION OF ALL WORKERS**

The Journey To Work Force 2000
Xerox Employment Representation

1978 Vs. 1988

| | 1978 | | | | | 1988 | | | | |
	Total	Minority #	%	Female #	%	Total	Minority #	%	Female #	%
Off/Mgrs	7,549	810	10.7	721	9.6	7,191	1,331	18.5	1,423	19.8
Profess'l	9,060	1,107	12.2	1,630	18.0	9,851	1,980	20.1	2,859	29.0
Sales	6,102	1,036	17.0	1,360	22.3	5,402	1,136	21.0	2,196	40.7
Technician	11,597	2,066	17.8	711	6.1	15,414	3,696	24.0	1,438	9.3
*Total	54,463	9,789	18.0	15,900	29.2	53,162	12,921	24.3	17,125	32.2

*Includes all job categories

XEROX   The Xerox Manager

Interpretive Information for Xerox Managers

Number 12
May 2, 1968

To All Xerox Managers:

We at Xerox are among those who are compelled to accept
the indictment of the National Advisory Commission on
Civil Disorders: "What white Americans have never fully
understood -- but what the Negro can never forget -- is
that white society is deeply implicated in the ghetto.
White institutions created it, white institutions maintain
it, and white society condones it."

We, like all other Americans, share the responsibility for
a color-divided nation; and in all honesty, we need not
look beyond our own doorstep to find out why.

In Rochester, one of the first American cities scarred by
racial strife, Xerox continues to employ only a very small
percentage of Negroes. In other major cities, including
some that have suffered even greater violence, we employ
no Negroes at all.

Thus, despite a stated policy that seeks to fulfill our
obligations to society -- and even though the significant
steps we have taken have been publicly praised -- our
performance is still far from a shining beacon of corporate
responsibility.

We know, of course, that many Negroes - fearing rejection -
simply don't apply to Xerox for jobs. And of those who do
apply, many fail to meet our usual standards of qualification.
But those factors obviously cannot be used as excuses. They
are, rather, the very problems which Xerox must and will attack
in the future.

In order to respond with concerted action to the Advisory
Commission's recommendations that American industry hire,
train and suitably employ one million Negroes within the
next three years, we are therefore going to adopt these
immediate courses of action:

Corporate Communications / Internal Communications

First, we will heavily intensify our recruiting of Negroes
and other minorities. If, as our past experience indicates,
they are reluctant to come to us, then we will go to them.

A special recruiting effort at University Microfilms in
Ann Arbor, Michigan has proved the validity of this approach
by substantially increasing minority employment in the space
of a few months. We will now extend that effort throughout
all the departments, divisions, and subsidiaries of Xerox.

Secondly, all managers responsible for hiring -- regardless
of geographical location -- will re-examine their selection
standards and training programs. Our past efforts, by and
large, have sought to find only the "best qualified" people
for Xerox, regardless of age, race or religion. But that
goal, however valid, has inadvertently excluded many good
people from productive employment.

We are, accordingly, going to change the selection standards
that screen out all but the most qualified people. We will
also begin devoting special attention to minority employees
of limited qualifications to make them genuinely productive
in the shortest possible time. Hopefully we can maintain
standards of performance throughout.

Effective immediately, therefore, all Xerox managers are
directed, on an individual basis, to begin this effort, pending a more systematic company-wide revision of standards.

Thirdly, we are planning to increase substantially our training of unqualified Negroes, and other minority members.

Although the Project Step Up Program to qualify people for
"entry level" jobs has been successful in the Rochester area,
we feel that its scope must be considerably broadened and the
entry requirements modified. We are presently planning to
incorporate the program into our present hiring process, and
to extend it to major Xerox facilities outside Rochester.

The full and unqualified cooperation of all Xerox managers
is expected in reaching our minority hiring goals. Corporate
Personnel has been given the responsibility for implementing
our plans, and for establishing an accountability system
through which top management -- beginning immediately -- can
regularly assess progress in all divisions, departments and
subsidiaries of the corporation.

Today there are 22 million Negroes in the United States.
The exclusion of many of them from our society is a malig-
nancy that the nation cannot endure. To include them as
integral to the nation, however, will mean even more than
the correction of an intolerable injustice. It will also
mean the creation of an enormous and affluent market for
new products and services, and of an equally enormous pool
of manpower to help meet the critical shortages predicted
for the future.

We are fully aware, of course, of the progress that Xerox
has already made in assisting the civil rights movement.

But it simply has not gone far enough.

We must do more because Xerox will not add to the misery of
the present condition of most Negroes. It will not condone
the waste of a great national resource. It will not compromise the conviction on which the success of this enterprise
and of the nation depends.

Reprinted by permission.

**American
Association For
Affirmative
Action**

PAUL C. BAYLESS
President

May 26, 1989

Mr. James Lynn
Chairman and Chief Executive Officer
The Aetna Life and Causalty Company
151 Farmington Avenue
Hartford, CT 06156

Dear Mr. Lynn:

The American Association for Affirmative Action is a nationwide, volunteer organization of over 1,000 individuals and employers, from both public and private sectors, who are dedicated to the development and enhancement of EEO/AA programs and to professional growth in the field.

We are pleased to announce that the Aetna Life and Casualty Company has been named the winner of our Association's **Corporate Friends of Affirmative Action** award for 1989.

Your company is being recognized for its longstanding support of affirmative action as evidenced by corporate public involvement in issues of equal access and equal opportunity, your outstanding record of minority hiring and upward mobility, the strong top-level commitment to educational outreach and development programs, and the company's excellent utilization of minority vendors and contractors.

A plaque will be presented during ceremonies at our upcoming 15th annual national conference, in the Imperial Ballroom of the Fairmont Hotel, New Orleans. For your information, a conference brochure is enclosed. The Awards Banquet will commence at 8:00 p.m., Tuesday, June 6, 1989. We certainly hope that you can be there in person to receive the commendation.

I congratulate you and The Aetna for your outstanding record and commitment to affirmative action. To confirm your acceptance of the award, please contact Ms. Jocelind Gant, our Awards Committee Chairperson. Ms. Gant is Director of Affirmative Action at the University of Massachusetts-Harbor Campus in Boston, and may be reached at (617) 929-7075.

Sincerely,,

Paul C. Bayless
AAAA President

PCB:
cc: Jocelind Gant, Awards Committee Chair
        Judi Burnison, Association Headquarters

RECEIVED

MAY 3 1 1989

CHAIRMAN'S OFFICE

Purdue University • 401 South Grant Street • West Lafayette. IN 47907 • (317) 494-7254

AMERICAN SOCIETY FOR
TRAINING AND DEVELOPMENT   NEWS

1630 Duke Street
Box 1443
Alexandria, VA 22313

703-683-8100

FOR RELEASE: NOT BEFORE AM JUNE 5   Contact: Helen Frank Bensimon
                                                   703/683-8123
                                                   June 4-8 call:
                                                   617/262-9600

AETNA RECEIVES CORPORATE AWARD
FROM ASTD

BOSTON, MA (June 5, 1989)--The Aetna Life and Casualty
Company today received the Corporate Award for excellence in
education, training and development programs from the
American Society for Training and Development (ASTD).

The award is presented annually by ASTD to a company
which has shown outstanding commitment to workplace
education and employee development.

The presentation to Aetna recognizes the company as a
leader both in creating innovative employee training and
development programs to meet the changing needs of the
financial services industry, and in educational outreach
within its communities to develop the employees of the
future.

Previous recipients of the award have included the Ford
Motor Company, the Dayton-Hudson Corporation, Motorola,
Inc., and IBM.

-more-

Accepting the award from Curtis E. Plott, executive vice president of ASTD was Richard A. McAloon, vice president for corporate human resources at Aetna. The presentation was made at ASTD's 45th National Conference here, which for the first time included a separate conference on training in the Financial Services industry.

"Aetna is a national leader in recognizing that its employees are its greatest asset, and has made a $40 million annual commitment to training and upgrading them," Plott said. "The company has made opportunities available to all levels of its workforce, including the use of innovative technology to reach the large number of employees in the field. But Aetna also has made a unique contribution to its communities, by pioneering outreach programs to train and develop new generations of employees."

In accepting the award McAloon said, "We are convinced that productivity and business growth at Aetna, and for the financial services industry, are rooted in the successful development and training of the employees on whom we rely to serve our customers. We've made major investments in these efforts because we know that to do otherwise would be to limit our ability to grow and prosper."

Aetna's commitment to education is most visible in the Aetna Institute for Corporate Education, through which more than 28,000 employees per year, at all levels of the company, participate in learning events on topics ranging from management education to basic literacy training.

-more-

Among Aetna's outstanding training and development
programs for employees are:

● The Aetna Management Process, which is the basis of
Aetna's education and training efforts. It trains
managers techniques used to systematically determine
business objectives and map out factors critical to
success in reaching those objectives.

● Technical training in insurance disciplines such as
underwriting, marketing, claims and systems, to enable
Aetna employees and agents to effectively confront
challenges in a rapidly changing business environment.

● The Effective Business Skills School, which provides
training to 1,500 employees a year to develop and
improve skills in reading, writing, mathematics, verbal
communications and computer skills.

● The Learning Design Process Model, a tool used by
Aetna to develop new training methods that are
progressive, timely and cost effective, and designed to
strengthen the competence of all employees.

Aetna takes advantage of the latest technological
advances, including computer-based instruction and direct
broadcast satellite television to bring training from its
home office directly to employees in 94 field locations
across the country.

● Stepping Up, a three-part program to deal with the
employability gap among disadvantaged groups in the
communities Aetna serves. Stepping Up comprises:

                         -more-

● Saturday Academy, an innovative program to provide
educational enrichment to inner city junior high school
students and their parents, which serves more than 400
youngsters and adults each year in Hartford, Connecticut and
Washington, D.C.

● Students at Work, which provides work/study
opportunities and motivation for high school students
who are at risk of dropping out. Students are
guaranteed regular full-time jobs with Aetna if they
complete the program and graduate from high school.
The program is now operating in Houston, Dallas,
Philadelphia, Atlanta, Sacramento, Seattle, and Walnut
Creek/Oakland.

● Hire and Train programs, which are aimed at youth and
marginally or unemployed adults in Aetna communities
who are identified by local community and government
agencies. The individuals have their educational needs
assessed and receive training tailored to their needs
to prepare them for entry-level jobs at Aetna.

The American Society for Training and Development is
the world's largest organization in the field of
employer-based training, representing 50,000 professionals.

-30-

APPENDIX D

SURVEYS

BNA Questionnaire (D-3)

Excerpts from Sirota Alper & Pfau Survey (D-7)

Excerpts from Korn/Ferry International's Executive Profile:
A Survey of Corporate Leaders in the Eighties (1986) (D-31)

Excerpts from Korn/Ferry International's Executive Profile:
A Survey of Corporate Leaders (1979) (D-39)

(Pages D-3 to D-5 contain the BNA questionnaire discussed in Chapter III of the report.)

GENERAL INFORMATION

1. Company location: _____
                                        (city and state)

2. Number of employees: _____

3. Industry (check one):

    _____ Manufacturing

    _____ Transportation, communication, utility

    _____ Retail trade

    _____ Banking, finance, insurance, real estate

    _____ Hospital, health care

    _____ Government

    _____ Other (specify): _____

4. Are any employees represented by a union? ___ Yes ___ No

5. Which of the following titles best describes your job duties?

    _____ EEO officer

    _____ Human resource/personnel officer

    _____ Chief executive officer/president

    _____ Other (specify): _____

ADVANCEMENT OF WOMEN

1. Approximately what percentage of your organization's management work force is composed of women? _____ %

2. How aggressive is your organization in seeking and training women for management positions?

   _____ very aggressive

   _____ somewhat aggressive

   _____ not very aggressive

   _____ not at all aggressive

3. To what extent do you think sexism is an obstacle to advancement of women in your organization?

   _____ to a great extent

   _____ to some extent

   _____ to little extent

   _____ not at all

   _____ don't know

4. In comparison with other employers, how would you rate your organization's record on advancement of female employees?

   _____ much better than other employers

   _____ somewhat better than other employers

   _____ about the same as other employers

   _____ much worse than other employers

   _____ no basis for judgment/don't know

5. How do you think the federal government should approach its role in promoting the advancement of women?

   _____ federal government should increase its efforts

   _____ federal government's role should remain about the same

   _____ federal government should decrease its efforts

MINORITY ADVANCEMENT

1. Approximately what percentage of your organization's management work force is composed of racial minorities (e.g., black, Hispanic, Asian)? _____ %

2. How aggressive is your organization in seeking and training minorities for management positions?

   ____ very aggressive

   ____ somewhat aggressive

   ____ not very aggressive

   ____ not at all aggressive

3. To what extent do you think racism is an obstacle to advancement of minorities in your organization?

   ____ to a great extent

   ____ to some extent

   ____ to little extent

   ____ not at all

   ____ don't know

4. In comparison with other employers, how would you rate your organization's record on advancement of minority employees?

   ____ much better than other employers

   ____ somewhat better than other employers

   ____ about the same as other employers

   ____ much worse than other employers

   ____ no basis for judgment/don't know

5. How do you think the federal government should approach its role in promoting the advancement of minorities?

   ____ federal government should increase its efforts

   ____ federal government's role should remain about the same

   ____ federal government should decrease its efforts

Reprinted with permission.

HOW THE INTERESTS OF

KEY CORPORATE CONSTITUENCIES

CONVERGE AND CONFLICT

DATA SUMMARY

SIROTA ALPER & PFAU

OUTLINE

Study Rationale

Study Objectives

Method:

- **Who-When-How**

- **Questions Asked:**

    • **Constituency Goals Examined by the Survey**

    • **Profit Distribution Fairness**

Results:

- **Views of Profit Distribution Fairness**
    • **Summary**

- **Goals and Priorities**
    • **Summary**

- **Gap Analysis: Goal Importance vs. Satisfaction for Each Stakeholder Group**
    • **Summary**

Conclusions

STUDY RATIONALE

- **Corporate Success Is Critically Affected by the Attitudes and Behavior of Key Corporate Constituencies:**

  - Employees
  - Customers
  - Communities
  - Investors

- **Vital for Companies to Strengthen Relationships With These Groups**

- **Scientific Diagnosis of Constituency Attitudes Is a Prerequisite of Effective Action**

STUDY OBJECTIVES

1. To Compare the Interests of Key Corporate Constituencies — How These Interests Converge or Conflict

2. To Examine How Well Corporations Meet Constituency Interests

METHOD

Who: National Random Samples of:

- Institutional Investors (100)

- Mayors (100)

- Procurement Executives, i.e., Business-to-Business Customers (100)

- Employees (350)

When: February 1989

How: Telephone Interviews

METHOD (Cont'd)

Questions Asked:

- Constituencies Were Asked How **Important** a Number of Characteristics are to Them in Their Dealings With Companies

Then

- How **Satisfied** They are With the Performance of Companies On Each of the Same Characteristics

METHOD (Cont'd)

Questions Asked: (Cont'd)

- **Constituencies Were Also Asked About Their Views of Profit Distribution Fairness:**

  When the Profits of Companies are Distributed, How Do You Feel About:

  - **The Amount of Compensation Top Management Receives**

  - **The Amount of Compensation the Rest of the Company's Employees Receive**

  - **The Amount of Dividends Stockholders and Other Investors Receive**

  - **The Amount of Money Reinvested in Activities Such as Research and Development, Plant Modernization, etc.**

  - **The Amount of Funds Distributed to the Community**

MAYORS' GOALS FOR CORPORATE PERFORMANCE

Rank	Goal	% Describing Goal as "Necessary"
1	Ethical Corporate Behavior	71
2	Environmental Protection	51
3	Honest Communication	44
4	Even-Handed Government Affairs	42
5	Competent Top Management	29
6	Quality Products and Services	20
7	Community Views Sought	19
8	Innovativeness	16
9	Active EEO	15
10	Industrial Develop. Assistance	15
11	Charitable Contributions	15
12	Upholding Human Rights	15
13	Steady Employment Growth	14
14	Stable Company Ownership	14
15	Workplace Efficiency	14

MAYORS' GOALS FOR CORPORATE PERFORMANCE (Cont'd)

Rank	Goal	% Describing Goal as "Necessary"
16	Educational Support	14
17	Social Problem Assistance	14
18	Profitability	14
19	Cultural Activity Support	13
20	Child Care Assistance	9
21	Civic Association Participation	8

MAYORS' GOALS FOR CORPORATE PERFORMANCE...IN SUM:

Most Important:

- **Ethical Corporate Behavior**
- **Environmental Protection**
- **Honest Communication with the Community**
- **Even-Handed Conduct of Governmental Affairs**

Least Important:

- **Civic Association Participation**
- **Child Care Assistance**
- **Cultural Activity Support**
- **Social Problem Assistance**
- **Profitability**

Ethical and Responsible Behavior More

Important Than "Giving" Activities (but

Latter Not Unimportant)

On the Following Page are the Total Distributions (i.e.,

Not Just "Necessary") for These Goals:

RESPONSIBLE CORPORATE BEHAVIOR VS. CORPORATE GIVING
(Total Distributions)

"How important is it in deciding whether you want a company to be part of your community that it..."

	Neces-sary	Quite Impor-tant	Some Impor-tance	Little/No Impor-tance
. Protects the environment	51	45	4	0
. Conducts its governmental affairs in a fair and responsible manner	42	45	11	2
. Contributes to community charities	15	46	31	8
. Supports community cultural activities	13	43	33	11

EMPLOYEE GOALS FOR CORPORATE PERFORMANCE

Rank	Goal	% Describing Goal as "Necessary"
1	Safe Working Conditions	54
2	Ethical Corporate Behavior	51
3	Good Benefits	50
4	Honest Company Communications	48
5	Respectful Treatment	47
6	Good Equipment and Resources	44
7	Competent Top Management	44
8	Quality Products and Services	40
9	Good Pay	39
10	Comfortable Working Conditions	35
11	Good Training	35
12	Job Security	33
13	Advancement Opportunity	32
14	Views Sought by Management	32
15	Recognition	31

EMPLOYEE GOALS FOR CORPORATE PERFORMANCE (Cont'd)

Rank	Goal	% Describing Goal as "Necessary"
16	High Performance Standards	29
17	Stability of Company Ownership	29
18	Fair Workload	28
19	Profitability	27
20	Workplace Efficiency	26
21	Innovativeness	25
22	Cooperative Atmosphere	24
23	Decision-Making Autonomy	24
24	Job Challenge	23
25	Active EEO	21
26	Child Care Assistance	14

EMPLOYEE GOALS FOR CORPORATE PERFORMANCE...IN SUM:

Most Important:

- Safe Working Conditions/Good Benefits/Respectful Treatment

- Ethical Corporate Behavior

- Honest Company Communications

- Good Equipment and Resources/Competent Top Management

- Quality Products and Services

EMPLOYEE GOALS FOR CORPORATE PERFORMANCE...IN SUM:
(Cont'd)

Least Important:

- Child Care Assistance

- Active EEO

- Job Challenge/Decision-Making Autonomy/Innovativeness

- Cooperative Atmosphere

- Workplace Efficiency/Company Profitability

The Following Pages Show the "Gaps" Between the Rated Importance of Each

Goal and the Rated Satisfaction (e.g., If a Goal is Rated Very High in

Importance -- Many Saying It is "Necessary" -- but Very Low in Satisfaction,

the "Gap" Would be Large and Negative. Conversely, Relatively Unimportant

Goals With Which There is High Satisfaction Could Have a Satisfaction

"Surplus"). The Idea of This Analysis is to Weight Satisfaction by

Importance.

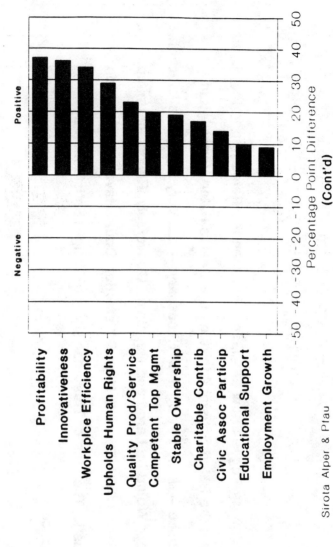

Gap Between Goal Importance
and Satisfaction for <u>Mayors</u>

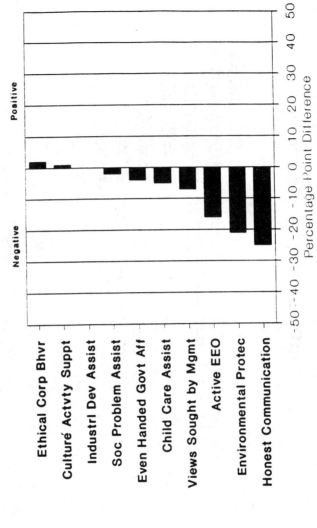

Gap Between Goal Importance and Satisfaction for Mayors *(Cont'd)*

Negative — Positive

Ethical Corp Bhvr
Culturé Actvty Suppt
Industrl Dev Assist
Soc Problem Assist
Even Handed Govt Aff
Child Care Assist
Views Sought by Mgmt
Active EEO
Environmental Protec
Honest Communication

Percentage Point Difference

-50 -40 -30 -20 -10 0 10 20 30 40 50

Sirota Alper & Pfau

MAYORS' "GAP" ANALYSIS...IN SUM:

- **Mayors Show Significant "Surplus" Satisfaction with Various Aspects of Corporate Performance:**

  - Profitability
  - Innovativeness
  - Efficiency
  - Upholding Human Rights
  - Quality of Products and Services

- **Their Widest Satisfaction "Gaps" Involve:**

  - Honesty of Company Communications
  - Environmental Protection
  - EEO

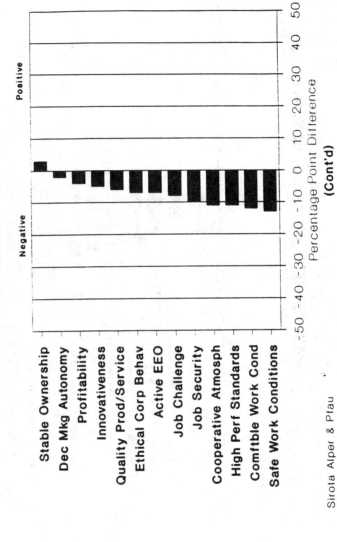

Gap Between Goal Importance
and Satisfaction for Employees

Sirota Alper & Pfau

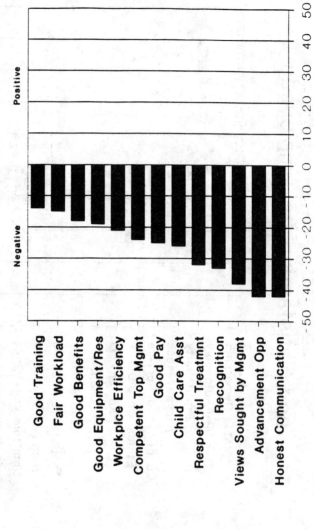

Gap Between Goal Importance and Satisfaction for Employees *(Cont'd)*

Sirota Alper & Pfau

EMPLOYEES' "GAP" ANALYSIS...IN SUM:

- Employees Show Narrowest "Satisfaction Gaps" Regarding:

  - Stability of Company Ownership

  - Decision-Making Autonomy

  - Profitability

  - Innovativeness

  - Quality of Products and Services

  - Ethical Corporate Behavior

  - EEO

  - Job Challenge

EMPLOYEES' "GAP" ANALYSIS...IN SUM: (Cont'd)

- Employees Show Widest "Satisfaction Gaps" Regarding:

    - Honesty of Company Communications

    - Advancement Opportunity

    - Management's Effort to Seek Employees' Views

    - Recognition

    - Respectful Treatment

"Korn/Ferry International's Executive Profile: A Survey of Corporate Leaders in the Eighties" (1986)

I. Background and Introduction

In 1979, Korn/Ferry conducted a survey of senior level executives of our nation's largest corporations. The results were published in "Korn/Ferry International's Executive Profile: A Survey of Corporate Leaders." The principal objective of the present study is to provide an updated and expanded version of the 1979 study.

Both studies were designed to gather data on the background and characteristics of a unique group of individuals—executives who occupy leadership positions in their companies and who are perceived by us and by the general business community as highly successful in their chosen fields.

We concentrated our attention on senior executives at large companies in the belief that they are the trend setters for the rest of the business community. Not only do these executives set the pace and direction for the corporate world, but they constitute a pool of talent upon which other companies tend to draw for both managerial expertise and guidance.

The objective of our study was to find out what these senior executives have in common regarding goals, attitudes, background and family life. We were interested in their motivation, their priorities and their paths to corporate success. In addition, we wanted to find out how these factors had changed in the six years since our last survey.

As in 1979, we have not included in our study chief executive officers and presidents because we feel that there is already ample data available on this much-publicized group. Instead, we have focused on the next level of responsibility—the group from which future CEOs and presidents will be selected—executive vice presidents, senior vice presidents, group vice presidents, functional vice presidents and corporate specialists. The data we have gathered present a detailed overview of this group, delineating the many features they share as well as providing clues to smaller but potentially significant trends now detectable within the group as a whole.

The study was designed to solicit information about the executives in four major areas of concern: business career, education, early background and personal life.

On the basis of the data gathered in the survey, we hoped to:
- produce a clear, accurate and timely description of the senior executive population;
- construct a composite profile of the typical senior executive;
- consider any changes in the description and profile since the 1979 study.

Prompted by the results of the 1979 survey, the following questions reflect areas of continued interest to us:
- How do executives define success?
- What single factor is most often identified as bringing about success?
- Which functional areas are seen as being the quickest route to upper management?
- Is academic background correlated to success?
- Are executives more or less mobile than they were in 1979?
- What do executives perceive to be the greatest threats to their careers?
- Have more women and minorities reached the senior executive ranks since 1979?

As in the previous survey, it was agreed that the study should include only senior level executives in large, publicly held corporations. Vice presidents were selected as the target population in order to isolate and define a specific level of corporate responsibility below the CEO and president but above middle management.

In 1979, the study's sample population was selected from the *Fortune* 500 Industrials and the *Fortune* Service 250. The decision to work with the *Fortune* executives, a clearly defined population, was consistent with our desire to have a basis for comparison with the 1979 study.

Since then, *Fortune* has expanded its service companies list to 500, and thus with the *Fortune* 500 Industrials more accurately reflects what we believe to be the current mix of companies in the economy. With a target of five executives per company, the survey population was raised from 3,750 to 4,350.

Relative to the type of company, our final tabulation of respondents was as follows:

Type of Company	Percent
Industrial	42%
Banking and Diversified Financial	13%
Insurance	8%
Transportation	6%
Retail	5%
Other	19%
No response	7%
Total	100%

Vice presidents were selected from specific functional areas as well as from general management. A conscious effort was made to include representatives from as many of the different functional areas as possible in each company.

Our final count of respondents showed that 44% considered themselves in general management, 23% in finance/accounting, 7% in marketing/sales, 6% in a professional/technical area, 6% in personnel, 2% in production/manufacturing and 1% in international.

In determining the sample size, our chief concern was that we receive a sufficient number of responses to make the data statistically valid. Of 4,350 questionnaires mailed, we received 1,362 responses, a 31% response rate.

Our report is arranged in the following manner: Section II is a composite profile of the typical senior executive who participated in our survey. Section III consists of a detailed analysis of the survey's findings. This section contains the data upon which the composite profile is built. The documentation of the findings is presented in the tables of Section IV.

II. The Executive Profile

In this section we present a profile of the typical senior executive. Based on survey responses, the profile reflects the way executives see themselves. The profile is not intended to be a scientific construction but rather an editorialized composite based on both mean responses and the dispersion of responses. Needless to say, it does not describe any one individual.

To the outside world, the executive considered in this study is, by definition, a successful businessman. He has managed to rise to a position of power and responsibility at the top of one of the country's most prominent corporations. He himself defines success as being able to enjoy his work and as having the ability to effect change. Money, position and power are all secondary considerations in his personal definition of success. Public recognition is not particularly important to him.

While he doesn't necessarily equate success with money, our executive is handsomely paid. His average current compensation is $215,000 annually. He first broke the $100,000-a-year barrier at or before age 35, as a vice president.

He reached the major turning point in his career at age 34. He attributes that breakthrough to timing—being in the right place at the right time—and to having made a move to a different area of functional responsibility. Taking on a high-risk project and changing companies were secondary factors in achieving his breakthrough. While he did not see alignment with the right people as particularly important, he viewed having a mentor as a valuable experience. In terms of career planning, he did not have a specific goal in mind at the beginning of his career.

Our composite executive has been with his present employer for 17 years and has worked for two companies in the course of his career. However, many of his younger colleagues are much more mobile and are willing to change jobs with increasing frequency. When he has changed employers, he has sought increased job responsibility and increased challenge. In changing companies, he was not influenced by the opportunity to move to a more desirable location. Our executive has relocated only three times in his career and has never been transferred overseas. When he has refused to relocate, he does not feel his decision has had an adverse effect on his career.

He has never really considered taking a leave of absence to enter government service, nor does he think the experience would advance his career. Neither has he taken time off to continue his education.

Our composite executive sees integrity as the most important element in a successful business career. Concern for results and a desire for responsibility are also deemed necessary. He does not attribute much importance to likability and appearance nor to formal business training. However, he does feel that general education can have a significant impact on career development.

In his own personal advancement, he firmly believes that hard work was the single most important factor in bringing about his success. Ambition and luck also figured prominently.

Our composite respondent is relatively satisfied with his job. If he were starting his career over, he would enter the same or a similar field, and even if he were financially independent, he would continue to work at his present position. He enjoys working for a large corporation and has little desire to own his own business. But despite his satisfaction, our executive is ambitious and aspires to his corporation's highest position—chief executive officer.

Although our executive is currently in general management, he began his career in finance / accounting. Most of his peers are also in general management, but they too started out in a different functional area, most likely in a professional / technical capacity or in marketing / sales. Despite his personal experience, he believes that marketing / sales is now the fastest route to the top in his organization. In 10 years, he believes that marketing / sales will still be the most viable fast-track option.

While he is well paid, enjoys his work and is ambitious enough to aspire to head his corporation, our executive believes that corporate reorganization could possibly threaten his career. On the other hand, he is not concerned about threats posed by subordinates, age discrimination or technical obsolescence.

His belief in the importance of hard work is reflected in the long hours he works. His average work week is 56 hours and he takes only 14 vacation days a year. He also spends about 49 days a year, or almost 10 full work weeks, out of town on business.

Although our typical executive considers himself a hard worker, he fully intends to retire at or before 65. Only a very small percentage of his peers would like to continue working as long as possible.

Our composite senior executive received a BS from a state university and, although many of his colleagues did not attend graduate school, he went on to earn an MBA from a large and prestigious private institution. He believes his education provided him with the general knowledge and technical skills required but does not feel that the social contacts developed at school proved to be all that useful.

He worked during undergraduate school and was able to cover about 55% of his expenses. After working and studying, he still found time to participate in a few extracurricular activities—most notably he belonged to a fraternity and was active in athletics.

Our composite respondent was a first child born in 1933. He spent most of his childhood in a mid-sized Midwestern city. Many of his peers also came from the Midwest, but an almost equal number grew up in the Northeast.

He lived with both parents during childhood, and his father worked in a white-collar job. His mother did not work outside the home. He was first employed at age 14.

Our typical respondent is a 51-year-old white male. He is married, has never been divorced and has three children. His wife, like his mother, does not work outside the home. His business associates are nearly all white, male and married.

He is a Protestant, although a growing number of his peers are Catholic and Jewish. Politically, he is a conservative and a registered Republican. Only a small number of his peers consider themselves Independents and even fewer are registered Democrats. While his opinions are moderate to conservative on social issues, he is strongly conservative on fiscal issues.

If he had more free time, he would prefer to spend it with his wife and children or on hobbies and recreational pursuits such as traveling. He is not interested in spending his extra free time on social relationships or on continuing his education.

He belongs to professional organizations as well as to a country club and another private club. He does not belong to a health club, and service organizations are not part of his life. He is not a member of his company's board of directors, but he is likely to sit on an outside corporate board.

Compared with the 1979 composite, our respondent is two years younger and is much better paid in real terms. He now sees marketing/sales as the fastest route to the top whereas six years ago he believed it was finance/accounting. Both the 1979 and our current composite executive view integrity, concern for results and desire for responsibility as factors that enhance an executive's chances for success.

Our 1985 respondent works harder than he did in 1979. He puts in three hours more a week and he takes fewer vacation days—only 14 days a year compared with 16 days in 1979.

Our current composite executive shares a similar background and education with the 1979 executive. He has similar aspirations, motivations and outlooks on retirement. Like his 1979 counterpart, he is satisfied with his career and would repeat it if he had to start over again. But in spite of his satisfaction, our 1985 composite is more ambitious than he was in 1979 and now aspires to the top position in his company—chief executive officer.

Personal Data

Ninety-eight percent of our senior executive respondents are men. While the percentage of women has increased from less than 1% in 1979 to 2%, there are still few women senior executives at our largest corporations. In absolute numbers, their ranks have increased from 8 in 1979 to 29 today (Table 23).

In our respondent population of 1,362 executives, four are Black, six are Oriental and three are of Hispanic origin. As in 1979, all non-white respondents taken together still constitute less than 1% of the total (Table 24).

In 1979, we observed that the country's very largest companies had not yet made a dent in solving the problem of women and minority representation at the senior corporate level. Six years later, despite industry and government efforts to promote opportunities for women and minority executives, the progress in this area is minimal.

Table 23

Sex

Response	1985 Freq.	%	1979 Freq.	%
Male	1,331	97.7	1,695	99.2
Female	29	2.1	8	0.5
No response	2	0.2	5	0.3
Total	1,362	100.0	1,708	100.0

Table 24

Ethnic Origin

Response	1985 Freq.	%	1979 Freq.	%
White	1,343	98.6	1,693	99.1
Black	4	0.3	3	0.2
Oriental	6	0.4	2	0.1
Hispanic	3	0.2	2	0.1
Other	—	—	2	0.1
No response	6	0.4	6	0.4
Total	1,362	100.0	1,708	100.0

"Korn/Ferry International's Executive Profile: A Survey of Corporate Leaders" (1979)

I. Background and Introduction

Korn/Ferry's principal objective in conducting this study was to be able to develop a composite "profile", of senior-level executives from our nation's very largest companies. In essence, we sought to document the background and characteristics of this unique group of individuals — executives perceived by us and the general business community as being highly successful in their chosen fields, and within leadership positions in their companies. To the best of our knowledge this documentation does not now exist.

We chose to examine executives from only the very largest companies (The "Fortune 500" and "Fortune 50's") because we, at Korn/Ferry, feel that it is these companies, and their respective senior-level executives, that often provide the direction and set the trends for the remainder of the business community. It is also most often from this group of executives that other companies seek the talent that they require to conduct their own operations in a more effective and efficient manner.

It was not our objective to profile this executive group so that others could blindly emulate their methods, or assume that the views of these executives would provide the ultimate "benchmarks" for success. Rather, we recommend that executives use the profile to enhance their understanding of the survey group and improve their insight into what this group is truly like as opposed to how it is perceived. Along these lines, this data should also be of considerable use to chief executives who seek to better understand the make-up and characteristics of their senior-level subordinates.

It should be noted that we have not included presidents and/or chief executive officers of the "Fortune" companies in our study because we believe that there is already ample data available for review of this group. We have chosen, instead, to study the next level of executives, i.e., executive vice presidents, senior vice presidents, group vice presidents, functional vice presidents and corporate specialists. We chose this group because we could find no studies that determine if a commonality exists between the backgrounds, philosophies and experiences of this much larger and, therefore, potentially more significant population. Also, the successors to today's CEO's are more than likely to be chosen from this group.

Of interest is that many of the commonalities found among chief executive officers of the nation's largest companies are also found among this next level of executives. There were also, however, many areas where definite differences in backgrounds and views did emerge.

The goals of this study were:
— To determine whether commonalities exist between the backgrounds, philosophies, and experiences of senior-level executives from the nation's largest corporations.
— To produce a clear, accurate and timely "profile" of these senior executives. This group would be described in terms of demographics (both present and historical), attitudes on career management, and lifestyle.
— To provide a "benchmark" study based on sound techniques, so that comparison with future studies would produce statistically valid findings. The study would *not* be designed to produce explanatory or predictive data at this time; rather, the data collected would be descriptive in nature.

Among the more intriguing questions pondered were:
1. Which qualities or character traits are believed most important in enhancing the chances for executive success?
2. Is an executive's early background indicative of how successful he will be?
3. Is an executive's life style indicative of how successful he will be?
4. Are most senior-level executives satisfied with their careers?
5. Are senior-level executives in our nation's largest companies desirous of reaching a higher level position?

Although executives from other types of companies, institutions and organizations could have been studied to provide a basis for comparison, it was agreed that this study include only senior-level executives in large, publicly-held corporations due primarily to the substantial amount of data already available on these executives. It was further decided to limit the scope of our study to executives from the "Fortune 500" and five of the "Fortune 50's" listings (commercial banking, life insurance, diversified financial, retailing and transportation companies). This decision was not only consistent with our goal of providing a descriptive, not a comparative, study but also provided us with a very clearly defined, isolated population.

Relative to the type of company, our final tabulation of respondents was categorized as follows:

Type of Company	Percent
Industrials	61%
Insurance	12%
Banking and Diversified Financial	11%
Transportation	7%
Retail	6%
Unclassified	3%
	100%

Because we sought to insure adequate representation from all functional areas in the population of "Fortune" company executives, we chose a stratified method of sample selection. This allowed us to choose approximately five executives from each "Fortune" company, with each executive potentially representing a different functional area. These executives were chosen from the listings and biographical data in Dun and Bradstreet's *Reference Book of Corporate Managements*, 1978-1979 edition.

A conscious effort was made to include a representative sample of senior-level executives from each of the fields of marketing/sales, finance/accounting, personnel, the international area, professional/technical, production/manufacturing and general management. Due to the fact that many executives were listed only as "VP", without designating their functional area, it was often difficult to identify whether the executive was in general management or a functional discipline.

Our final tabulation of respondents shows that forty-four percent considered themselves to be in general management, twenty-two percent in finance/accounting, twelve percent in a professional/technical area, eight percent in marketing/sales, seven percent in personnel, two percent in international, two percent in production/manufacturing and three percent in all other areas.

In selecting the sample size, our chief concern was that we receive a sufficient number of responses to make the data statistically valid. We chose a rather large sample size of 3,640 to insure receiving at least a ten to twenty percent response. As it turned out, the response rate was a surprisingly high forty-seven percent, giving us 1,708 valid questionnaires.

We have arranged our report in the following manner: first we "profile" the participating senior-level executive or "composite respondent" within the nation's largest companies; we then follow with a summary and analysis of the major findings of the study which form the basis for the "profile" section; lastly, we expand upon the methodology used in this study. We include documentation of the findings within the "Exhibits" section.

II. The Executive Profile

This section presents a profile of our survey respondents as they perceive themselves, and it should serve to enhance understanding of the survey results. The profile is not a description of any one individual, but rather is an editorialized composite, based upon survey responses, of the more common characteristics of all the executives. The result is an overall image of the responding group. While this image may be helpful in understanding the detailed data, and in formulating hypotheses to be tested in future studies, it is of itself only descriptive of our sample. No other similar data was available for comparative purposes, and we hope that this study will, in fact, pave the way for future research so comparisons, over the passage of time, can be made.

Our composite respondent is a most successful business executive if we use yearly income and company position as indicators of success. His annual cash compensation (base salary and bonus) is well in excess of $100,000 per year, which does not include the normal fringe benefits provided to senior-level management within the corporate environment. Within the hierarchical structure of a company, he is one of relatively few executives who have reached a high level or position of power and prestige. He has achieved this level of success through "hard work" and firmly believes that it is "what he knows" rather than "who he knows" that has brought about his achievements.

Although he believes in executive mobility and that an executive's chances for advancement are greater if he does *not* remain with one company for his entire career, he has remained with his present employer for almost twenty years. In fact, many of his business peers have never worked for another company since their graduation from college! If he has changed positions during his career, the factors that were most influential in his decision to do so were: an opportunity for increased responsibility and challenge, and perhaps, although not necessarily, a better compensation package. He was *not* influenced by the chance for increased status or a more desirable living location for his family. He was also *not* influenced by the chance to be more creative in his work.

Although he is *not* a "workaholic", his average work week is over fifty hours long and he has found that his hours have remained constant or increased as he has risen within the corporate structure. He, unfortunately, has to spend over ten weeks out-of-town on business each year and has found that the amount of out-of-town time has also remained constant or increased as he has progressed. Interestingly, he does feel that he is still able to spend an adequate amount of time with his family, although the study did not attempt to confirm that response with his wife and children.

Last year, he was able to take three weeks of vacation although a good many of his peers only took two weeks or less. Despite the three week vacation, he feels that he has less time to devote to leisure activities.

Although he often hears about other executives having to relocate their families almost on a constant basis, he has only had to relocate his family three times during his entire business career. In fact, he knows of many executives within his own company and circle of friends who have never had to relocate! He is beginning to wonder if this question of constant relocation in order to advance in one's company is really a myth. Although he may have thought about transferring to one of his company's overseas operations for a brief period of time because he considers overseas experience valuable in terms of his professional growth, he has never been asked to do so by top management.

He has never really considered taking a leave of absence from his company to participate in government service. He also does not think that, if he did go into government service for a period of time, it would enhance his chances for corporate success. As he never really had much interest in government service, the "Watergate" era had little or no effect on his desire to serve in government.

Our composite respondent began his career in a functional as opposed to general management discipline, as did most of his peers. Finance/accounting, and professional or technical positions were the entry areas where he and his peers most often began their careers. Marketing/sales positions were also popular choices. Few of the junior executives that he began working with chose production or personnel, or sought the limited number of international positions offered, to start their careers. Still fewer were offered general management positions at the entry level. As his peers progressed within the company, many, including himself, began leaving their specialty functions and were promoted into positions within the ranks of general management. At present, with the exception of some who chose the finance/accounting route and one or two technical specialists, almost all of the executives who are at this level within the corporate structure are within the ranks of general management.

When asked which functional area he believes *currently* provides the fastest "route to the top" in his company, our composite respondent and his peers mention finance/accounting, marketing/sales and general management. Few see personnel, production, the professional/technical or international areas as providing a "fast track." As to a *future* fast "route to the top", our composite respondent and his peers continue to favor finance/accounting, were less confident of the marketing/sales route, and more confident of the general management route. A few of his peers cautiously predict, however, that the professional/technical area, and possibly the international area, *may* be future fast routes to senior-level management.

A "concern for results", first and foremost, is the character trait our composite respondent believes most enhances an executive's chance for success.

Other traits that he feels are very important are "integrity" and a desire for "greater responsibility". "Getting along with people" also rates high. "Ambition" and "creativity" are "secondary" success traits in the mind of our composite respondent. He also has little regard for such factors as "appearance", "social skills", "exceptional intelligence", and "aggressiveness" as being predictive of a successful career. Although he did *not* consider "loyalty" of prime importance, he, himself, has remained loyal to his present company for almost twenty years!

As our composite respondent does not consider "ambition" and "aggressiveness" to be prime traits for enhancing success, it is not surprising that he is most satisfied with his current position and has few aspirations for a higher position within his company. Also, even if he were financially independent, he stated that, "he would continue to work at his present position."

Contrary to what he has read, he, along with many of his peers, would like to retire at or before age sixty-five. He feels that, at age fifty-three, he still should be making a contribution to society through his work efforts even if he had enough money not to have to work. He feels that he will well deserve retirement in the not-to-distant future and has no intention to continue working after age sixty-five, although he knows that a small group of his peers would like to do so.

As a final indication of job satisfaction, our composite respondent stated that "if he were starting over", he would pursue the very same or a similar career.

Our composite respondent was born in 1926, was his parents' first child and spent the major portion of his childhood in a midwestern city with a population of about 100,000 people. Many of his business peers also came from the urban midwest, although almost as many grew up in the northeast and/or in a suburban environment.

Our composite respondent had what is often referred to as a "normal" upbringing, living with both parents, a sister and a brother during his formative years. His father was employed in a "white collar" capacity (professional/ technical, managerial, sole proprietor) and his mother did *not* work outside the home. He attended public schools for his primary education.

Our composite respondent received a bachelor of arts degree from a large public institution. Although many of his business peers did not attend graduate school, he did, and obtained an MBA degree from a large, well known private school. As an undergraduate, our composite respondent was gainfully employed and was able to cover about one-half of his college expenses by himself. On occasion, and as time permitted, he did participate in team sports. In general, he believes that his formal education was "very worthwhile as it applied to his career."

Our composite respondent has a high regard for the traditional American values of "hard work, family, education, and honesty."

He is fifty-three years old, white, male, married (and never divorced) with three children. As was the case with his own mother, his wife is not employed outside the home. His corporate peers are virtually all male, all white, and all married. Religion plays a moderate role in his daily life and he is of the Protestant faith. His peers are also mostly Protestants, a few are Catholic, and a small number are Jewish.

Our composite respondent is a registered Republican as are the vast majority of his peers. He almost always votes and considers himself to be conservative on fiscal issues and moderate to conservative on social issues. Very few of his business peers are "liberal" in their political thinking.

Our composite respondent does not now smoke or use tranquilizers. He does, however, drink "moderately" and finds that several of his colleagues drink "often".

According to our survey there are very few females employed in senior management capacities at this time within "Fortune 500" and "Fortune 50" companies. Of the 1,708 respondents, only eight, or less than one percent, are female. It will be of considerable interest for future studies to review this percentage. (Exhibit 50)

Also of considerable significance is that of the same respondent population of 1,708, only three senior-level executives are black, two are Oriental, and two are of Hispanic origin. In total, less than one percent of all respondents are non-white. (Exhibit 51)

The above figures are overwhelming, given the present emphasis by industry and government in enhancing the position of the female and minority executive. According to our data, the country's very largest companies have not, as yet, made even the slightest dent in solving the problem of female and minority employment at the senior corporate levels. However, we at Korn/ Ferry believe that figures for middle management would show a much greater minority representation.

Exhibit 50

Indicate your sex.

Sex	Absolute Freq.	Relative Freq. (Pct.)
Male	1695	99.2
Female	8	0.5
No Response	5	0.3
Total	1708	100.0

Exhibit 51

Indicate your ethnic origin (race).

Ethnic Origin	Absolute Freq.	Relative Freq. (Pct.)
White	1693	99.1
Black	3	0.2
Oriental	2	0.1
Hispanic	2	0.1
Other	2	0.1
No Response	6	0.4
Total	1708	100.0

APPENDIX E

An Analysis by the NAACP Legal Defense Fund On the Impact of the Supreme Court's Decision In *Patterson v. McLean Credit Union* (E-3)

AN ANALYSIS BY THE NAACP LEGAL DEFENSE FUND OF THE IMPACT OF THE SUPREME COURT'S DECISION IN *PATTERSON v. McLEAN CREDIT UNION*

SUMMARY

This study assesses the impact in the lower federal courts of the June 15, 1989 decision in *Patterson v. McLean Credit Union*. Between June 15, 1989, and November 1, 1989, at least 96 section 1981 claims were dismissed because of *Patterson*. Although the central holding of *Patterson* was that racial harassment was not forbidden by section 1981, most of the dismissals have involved forms of discrimination other than racial harassment.

Type of Discrimination	Claims Dismissed
Discharge	31
Promotion	16
Retaliation	8
Demotion	6
Miscellaneous Employment	6
Non-Employment	7
Harassment	22

These dismissal orders were entered in a total of 50 different cases.

The dismissals were not limited to claims of discrimination against blacks. Also dismissed were race discrimination claims by Hispanic, Chinese, Filipino, Hawaiian and Jewish plaintiffs. None of the claims thrown out under *Patterson* were class actions, none were based on a discrimination effect theory, and none—so far as can be ascertained from the opinions—was seeking quota or other affirmative action remedies. The only affirmative action dispute affected by *Patterson* was *Torres v. City of Chicago*, in which a federal court dismissed because of *Patterson* a lawsuit challenging a Chicago minority set aside program.

The decision in *Patterson* has raised a host of novel and difficult legal issues regarding the scope of section 1981. The lower courts are already sharply divided about those questions, and resolution of these complex problems is likely to require years of litigation. The ability of private attorneys to litigate these issues has been impaired by a pattern of *sua sponte* dismissals, and by a well-founded fear of Rule 11 sanctions.

For unexplained reasons, approximately one third of all dismissals and dismissal orders have been issued by the federal court in Chicago.

Introduction

On June 15, 1989, the United States Supreme Court in *Patterson v. McLean Credit Union*[1] abruptly and substantially reduced the protections which federal law had until then afforded against intentional discrimination on the basis of race. The statute at issue in *Patterson*, 42 U.S.C. § 1981, which derives from the 1866 Civil Rights Act, prohibits racial discrimination in the making and enforcement of contracts. Until the *Patterson* decision federal district and appellate courts had been virtually unanimous in construing section 1981 to forbid all forms of intentional racial discrimination in contractual relations, including all forms of racial discrimination in employment. *Patterson* effectively overruled or limited many if not most of the lower court decisions of the last two decades regarding the meaning and scope of section 1981.

Patterson itself involved, *inter alia*,[2] a claim of racial harassment in employment. The plaintiff, a black female former employee of a Raleigh, North Carolina credit union, alleged that she had been subjected to a long series of abusive comments and treatment because of her race. Ms. Patterson claimed that the firm's president repeatedly admonished her that "blacks are known to work slower than whites by nature," because "some animals [are] faster than other animals."[3] Ms. Patterson also asserted that she was regularly given more work than white employees, and that she was required to do demeaning tasks never asked of whites.[4] The minority opinion in *Patterson* held that such intentionally discriminatory practices were permitted by section 1981. The majority insisted that the section 1981 guarantee of non-discrimination in the making of a contract "extends only to the formation of a contract, but not to problems that may arise later from the conditions of continuing employment."[5] The Court reasoned that the section 1981 right to non-discrimination in the enforcement of a contract did not apply to the racially motivated breach of a contract, but encompassed only "protection of a legal process ... that will address and resolve contract-law claims without regard to race."[6]

The *Patterson* decision gave rise to a dispute as to the practical significance of this new construction of section 1981. Justice Kennedy, writing for the majority, insisted, "Neither our words nor our decisions should be interpreted as signaling one inch of retreat from Congress' policy to forbid discrimination in the private, as well as the public, sphere."[7] Justice Brennan objected, on the other hand, that "[w]hat the Court declines to snatch away with one hand, it takes away with the other."[8] Justice Stevens argued that the majority's interpretation of section 1981 was "dramatically askew" from prior decisions, "replacing a sense of rational direction and purpose in the law with an aimless confinement to a narrow construction."[9] The Administration expressed an unwillingness to support legislation to overturn *Patterson* until and unless experience demonstrated that the decision was having a significant impact.

This study undertakes to assess what the practical impact of *Patterson* has been on civil rights litigation in the federal courts during the first four and one half months since that decision was handed down. Among the federal court decisions applying *Patterson* since June 15, only a small minority are yet officially reported. A much larger number of those decisions can be found through LEXIS and FEP Cases (BNA). Also included in the study were several slip opinions which have not yet appeared in LEXIS or any official or unofficial reporter. The assessment which follows draws, as well, on interviews with several dozen attorneys handling existing section 1981 claims.

The Number of Dismissals

The impact of *Patterson* can be measured most readily by considering the number of race discrimination claims that have been dismissed by the lower courts, without ever being tried[10] and resolved on the merits, solely because of the *Patterson* decision. Between June 15, 1989 and November 1, 1989,[11] at least 96 such race discrimination claims have been dismissed by federal judges because of *Patterson*.[12] These dismissal orders were entered in a total of 50 different cases. The actual number of dismissed claims is, for a number of reasons,[13] higher than 96, but the precise figure cannot readily be ascertained. A list of cases in which section 1981 claims have been dismissed under *Patterson* is set forth at the end of this report.

The race discrimination claim dismissed in *Patterson* itself involved racial harassment; there is, as is explained below, considerable confusion regarding what other forms of racial discrimination are and are not forbidden by section 1981. Somewhat surprisingly, however, the largest category group of claims dismissed under *Patterson*, are not harassment claims at all. The largest group of claims that have been thrown out as a result of *Patterson* concerns allegations that a plaintiff was fired because of his or her race; some 31 of the dismissals are of this sort. A total of 22 racial harassment claims have been dismissed in the wake of *Patterson* as have 16 claims alleging that promotions or transfers were denied on account of race. *Patterson* has lead, as well, to the dismissal of 8 retaliation claims, and 6 demotion claims.[14]

The Characteristics of the Dismissed Claims

Prior to *Patterson*, the lower courts and the Supreme Court had interpreted section 1981 to protect not just blacks, but all racial and ethnic groups.[15] Thus, the decision in *Patterson*, narrowing the types of discrimination forbidden by section 1981, has affected claims by a wide range of plaintiffs. Among the section 1981 claims dismissed under *Patterson* have been allegations of racial discrimination against Hispanic,[16] native Hawaiian,[17] Chinese,[18] Filipino,[19] Cuban,[20] and Jewish[21] plaintiffs. In a significant number of the dismissed racial harassment claims, the plaintiffs were black women who also alleged they had been the victims of both racial and sexual harassment;[22] because of the practical difficulty of distinguishing between these two forms of discrimination, racial harassment claims prior to *Patterson* may have provided an indirect but potentially important adjunct to the limited and often inadequate remedies available under Title VII for sexual harassment.

Although involving a variety of different types of claims and plaintiffs, the dismissed claims have a number of common characteristics. First, all alleged *intentional* discrimination on the basis of race. This was to be expected, since the Supreme Court held in 1982 that section 1981 forbids solely intentionally discriminatory practices, and has no application to practices with only a discriminatory effect.[23] Second, all of the dismissed claims were individual actions, although in a few instances several aggrieved individuals joined in the same lawsuit. The decisions provide no basis for ascertaining why no class actions were involved. Third, there is no indication in these decisions that the plaintiffs were seeking as a remedy any form of affirmative action; for practical and legal reasons such affirmative action remedies in employment discrimination cases are sought primarily in class actions.

One of the dismissed claims did involve affirmative action, but not as a court ordered remedy. In *Torres v. City of Chicago*, 1989 U.S. Dist. LEXIS 9503 (N.D. Ill. 1989), *Patterson* was invoked to prevent a plaintiff from challenging the legality of a minority set aside program. The district court explained:

> The relevant facts are not in dispute. Torres is a black Hispanic female who owns and operates Legal Secretarial Services, Ltd. On July 2, 1984, Torres entered into a written contract with the City in which Legal Secretarial Services agreed to provide the City with temporary telephone switchboard operators on an "as required" basis.... On November 4, 1984, Torres received a telephone call from Francisco DuPrey, then the Deputy Director of the Mayor's Office of Inquiry and Information. During their conversation, DuPrey informed Torres that unless she could prove that black Americans control 51 percent or more of her business, the City would cancel her contract.... On November 6, 1984, DuPrey informed Torres that the City terminated her contract because s[h]e was Hispanic rather than black.

1989 U.S. Dist. LEXIS 9503 at 1-2. The district court dismissed Torres' complaint on the ground that, under *Patterson*, "Section 1981 ... does not apply to post-formation conduct where, as here, a contract allegedly is breached." *Id.* at 3.

The decisions handed down since Patterson illustrate the egregious nature of the forms of harassment, and other discrimination, for which section 1981 no longer provides a remedy. The action in *Brooms v. Regal Tube Co.,* 881 F.2d 412 (7th Cir. 1989), was brought by a 36 year-old black female who had been employed as an industrial nurse at Regal Tube Company for 16 months beginning in 1983. The district court found that during the course of her employment Brooms' supervisor, Charles Gustafson, subjected her to repeated explicit racial and sexual remarks, and in one instance directly propositioned her. On two occasions Gustafson displayed to Brooms illustrations of interracial sexual acts, and told her that she was hired to perform the kind of sexual acts depicted. On the second occasion, after Gustafson threatened to kill her, Brooms fled screaming and suffered a fall down a flight of stairs. She thereafter left Regal Tube and received two months of disability pay for severe depression brought on by the repeated harassment, which left her unable to work on a permanent basis for several years. The litigation was pending in the Seventh Circuit when

Patterson was decided; the court of appeals summarily dismissed the complaint, reasoning that the alleged harassment was lawful under section 1981.

> It is undisputed that Brooms' section 1981 claim does not relate to "conduct at the initial formation of the [employment] contract" or to "conduct which impairs the right to enforce contract obligations...." Thus, Brooms' section 1981 claims appear to be foreclosed by *Patterson* and the claim must be dismissed.

881 F.2d at 424.

In *Leong v. Hilton Hotels,* 50 FEP Cas. 738 (D. Hawaii 1989), the district court applied *Patterson* to dismiss the complaint of B. Kishaba, a Hawaiian woman of Asian extraction:

> It is undisputed that [Kishaba's supervisor] McDonough made many derogatory and discriminatory remarks about various ethnic groups.... McDonough referred to a Japanese person as a "Jap" and compared local people to "the spics in New York," stating that locals are "not capable of being supervisors" and are "incompetent".... Kishaba witnessed racist behavior of a more subtle kind. When a Jewish group attempted to contact the executive office, McDonough told her to have D'Rovencourt take care of it because "he's our resident." She asserts that there was no doubt from his manner that he meant "resident Jew".... McDonough told her..."in a contemptuous way" that "I have to have the only secretary who does the hula." Additionally, McDonough frequently used the term "you people" in such phrases as "what's the matter with you people" or "if you people don't shape up, I'll get rid of all of you." Kishaba states that "there was no doubt whatever that his references to "people" were to local Asians and Hawaiians.... McDonough adopted a rude and aggressive behavior with Kishaba, yelling at her frequently and demeaning her in front of other employees.

50 FEP Cas. at 739. The district court held that *Patterson* required dismissal of Kishaba's claim, reasoning that racial harassment, even racial harassment resulting in constructive discharge, was legal under section 1981.

In *Mason v. Coca-Cola Bottling Co.,* 1989 U.S. Dist. LEXIS 10533 (D.Kan. 1989), the defendant conceded that co-workers of its employee, Mr. Mason, had told "numerous racial jokes and used frequently racial epithets toward [him] and that plaintiff let it be known that these racially offensive practices upset him." Among the more recent incidents was a co-worker's comment that he had "never seen a depressed nigger before," after Mason's wife gave birth to a still-born child. A supervisor of Mason had also empathized with a customer's complaints that Mason, a black man, was serving her, saying "you know how they are." The district court dismissed Mason's section 1981 claims in light of *Patterson.* In *Dangerfield v. Mission Press,* 50 FEP Cas. 1171 (N.D. Ill. 1989), several black plaintiffs claimed that their employer alternately harassed, demoted and terminated them in violation of section 1981. Two of the plaintiffs alleged that officials of Mission Press refused to assign work to them, or assigned work for which they were not trained, and then verbally abused them as "stupid" and "lazy." One plaintiff claimed that the defendant demoted him while allowing a lateral transfer for a white employee in a comparable position. All three claimed that Mission Press subjected them to intense supervision not given to white employees. The district court held that "[s]uch conduct is contemptible. After *Patterson,* however, it is not actionable. At least, not under § 1981." 90 FEP Cas. at 1172.

The majority in *Patterson* insisted on a narrow construction of section 1981 in order to avoid overlapping the separate prohibitions and remedies of Title VII.

> Interpreting § 1981 to cover post-formation conduct unrelated to an employee's right to enforce her contract, such as incidents relating to the conditions of employment ... would ... undermine the detailed and well-crafted procedures for conciliation and resolution of Title VII claims ... where conduct is covered by both § 1981 and Title VII, the detailed procedures of Title VII are rendered a dead letter.... We should be reluctant ... to read an earlier statute broadly where the result is to circumvent the detailed remedial scheme constructed in a later statute.[24]

A significant number of the claims that have been dismissed in the wake of *Patterson,* however, involved discriminatory practices that were not covered by Title VII at all. In *Gonzalez v. The Home Insurance Co.,* 1989 U.S. Dist. LEXIS 8733

(S.D.N.Y. 1989), the complaint alleged that the defendant insurance companies had refused to be represented by the plaintiff insurance agency because the owners of the agency were Hispanic. In *Nolan's Auto Body Shop, Inc. v. Allstate Insurance Co.,* 718 F.Supp. 721 (N.D. Ill. 1989), the plaintiffs claimed that Allstate had cancelled an agreement for insurance repair work to be done at a garage because its owners were black. The plaintiff in *Clark v. State Farm Insurance Co.,* 1989 U.S. Dist. LEXIS 10666 (E.D. Pa. 1989), asserted that State Farm had refused to pay her legitimate insurance claim because she was black. *See also Ragin v. Steiner, Clateman and Associates,* 714 F.Supp. 709, 713 (S.D.N.Y. 1989) (racially oriented advertisement); *Torres v. City of Chicago,* 1989 U.S. Dist LEXIS 9503 (N.D. Ill. 1989). In all of these cases Title VII was plainly inapplicable. The only federal statute which arguably forbad the alleged discrimination was section 1981, but in each case the claim was nonetheless dismissed under *Patterson.*

A number of other dismissals involved employment discrimination claims which, for a variety of reasons, were not actionable or could not be remedied under Title VII. In *Guerra v. Tishman East Realty,* 1989 U.S. Dist. LEXIS 6744 (S.D.N.Y. 1989), the district court held, in light of *Patterson,* that it was legal under section 1981 for a racially motivated third party to coerce or induce an employer to fire a black worker. In *Washington v. Lake County, Illinois,* 717 F.Supp. 1310 (N.D. Ill. 1989), the judge who threw out the plaintiff's section 1981 claim also held that the plaintiff could not sue his allegedly racially motivated supervisor under Title VII because the supervisor was not an "employer" within the meaning of Title VII. In *Mason v. Coca-Cola Bottling Co.,* 1989 U.S. Dist. LEXIS 10533 (D. Kan. 1989), the district court not only dismissed the plaintiff's section 1981 harassment claims, despite acknowledging the undisputed racial harassment that had occurred, but also dismissed the plaintiff's Title VII claim on the ground that, in the court's view, Title VII did not provide a remedy for all racial harassment, but only for racial harassment that "destroy[ed] the emotional and psychological stability of the [plaintiff]."

The majority in *Patterson* assumed that the availability of a section 1981 remedy would induce plaintiffs to deliberately disregard the conciliation procedures established by Title VII. Frequently, however, the plaintiffs whose claims were dismissed under *Patterson* had indeed attempted to invoke those very Title VII procedures. In *Sofferin v. American Airlines*, 717 F.Supp. 597 (N.D. Ill. 1989), and *Hall v. County of Cook, Illinois*, 719 F.Supp. 721 (N.D. Ill. 1989),[25] the plaintiffs inadvertently forfeited their Title VII claims by filing their administrative charges with the wrong agency. In three cases the plaintiffs properly filed their administrative charges with EEOC, but were held to have delayed too long in doing so. *Byrd v. Pyle*, No. 87-3547 (CRR), D.D.C. (slip opinion, Sept. 1, 1989); *Brackshaw v. Miles*, 1989 U.S. Dist. LEXIS 12820 (N.D. Ill. 1989); *Mason v. Coca-Cola Bottling Co.*, 1989 U.S. Dist. LEXIS 10533 (D. Kan. 1989). In some cases the plaintiff carefully filed proper Title VII charges before suing under both Title VII and section 1981 because of the more efficacious remedies at times available under section 1981. Section 1981 is particularly important in harassment cases, since monetary relief often cannot be obtained in a harassment case brought under Title VII alone; in a number of the section 1981 harassment cases the plaintiff had also filed a timely Title VII claim.[26] In several other cases a section 1981 claim appears to have been joined with a Title VII claim for the purpose of obtaining a jury trial.[27]

Lower Court Opinions Interpreting *Patterson*

The impact of *Patterson* is complicated considerably by the fact that the majority opinion raises far more questions than it resolves. Prior to *Patterson* the federal courts had held that virtually all forms of racial discrimination in employment violated section 1981. The decision in *Patterson* leaves clear only two things about the scope of section 1981: a racially motivated refusal to hire violates an employee's rights under section 1981, and a practice of racial harassment, adopted after an employee was hired, does not. The Supreme Court's decision leaves in an entirely confused state the application of section 1981 to other discriminatory employment practices. The majority opinion apparently contemplates that some but not all promotion claims will remain within the scope of section 1981; whether few or many promotion decisions are still covered by section 1981, and how the line is to be drawn, are entirely unclear. The majority opinion makes no reference, favorable or unfavorable, to the large number of pre-*Patterson* section 1981 employment cases, including, for example, the Court's own prior decisions applying section 1981 to claims of discriminatory discharges.[28] *Patterson,* as a consequence, has spawned a host of novel and unprecedented new issues about the meaning of section 1981, issues which in the ordinary course of litigation could easily require a decade or more to resolve, and which will breed conflict and confusion among the lower courts.

The disagreements and uncertainty that will inevitably flow from the *Patterson* decision became apparent within a matter of months. In Colorado, for example, District Judge Arraj concluded in *Padilla v. United Air Lines,* 716 F.Supp. 485 (D. Colo. July 5, 1989), that racially discriminatory dismissals still violate section 1981 because "termination affects the existence of the contract, not merely the terms of its performance," and that the plaintiff's § 1981 discriminatory firing claim was therefore good after *Patterson.* Judge Babcock of the same District Court, on the other hand, expressly rejected Judge Arraj's interpretation of section 1981 and *Patterson,* dismissing a § 1981 termination claim case similar to that in *Padilla.* "I respectfully disagree with my colleague's rationale ... [d]iscriminatory discharge occurs after the commencement of the employment relationship and does not affect the employee's right to make or enforce contracts." *Rivera v. A.T. & T. Information Systems,* 719 F.Supp. 962 (D. Colo. 1989).

On August 14, 1989, Judge Rovner of the federal District Court in Chicago held that section 1981 does not forbid an employer from dismissing an employee in retaliation for having complained about racial discrimination. "Because [this] Court has determined that plaintiff's discharge is not actionable under section 1981, the fact that the discharge may have been retaliatory has no impact on the Court's holding." *Hall v. County of Cook, Illinois*, 719 F.Supp. 721 (N.D. Ill. August 14, 1989). *The next day* Judge Duff, also of the District Court in Chicago, reached the opposite conclusion, holding that discriminatory discharges do violate section 1981, ruling in a case in which two white plaintiffs were allegedly terminated in retaliation for their complaints to company management about racial discrimination in hiring. *English v. General Development Corporation*, 717 F.Supp. 628 (N.D. Ill. 1989). The Ninth Circuit, and one opinion in the Southern District of New York agree with Judge Rovner.[29] The Seventh Circuit, and a district court opinion in Colorado agree with Judge Duff.[30]

In *Patterson* the Supreme Court held that "[o]nly where the promotion rises to the level of an opportunity for a new and distinct relation between the employee and the employer is such a claim actionable under section 1981." 105 L.Ed.2d at 156. This "new and distinct relation" was entirely a novel concept in the law, and is certain to elicit imaginative and divergent theories among the lower courts.[31] As of today there appear to be several different interpretations of this phrase. The Fourth Circuit holds that the combination of increased responsibility and increased salary render a promotion a "new and distinct relation".[32] Judge Posner, in a recent Seventh Circuit opinion, argued that a promotion involved a "new and distinct relation" if the position was one for which a non-employee could also have applied.[33] A Colorado district court opinion holds that whether a promotion would rise to the level of a "new and distinct relation" is a question of fact for the jury or other trier of fact.[34] Another group of decisions holds that an ordinary promotion is not actionable under section 1981, and limits "new and distinct relation" to changes like that occurring when a law firm associate becomes a partner, "a transformation from employee to employer."[35] *Anderson v. United Parcel Service*, 1989 U.S. Dist. LEXIS 12195 (N.D. Ill. 1989), rejected a section 1981 promotion case because the promotion involved a significant change in duties, but only a minor increase in salary; *Williams v. National Railroad Passenger Corp.*, 716 F.Supp. 49 (D.D.C. 1989), rejected a section 1981 promotion claim because the promotion involved a significant increase in salary, but only a minor change in responsibilities. Two district court judges have expressly disapproved the standard advocated by Judge Posner in *Malhotra*; both of these judges, somewhat surprisingly, sit within the Seventh Circuit.[36] A number of other district opinions dismiss section 1981 promotion claims without ever articulating any standard at all regarding what constitutes a "new and distinct relation."[37]

There has been a divergence, as well, in the more general approach the lower courts have taken to the problems and issues raised by *Patterson*. Judge Richard Posner, a Reagan-appointee of a fairly conservative persuasion, has expressed concern as to "[h]ow many plaintiffs can successfully negotiate the treacherous and shifting shoals of present- day federal employment discrimination law." *Malhotra v. Cotter & Co.*, 50 FEP Cas. 1474 (7th Cir. 1989). Several lower court decisions have recognized the need to allow section 1981 plaintiffs to amend their complaints to include additional allegations that may now be required by *Patterson*.[38] Other courts, however, have in the wake of *Patterson* dismissed section 981 claims with an alacrity bordering on enthusiasm. Between June 15 and July 31, 1989, a majority of the orders dismissing *Patterson* claims were issued *sua sponte*; the defendants never filed any request for dismissal, and the plaintiffs were neither notified that dismissal was being considered by the court nor afforded any opportunity to submit a brief on the meaning of *Patterson*.[39] *Sua sponte* dismissals of civil claims are a debatable practice even when the law is crystal clear; in section 1981 cases, given the ambiguity of *Patterson* and the possibility that plaintiffs might be able to offer material additional allegations, *sua sponte* dismissals seem uniquely inappropriate.

A number of lower court decisions read as though the central purpose of *Patterson* was simply to throw out as many section 1981 race discrimination cases as possible. In *Sofferin v. American Airlines, Inc.,* 717 F.Supp. 597 (N.D. Ill. 1989), the plaintiff contended that promotion from a "probationary" to a "tenured" position involved a new and distinct relation within the meaning of *Patterson.* Judge Norgle rejected that contention, in part, on the ground that it would permit too many promotion claims to remain actionable under section 1981:

> Plaintiff's [contention] ... would create an exception which would swallow up the rule announced in *Patterson,* subjecting *innumerable* claims of discriminatory working conditions, which *the Court considered* better addressed by Title VII's comprehensive scheme, to review under § 1981.

(Emphasis added) In *Nolan's Auto Body Shop, Inc. v. Allstate Insurance Co.,* 718 F.Supp. 721 (N.D. Ill. 1989), the plaintiffs alleged that, after their first contract with Allstate was terminated for racial reasons, they asked Allstate to enter into a new contract, and that this request was denied because they were black. The district court did not suggest that a race based refusal to make such a new contract would somehow fall outside the literal language of section 1981 itself. Rather, Judge Bua dismissed this claim because of his fear that too many contract termination cases could successfully be repleaded in this manner:

> *Patterson's* distinction between preformation discrimination — actionable under § 1981 — and postformation discrimination — not actionable under § 1981 — would be obliterated under plaintiffs' theory of recovery. Discrimination plaintiffs could turn postformation conduct into preformation conduct simply by *alleging* that they sought a "new" contract reinstating the terms of a prior agreement.

(Emphasis added). The court evidently regarded as irrelevant the possibility that such an allegation might indeed be true. In

Dangerfield v. The Mission Press, 50 FEP Cas. 1171, the plaintiffs alleged that their employer intended, at the time it contracted with them, to imposed on them discriminatory terms of
employment. Judge Hart insisted that such discrimination be
regarded as legal under section 1981, fearful that it would otherwise be too easy for a plaintiff to state a cause of action:

> If a plaintiff can rely on post formation conduct to show the
> employer's state of mind at the time of contracting, and thereby sue
> under § 1981, then *Patterson* is essentially a nullity. In every suit, a
> plaintiff could *allege* that the employer intended all along to dis-
> criminate based on race, end that the post formation conduct is
> proof of unspoken intent. Section 1981 would in that case be used
> *to expose the exact same conduct as Patterson disallows....* Plaintiff,
> in other words, would accomplish indirectly what *Patterson directly
> prohibits.*

(Emphasis added). This passage reads as though *Patterson* had
declared that on-the-job discrimination end racial harassment
were forms of protected activity with which the federal courts,
at least in a section 1981 case, were not to interfere.

There has been an inexplicable flurry of dismissals in the
federal district court in Chicago. Approximately one-third of
all orders dismissing section 1981 claims have been issued by
federal judges in Chicago, four times as many orders as in the
next largest city, the two district courts for New York City.
More dismissal orders have been entered in Chicago, and
more section 1981 claims have been dismissed there, than in
the next six largest (in terms of dismissals) cities combined.
This has occurred, in part, because a majority of all *sua sponte*
dismissal orders in the country have been issued by Chicago
federal judges.[40] It is unclear whether these orders, or the
other Chicago federal court dismissals,[41] are the result of some
coincidence of benign factors, or reflect a substantive view of
section 1981 or civil rights claims in general.

The Broader Impact of Patterson

The judicial decisions described above are necessarily limited to the race discrimination claims of individuals who are

able to find an attorney who would take on their cases, and continue to pursue them, despite the decision in *Patterson*. Our discussions with attorneys across the country indicate that *Patterson* has had a palpable deterrent effect on attorneys asked to represent, or already representing, civil rights plaintiffs. In the wake of *Patterson* private practitioners are substantially and avowedly less willing to handle section 1981 cases, regardless of whether they may be convinced that they could prove that racial discrimination had indeed occurred. Lawyers who were already handling section 1981 cases when *Patterson* was filed are encouraging their clients to abandon those claims. In the long term this deterrent effect of *Patterson* is likely to be more important, and far reaching, than lower court opinions interpreting that decision.

Patterson has had this impact, in part, because it is perceived as reflecting or presaging an unwillingness on the part of the federal courts to award relief in section 1981 cases, if not civil rights cases generally. In most of the possible section 1981 cases considered by private attorneys, the meaning of *Patterson* and section 1981 are far from clear. But that very turmoil is often sufficient, for inexorable economic reasons, to dissuade counsel from handling these cases. Private attorneys who handle civil rights cases, of course, do not get paid unless the claim is successful. Success need not be a certainty, but when the probability of success falls too low, it makes no financial sense for a lawyer to take or pursue the case. *Patterson* has not guaranteed the failure of section 1981 promotion, transfer, discharge, dismissal, retaliation or salary claims, but the confusion wrought by *Patterson* has created a legal environment in which today, and for the foreseeable future, some meritorious section 1981 cases will not be brought simply because of that turmoil. *Patterson* will affect, as well, private enforcement of Title VII, because there are forms of discrimination, such as racial harassment, which Title VII forbids, but for which Title VII itself provides no substantial monetary remedy. Doubts created by *Patterson* are likely to discourage the filing of combined Title VII - section 1981 harassment claims; without the section 1981 element of those cases, the remaining Title VII claim will often not be worth pursuing, for either plaintiffs or their counsel. The extent to which *Patterson* has deterred or discouraged lawyers in pending litigation is reflected in cases in which plaintiffs' counsel conceded that their section 1981 claims were no longer viable,[42] or in which plaintiffs' counsel simply did not respond when the viability of those claims were challenged by the defendant or the court.[43]

Private attorneys are also being deterred from handling or pursuing these cases because of fear that the federal courts will impose sanctions on them under Rule 11 of the Federal Rules of Civil Procedure. Rule 11 sanctions are limited, at least in theory, to the filing or pursuit of frivolous claims. But in the wake of *Patterson* it is far from clear which section 1981 claims will be regarded by the courts as frivolous. In *Nolan's Auto Body Shop v. Allstate Insurance Co.*, 718 F.Supp. 721 (N.D. Ill. 1989), for example, Judge Bua denounced as a "disingenuous pleading" an allegation that a plaintiff, who originally complained of contract termination, had sought to reinstate that contract. Several other cases, however, hold that termination claims may be recast in just this manner to conform to the requirements of *Patterson.*[44] In *Matthews v. Freedman, Darryl and McCormick, Taylor & Co.*, 882 F.2d 83 (3d Cir. 1989), the Third Circuit imposed sanctions on an attorney who failed to withdraw an appeal in a section 1981 discharge case, asserting that *Patterson* "was patently dispositive of the issues" and that the appeal, in the wake of *Patterson*, was obviously "frivolous." A number of district courts, on the other hand, continue to sustain discharge claims after *Patterson.*[45] Rule 11 sanctions are not, of course, a certainty after *Patterson*; a defense motion for sanctions was recently denied, for example, in *Dicker v. Allstate Insurance Co.*, 1989 U.S. Dist. LEXIS 12482 (N.D. Ill. 1989). But the possibility that they will be sought in a given case will almost inevitably color the judgment of counsel.

The decision in *Patterson*, and the confusion which it has created, have also diminished significantly the possibility of settling section 1981 claims. In a number of pending section 1981 cases, settlement negotiations, or settlements tentatively arrived at, have collapsed as a result of *Patterson*. The settlement of a meritorious civil rights claim ordinarily requires that the relevant law and fact be reasonably clear, so that counsel for the parties can arrive at a similar assessment of the likely outcome of further litigation. In the wake of *Patterson*, however, the scope of section 1981 is an open question; today a civil rights defendant has good cause to hope that virtually any section 1981 claim will be dismissed, if not in the district court then on appeal. As a consequence, section 1981 cases which would have been settled but for *Patterson* will now be tried instead.

CONCLUSION

It is not our intent to reargue the technical legal issues addressed by the Supreme Court in *Patterson*. The majority opinion, whether or not one agrees with it, is at the least an ingenious academic exercise in the conceivable. But is an exercise that has had very serious and regrettable consequences for the men and women who have to live with the intractable realities of racial discrimination.

Patterson has not in a single blow returned the nation to the deplorable ideas and practices embraced by the Supreme Court in *Plessy v. Ferguson*. But our entire legal system is correctly premised on a recognition that individuals and officials shape their conduct in light of the likely legal consequences of those actions. When the Supreme Court reduces the likelihood that discriminatory employers can be called to account for their practices, or restricts the remedies that even a successful civil rights plaintiff can win, the Court shifts the balance of considerations that affect how employers will act.

The majority in *Patterson* insisted it had not retreated so much as one inch from the national policy to forbid intentional racial discrimination. But effective protection against invidious discrimination, like effective protection of the national security, can be imperiled as much by a weakened defense as by an overt policy of tolerating repeated assaults. This is not time for tampering with the arsenal of remedial measures that have made possible the civil rights progress of the last two decades. Creativity and flexibility continue to have an important role to play in the evolution of the law. But the hard won right of black Americans, of all Americans, to equal opportunity should not be subject to rehearing or reconsideration, even in the highest court in the land.

Eric Schnapper

Cases Dismissed Under
Patterson v. McLean Credit Union

As of November 1, 1989

Key:

H	Harassment
D	Discharge/Termination
DM	Demotion
P	Promotion/Transfer
R	Retaliation
N7	Discriminatory practice not covered by Title VII
M	Miscellaneous discriminatory treatment

Summary

Number of Claims Dismissed, by Type

Harassment	22
Demotion	6
Retaliation	8
Misc. employment	6
Discharge	31
Promotion/Transfer	16
No Title VII Coverage	7
TOTAL	96

D DM R   *Alexander v. New York Medical College*, 50 FEP Cas. 1729 (S.D.N.Y. 1989).

D   *Alvarez v. Norden Systems, Inc.*, 1989 U.S. Dist. LEXIS 9954 (S.D.N.Y. August 24, 1989).

P (5)   *Anderson v. United Parcel Service*, 1989 U.S. Dist. LEXIS 12195 (N.D.Ill. October 5, 1989). (5 plaintiffs).

H D   *Becton v. Burlington Northern Railroad Co.*, 878 F.2d 1436 (6th Cir. 1989).

H P D   *Brackshaw v. Miles, Inc.*, 1989 U.S. Dist. LEXIS 12820 (N.D.Ill. 1989).

H   *Brooms v. Regal Tube Company*, 881 F.2d 412 (7th Cir. 1989).

D P   *Brown v. Avon Products*, 1989 U.S. Dist. LEXIS 12142 (N.D.Ill. 1989).

H   *Bunyan v. Fleming Food Co.*, No. 88-9652 (E.D.Pa.)(order from the bench, September 27, 1989).

H(2) D   *Busch v. Pizza Hut, Inc.*, 1989 U.S. Dist. LEXIS 11974 (N.D.Ill. 1989).

D   *Bush v. Union Bank*, 1989 U.S. Dist. LEXIS 10936 (W.D.Mo. 1989). (3 plaintiffs)

P   *Byrd v. Pyle*, No. 87-3547 (CRR) (D.D.C.) (Slip opinion, September 1, 1989).

D   *Carroll v. General Motors*, 1989 U.S. Dist. LEXIS 10481 (D.Kans. 1989).

D   *Carter v. Aselton*, 50 FEP Cas. 251 (M.D.Fla. 1989).

N7   *Clark v. State Farm Insurance*, 1989 U.S. Dist. LEXIS 10666 (E.D.Pa. 1989).

D   *Conley v. University of Chicago Hospitals*, 50 FEP Cas. 1145 (N.D.Ill. 1989).

D   *Copperidge v. Terminal Freight Handling*, 50 FEP Cas. 812 (W.D. Tenn. 1989).

H D P   *Crader v. Concordia College*, 1989 U.S. Dist. LEXIS 12114 (N.D.Ill. 1989).

H D DM R (3)   *Dangerfield v. Mission Press*, 50 FEP Cas. 1171 (N.D.Ill. 1989). (3 plaintiffs)

P (3)   *Dicker v. Allstate Life Insurance Co.*, 1989 U.S. Dist. LEXIS 12482 (N.D.Ill. 1989). (3 plaintiffs)

N7 (2)   *Gonzalez v. Home Insurance Co.*, 50 FEP Cases. 1173 (S.D.N.Y. 1989).

D P M   *Greggs v. Hillman Distributing*, 719 F.Supp. 552; 50 FEP Cas. 49 (S.D.Tex. 1989).

H M N7   *Guerra v. Tishman East Realty*, 1989 U.S. Dist. LEXIS 6744 (S.D.N.Y. 1989).

D   *Hall v. County of Cook, Illinois*, 719 F.Supp. 721 (N.D.Ill. 1989).

H   *Harris v. Home Savings Association*, 1989 U.S. Dist. LEXIS 7015 (W.D.Mo. 1989).

D M   *International City Management Assoc. Retirement Corp. v. Watkins*, 1989 U.S. Dist. LEXIS 12201 (D.D.C. 1989).

D   *Jackson v. Commonwealth Edison*, 1989 U.S. Dist. LEXIS 10514 (N.D.Ill. 1989).

D   *Jones v. Alltech Associates*, 1989 U.S. Dist. LEXIS 10422 (N.D.Ill. 1989).

DM   *Jordan v. U.S. West Direct Co.*, 50 FEP Cas. 633 (D.Colo. 1989).

H(2) D DM   *Leong v. Hilton Hotels*, 50 FEP Cas. 738 (D.D.C. 1989).

H   *Mason v. Coca-Cola Bottling Co.*, No. 88-2636, U.S. Dist. LEXIS 10533 (D.Kans. 1989).

H M   *Mathis v. Boeing Military Airplane Co.*, 719 F.Supp. 991; 50 FEP Cas. 689 (D.Kans. 1989).

H D   *Matthews v. Freedman, Darryl and McCormick, Taylor & Co.*, 882 F.2d 83, 50 FEP Cas. P874 (3rd Cir. 1989).

R   *Matthews v. Northern Telecom, Inc.*, 1989 U.S. Dist. LEXIS 12926 (S.D.N.Y. 1989).

H   *Miller v. Aldridge*, 1989 U.S. Dist. LEXIS 9747 (1989).

D   *Morgan v. Kansas City Area Transportation Authority*, 1989 U.S. Dist. LEXIS 10482 (W.D.Mo. 1989).

P   *Newman v. University of the District of Columbia*, 1989 U.S. Dist. LEXIS 12201 (D.D.C. 1989).

N7   *Nolan's Auto Body Shop v. Allstate Insurance*, 718 F.Supp. 721 (N.D.Ill. 1989).

H   *Obago v. Union of American Hebrew Congregations*, 1989 U.S. Dist. LEXIS 9055 (S.D.N.Y. 1989)

R   *Overby v. Chevon USA, Inc.*, 884 F.2d 470, 50 FEP Cas. 1211 (9th Cir. 1989).

D   *Prather v. Dayton Power & Light*, 1989 U.S. Dist. LEXIS 10734 (S.D.Ohio 1989).

N7   *Ragin v. Steiner, Clateman & Assoc.*, 714 F.Supp. 709 (S.D.N.Y. 1989).

H   *Riley v. Illinois Dept. of Mental Health*, 1989 U.S. Dist. LEXIS 7686 (N.D.Ill. 1989).

H   *Risinger v. Ohio Bureau of Workers' Compensation*, 883 F.2d 475 (6th Cir. 1989).

D   *Rivera v. AT&T Information Systems*, 719 F.Supp. 962 (D. Colo. 1989).

P D   *Sofferin v. American Airlines, Inc.*, 717 F.Supp. 597 (N.D.Ill. 1989).

N7   *Torres v. City of Chicago*, 1989 U.S. Dist LEXIS 9503 (N.D.Ill. 1989).

H D   *Washington v. Lake County*, 717 F.Supp. 1310; 50 FEP Cas. 1247 (N.D.Ill. 1989).

D (2)   *Williams v. Edsal Manufacturing Co.*, 1989 U.S. Dist. LEXIS 12606 (N.D.Ill. 1989).(2 plaintiffs)

P M R   *Williams v. National Railroad Passenger Corp.*, 716 F.Supp. 79 (D.D.C. 1989).

M R   *Woods v. Miles Pharmaceuticals*, 1989 U.S. Dist. LEXIS 7642 (N.D.Ill. 1989).

ENDNOTES

[1] 105 L.Ed.2d 132, 109 S.Ct. 2363, 57 U.S.L.W. 4705 (1989).

[2] The plaintiff also alleged that she had been denied a promotion because of race. The *Patterson* majority held that some but not all promotion claims could still be brought under section 1981.

[3] 105 L.Ed.2d at 174 (Brennan J., concurring and dissenting).

[4] *Id.*

[5] 105 L.Ed.2d at 150.

[6] 105 L.Ed.2d at 151.

[7] 105 L.Ed.2d at 158.

[8] 105 L.Ed.2d at 158-59.

[9] 105 L.Ed.2d at 180.

[10] A few of the cases discussed below were dismissed under *Patterson* after having been tried on the merits. E.g. *Morgan v. Kansas City Area Transportation Authority,* 1989 U.S. Dist. LEXIS 10482 (W.D. Mo. 1989) (overturning $60,000 jury verdict for victim of discrimination discharge).

[11] Excluding Saturdays, Sundays, Holidays, the federal courts were open a total of 97 days during this period.

[12] In ascertaining the number of section 1981 claims that have been dismissed, we have considered as distinct the claims of several different plaintiffs in the same lawsuit, e.g. *Anderson v. United Parcel Service,* 1989 U.S. Dist. LEXIS 12195 (N.D. Ill. 1989), and different types of discrimination claims brought in one suit by a single plaintiff, e.g. *Dangerfield v. The Mission Press,* 50 FEP Cas. 1171 (N.D. Ill. 1989). We treated as involving only a single claim cases in which a plaintiff sued several defendants because of a single discriminatory act, e.g. *Sofferin v. American Airlines,* 717 F.Supp. 597 (N.D. Ill. 1989), or in which several plaintiffs were allegedly injured by a single discriminatory act, e.g. *Gonzalez v. The Home Insurance Co.,* 1989 U.S. Dist. LEXIS 8733 (S.D.N.Y. 1989).

[13] There are a number of decisions which dismiss multiple claims, but do not specify how many there were or what their nature might have been. E.g. *Woods v. Miles Pharmaceuticals,* 1989 U.S. Dist LEXIS 7642 (N.D. Ill. 1989). There appear to be a significant number of instances in which section 1981 claims have been dismissed without written opinions in one line orders, or have been dismissed by judges from the bench.

[14] The cases in each category can be ascertained from the table printed at the end of the study.

[15] *St. Francis College v. Al-Kharaji*, 481 U.S. 604 (1987); (Arabs); *Shaare Tefila Congregation v. Cobb*, 481 U.S. 615 (1985) (Jews); *McDonald v. Santa Fe Trail Transportation Co.*, 427 U.S. 273 (1976) (Whites).

[16] *Gonzalez v. The Home Insurance Co.*, 1989 U.S. Dist. LEXIS 8733 (S.D.N.Y. 1989).

[17] *Leong v. Hilton Hotels*, 50 FEP Cas. 738 (D. Hawaii, 1989).

[18] *Risinger v. Ohio Bureau of Workers' Compensation*, 883 F.2d 475 (6th Cir. 1989).

[19] *Brackshaw v. Miles, Inc.* 1989 U.S. Dist. LEXIS 12820 (N.D. Ill. 1989).

[20] *Alverez v. Norden Systems, Inc.*, 1989 U.S. Dist. LEXIS 9954 (S.D.N.Y. 1989).

[21] *Sofferin v. American Airlines, Inc.*, 1989 U.S. Dist. LEXIS 9632 (N.D. Ill. 1989).

[22] E.g., *Dangerfield v. The Mission Press*, 50 FEP Cas. 1171 (N.D. Ill. 1989) (plaintiff Kimble); *Busch v. Pizza Hut, Inc.*, 1989 U.S. Dist. LEXIS 11974 (N.D. Ill. 1989); *Brooms v. Regal Tube Co.*, 881 F.2d 412 (7th Cir. 1989); *Harris v. Home Savings Ass'n*, 1989 U.S. Dist. LEXIS 7015 (W.D. Mo. 1989); *Matthews v. Freedman, Darryl and McCormack, Taylor, & Co.*, 882 F.2d 83 (3d Cir. 1989); *Mathis v. Boeing Military Airplane Co.*, 50 FEP Cas. 688 (D. Kan. 1989).

[23] General Building Contractors v. Pennsylvania, 458 U.S. 375 (1982).

[24] 105 L.Ed.2d at 153.

[25] Telephone Interview, November 1, 1989, with Thomas Buess, Chicago, Illinois, counsel for plaintiff.

[26] *Brackshaw v. Miles, Inc.*, 1989 U.S. Dist. LEXIS 12820 (N.D. Ill. 1989); *Harris v. Home Savings Ass'n*, 1989 U.S. Dist. LEXIS 7015 (W.D. Mo. 1989); *Washington v. Lake County, Illinois*, 717 F.Supp. 1310 (N.D. Ill. 1989).

[27] *Bush v. Union Bank*, 1989 U.S. Dist. LEXIS 10936 (W.D. Mo. 1989); *Cooperidge v. Terminal Flight Handling*, 50 FEP Cas. 812 (W.D. Tenn. 1989).

[28] *Johnson v. Railway Express Agency*, 421 U.S. 454, 459-60 (1975); *McDonald v. Santa Fe Trail Transportation Co.*, 427 U.S. 273, 275 (1976); *Delaware State College v. Ricks*, 449 U.S. 250 (1980); *St. Francis College v. Al-Khazraji*, 481 U.S. 604 (1987); *Goodman v. Lukens Steel Co.*, 482 U.S. 656 (1987). Virtually every federal circuit court of appeals prior to *Patterson* had affirmatively stated that terminations were covered by section 1981. E.g. *Estes v. Dick Smith Ford, Inc.*, 856 F.2d 1097, 1100-01 (8th Cir. 1988); *Connor v. Fort Gordon Bus. Co.*, 761 F.2d 1495, 1498-99 (11th Cir. 1985).

[29] *Overby v. Chevron USA, Inc.*, 882 F.2d 470 (9th Cir. 1989) ("Though an argument could be concocted that [retaliation] impedes, in some broad sense,

Overby's access to the EEOC, the court in *Patterson* counseled against stretching the meaning of section 1981..."); *Alexander v. New York Medical College*, 50 FEP Cas. 1729 (S.D.N.Y. 1989) ("retaliatory discharges...take place after the initial employment contract is made").

[30] *Malhotra v. Cotter & Co.*, 50 FEP Cas. 1474 (7th Cir. 1989) ("clearly, when an employer punishes an employee for attempting to enforce her rights under section 1981, this conduct impairs the employee's ability to enforce her contract rights") (section 1981 would become "meaningless" if such claims were excluded) (Cudahy, J., concurring); *Jordan v. U.S. West Direct Co.*, 50 FEP Cas. 633 (D. Colo. 1989) (section 1981 protects an employee subjected to retaliatory harassment because of his instigation regarding discrimination).

[31] One district judge observed that this language in *Patterson* was "certain to generate substantial litigation before the line is marked out with any precision." *Crader v. Concordia College*, 1989 U.S. Dist. LEXIS 12114 (N.D. Ill. 1989).

[32] *Mallory v. Booth Refrigeration Supply Co.*, 882 F.2d 908 (4th Cir. 1989); see also *Green v. Kinney Shoe Corp.*, 1989 U.S. Dist. LEXIS 10736 (D.D.C. 1989).

[33] *Malhotra v. Cotter & Co.*, 1989 U.S. App. LEXIS 13843, p. 13 (7th Cir. 1989).

[34] *Luna v. City and County of Denver*, 718 F.Supp. 85 (D.Colo. 1989).

[35] *Sofferin v. American Airlines*, 717 F.Supp. 597 (N.D. Ill. 1989); see also *Dicker v. Allstate Life Insurance Co.*, 1989 U.S. Dist LEXIS 12482 (N.D. Ill. 1989); *Crader v. Concordia College*, 1989 U.S. Dist. LEXIS 12114 (N.D. Ill. 1989).

[36] *Dicker v. Allstate Insurance Co.*, 1989 U.S. Dist. LEXIS 12482 (N.D. Ill. 1989); *Crader v. Concordia College*, 1989 U.S. Dist. LEXIS 12114.

[37] *Greggs v. Hillman Distributing Co.*, 50 FEP Cas. 429 (S.D. Tex. 1989); *Brown v. Avon Products, Inc.*, 1989 U.S. Dist. LEXIS 12142 (N.D. Ill. 1989); *Newman v. University of the District of Columbia*, 1989 U.S. Dist. LEXIS 12346 (D.D.C. 1985).

[38] E.g. *Hannah v. The Philadelphia Coca-Cola Bottling Co.*, 1989 U.S. Dist. LEXIS 7200 (E.D.Pa. 1989); *Prather v. Dayton Power & Light Co.*, 1989 U.S Dist. LEXIS 10756 (S.D. Ohio 1989); *English v. General Development Corp.*, 717 F.Supp. 628 (N.D. Ill. 1989).

[39] See *Sofferin v. American Airlines, Inc.*, 717 F.Supp. 597; *Guerra v. Tishman East Realty*, 1989 U.S.App. Dist. LEXIS 6744 (S.D.N.Y. 1985); *Woods v. Miles Pharmaceuticals*, 1989 U.S. Dist. LEXIS 7643 (N.D. Ill. 1989); *Riley*

v. Illinois Dept. of Mental Health, 1989 U.S. Dist. LEXIS 7686 (N.D.Ill. 1989).

[40] *Conley v. University of Chicago Hospitals,* 50 FEP Cas. 1145 (N.D. Ill. 1989); *Riley v. Illinois Dept. of Mental Health,* 1989 U.S. Dist. LEXIS 7688 (N.D. Ill. 1989); *Sofferin v. American Airlines,* 717 F.Supp. 597 (N.D. Ill. 1989); *Woods v. Miles Pharmaceuticals,* 1989 U.S. Dist. LEXIS 7042 (N.D. Ill. 1989).

[41] *Anderson v. United Parcel Service,* 1989 U.S. Dist. LEXIS 9954 (N.D. Ill. 1989); *Bush v. Pizza Hut, Inc.,* 1989 U.S. Dist. LEXIS 11974 (N.D. Ill. 1989); *Dangerfield v. Mission Press,* 50 FEP Cas. 1171 (N.D. Ill. 1989); *Brown v. Avon Products,* 1989 U.S. Dist. LEXIS 17142 (N.D. Ill. 1989); *Hall v. County of Cook,* 719 F.Supp. 721 (N.D. Ill. 1989); *Nolan's Auto Body Shop v. Allstate Insurance,* 718 F.Supp. 721 (N.D. Ill. 1989); *Torres v. City of Chicago,* 1989 U.S. Dist. LEXIS 9503 (N.D. Ill. 1989); *Dicker v. Moore,* 1989 U.S. Dist. LEXIS 12482 (N.D. Ill. 1989); *Brackshaw v. Miles, Inc.,* 1989 U.S. Dist. LEXIS 12820 (N.D. Ill. 1989); *Williams v. Edsal Mfg.,* 1989 U.S. Dist. LEXIS 12602 (N.D. Ill. 1989); *Crader v. Concordia College,* 1989 U.S. Dist. LEXIS 12114 (N.D. Ill. 1989).

[42] *Brackshaw v. Miles, Inc.,* 1989 U.S. Dist. LEXIS 12820 (N.D. Ill. 1989); *Torres v. City of Chicago,* 1989 U.S. Dist. LEXIS 9503 (N.D. Ill. 1989).

[43] *Carroll v. General Motors,* 1989 U.S. Dist. LEXIS 10481 (D. Kan. 1989); *Copperidge v. Terminal Freight Handling,* 50 FEP Cas. 812 (W.D. Tenn. 1989); *Mason v. Coca-Cola Bottling Co.,* 1989 U.S. Dist. LEXIS 10533 (D. Kan. 1989); *Matthews v. Freedom, Darryl, McCormick, Taylor & Co.,* 882 F.2d 83 (3d Cir. 1989).

[44] *Padilla v. United Airlines,* 716 F.Supp. 485 (D. Colo. 1989); *Jones v. Pepsi-Cola General Bottlers,* 1989 U.S. Dist. LEXIS 10407 (W.D. Mo. 1989).

[45] In addition to the cases cited in the previous footnotes, see *Birdwhistle v. Kansas Power and Light Co.,* 1989 U.S. Dist. LEXIS 9227 (D. Kan. 1989); *Gamboa v. Washington,* 716 F.Supp. 353 (N.D. Ill. 1989).